THE POPE AND THE DUCE

THE POPE AND THE DUCE

The International Impact of the Lateran Agreements

Peter C. Kent

BX
1545
.K+
1981
cop.2

© Peter C. Kent 1981

First published 1981 by
THE MACMILLAN PRESS LTD
London and Basingstoke
Companies and representatives
throughout the world

ISBN 0 333 27774 0

Typeset in Great Britain by
REDWOOD BURN LIMITED
Trowbridge & Esher
and printed in Hong Kong

Contents

List of Plates

Preface

This is a study of the impact of the Lateran Agreements of 1929 on Italian foreign policy and of the effect of Church–State relations on the development of that policy between 1929 and 1935. It is offered as a contribution to the historical debate on the nature of Mussolini's governance of Italy. As it relates to Fascist foreign policy, this debate has centred on the question of whether Mussolini was completely opportunistic or whether he operated in accordance with a policy of some consistence and coherence. Did Mussolini only respond to crises and opportunities as they arose, seeking transitory propaganda victories, or did he develop and act on any conception of a more long-range Italian interest? The current study contends that Mussolini certainly had a coherent foreign policy between 1927 and 1935 and, moreover, that he would not permit this policy to be deflected for the momentary political advantages offered by such a major international phenomenon as his reconciliation with the Vatican.

I have also sought to examine the impact of the Great Depression on the policies of Pope Pius XI, especially the way in which the papacy's anti-Communist crusade did not develop so much as a direct result of the 1917 Russian revolution as of the breakdown of European society in the early 1930s. This onset of a holy 'Cold War' in 1930 meant that the concordat signed with Hitler in 1933 was conceived in a totally different context from that which had been concluded with Mussolini in 1929; it also helps to explain the ambiguities in the relationship of the Vatican with the Fascist and Nazi regimes in the 1930s and 1940s.

The study was originally written as a doctoral thesis for the University of London. Esmonde M. Robertson of the Department of International History of the London School of Economics was my supervisor. Not only did he suggest the original topic of my research but, through his continued guidance and encourage-

PREFACE

ment, he saw me through to its completion. I am very much indebted to him.

My research was made possible by grants from the Canada Council, the William Lyon MacKenzie King Scholarship Trust, the Province of New Brunswick and the University of New Brunswick.

In the course of my research, useful assistance, information and advice has been gratefully received from the following individuals: Gordon Brook-Shepherd, Alan Cassels, Paul Corner, Renzo De Felice, Peter Edwards, Father Robert Graham, James Joll, Monsignor Kasteel and Father Lizzoli of the Congregation of the *Propaganda Fide*, Hilda Lee, Adrian Lyttelton, Jens Petersen, Sir Alec Randall, Anthony Rhodes, Father Michael Richards, Christopher Seton-Watson, Hon. Mabel Strickland and Dr Otto von Habsburg.

I also wish to acknowledge the help of the staffs of the Public Record Office in London, the Archivio Centrale dello Stato in Rome, St Antony's College, Oxford, and the Library of the University of Birmingham.

I received assistance with translations from Valli Persello, Mariano Piquer, Rosaria Quartararo and R. Steven Turner. Several of my colleagues in the History Department of the University of New Brunswick, and particularly D. M. Young and T. W. Acheson, have read and commented on parts of the manuscript. I wish to thank both my colleagues and my students at the University of New Brunswick for their encouragement in this project, and also Sherry Woodman and Catherine Orchard who helped with typing the manuscript.

Finally, I wish to record my gratitude to my in-laws, Doris and Worthy Preece, for their support, especially during our years in England and, of course, to my wife, Wendy, who has put up with all this and has read the manuscript.

Fredericton, New Brunswick
July 1979

P.C.K.

List of Abbreviations

ACS	Archivio Centrale dello Stato, Rome
De Felice III	Renzo De Felice, *Mussolini il fascista*, vol. II, *L'organizzazione dello stato fascista, 1925–1929*
De Felice IV	Renzo De Felice, *Mussolini il duce*, vol. I, *Gli anni del consenso, 1929–1936*
DDF	*Documents diplomatiques français*
DDI	*Documenti diplomatici italiani*
DGFP	*Documents on German Foreign Policy*
FO	Papers of the British Foreign Office, Public Record Office, London
Opera Omnia	Edoardo and Duilio Susmel (eds), *Opera Omnia di Benito Mussolini*
SPD	Segreteria Particolare del Duce, Carteggio Riservato
StA	Collection of Italian Documents, St Antony's College, Oxford

1 'A Very Determined Antagonist'

In the first public gesture of his pontificate on 6 February 1922, Pope Pius XI made a deliberate break with papal tradition. Having announced to the conclave upon his election that he would style himself Pius XI, Achille Cardinal Ratti, the Archbishop of Milan, then declared

> ... I wish my benediction to go out, as a pledge of that peace for which humanity is yearning, not only to Rome and to Italy, but to the whole Church and the whole world. I will therefore give the benediction from the outer balcony of St. Peter's.[1]

It was the first time since the election of Pius IX in 1846 that the papal blessing to the City and to the world – *urbi et orbi* – had been given outside rather than inside St Peter's.

By this gesture, the new Pope sought to underline his intention to end the conflict between the Holy See and the kingdom of Italy, a conflict referred to as the 'Roman Question'. The Papacy had had no official relationship with the Italian Government since Italian troops occupied Rome in 1870. Pius XI also demonstrated his intention to take the message of the Church into the contemporary world which was still suffering in the moral, spiritual and political chaos of the aftermath of the first mechanized total war. The new Pope differed from his predecessor, Benedict XV, in the public way in which he demonstrated these intentions; Benedict had sought similar ends but in a subtler fashion. The gesture was symbolic of the priorities which Pius XI would establish for his pontificate. Moreover, in the peremptory and decisive manner in which Pius XI acted on 6 February 1922, was foreshadowed the authoritarian militancy of this new pontiff.

The Italian Government did not respond to such papal initiatives until Benito Mussolini became Prime Minister in October of the same year but, seven years later, these initiatives culminated in the *Conciliazione*, the reconciliation between Church and State incorporated in the signing of the Lateran Agreements on 11 February 1929. These agreements were signed in the Lateran Palace in Rome by Mussolini and Pietro Cardinal Gasparri, the Vatican Secretary of State, and consisted of three documents. The first was a treaty which officially settled the Roman Question by offering an Italian recognition of the sovereignty of the Pope within the Vatican City in return for papal recognition of the kingdom of Italy and by arranging for the exchange of ambassadors. The second was a financial agreement whereby Italy paid the Holy See an indemnity which settled accounts outstanding since 1870. The third document was a concordat regulating the position of the Church in Italy. Not only would this settlement prove to be the most significant event in the pontificate of Pius XI, but it would also be the most positive achievement and the most lasting contribution of the Fascist regime to the history of modern Italy.

In its immediate political context, the *Conciliazione* was recognized as marking the culmination of Mussolini's 'seizure of power', completing, as it did, the matrix of supporting institutional structures for his dictatorial regime and freeing him from his dependence on the Fascist party.[2] Mussolini had based his dictatorship on a series of compromises with the traditional institutions of the Italian State: the monarchy, the armed forces, the civil service, the industrial community and the Roman Catholic Church. Moreover, the genuine popular enthusiasm for the Lateran Agreements, manifested in the public response to the plebescite of 24 March 1929, helped to obscure the memory of the murder of the Socialist Giacomo Matteotti in 1924 which had served to set Mussolini on his path to dictatorship. The Lateran Agreements, first and foremost, represented an historic domestic victory for Mussolini; he had succeeded where Cavour had failed and, with this eventual integration of all the institutions of the State, the process of Italian unification could now be said to be complete. In thus draping the historical mantle of the *Risorgimento* over his regime, Mussolini established its legitimacy both within and without Italy in a way that few of his earlier programmes and policies had done.[3] The *Conciliazione* served to usher in that period of broad popular support for Mussolini and Fascism which characterized Italy in the early 1930s.

The domestic dimension of the Lateran Agreements has,

rightly, received all the scholarly attention which has been devoted to the subject, from D. A. Binchy's pioneering work of 1941, *Church and State in Fascist Italy*, through A. C. Jemolo's *Church and State in Italy in the Last Hundred Years* (1948) and Richard Webster's *The Cross and the Fasces* (1960), to the more recent studies of Francesco Margiotta Broglio, *Italia e Santa Sede dalla grande guerra alla conciliazione* (1966), Pietro Scoppola's *La chiesa e il fascismo* (1971) and Renzo De Felice's most recent volumes in his comprehensive biography of Mussolini.[4]

What has not been studied is the international dimension of the *Conciliazione*. Because the Roman Catholic Church is an international institution, the significance of the Lateran Accords was not restricted to the frontiers of Italy. For example, Cardinal Rouleau, Archbishop of Quebec, on the day of the signing of the Agreements, claimed that 'This historic event, prepared by the providential meeting of a great minister with a great Pope, can only augment the prestige of the Papacy and favour the expansion of Catholicism.'[5] The settlement of the Roman Question was warmly received by Roman Catholics throughout the world when the spiritual independence of their Pontiff was guaranteed by the restoration of temporal power over his immediate surroundings in the Vatican City. Mussolini and Fascism rightly enjoyed extensive international acclaim as a result of having hammered out this compromise with the Church.[6] Yet, although enjoying such international approbation, Mussolini also had his foreign policy priorities to consider. The question at issue, then, is how this conclusion of the Lateran Agreements affected the subsequent conduct and development of Italian foreign policy.

Such a study must, of necessity, be conducted on two levels which frequently overlap and intersect. On one level, there is the relationship between the Italian Government and the Holy See in foreign affairs. Did the Lateran Agreements lead to close support of one anothers' foreign policy objectives? Was there any direct collusion in policy? Or, on the contrary, did domestic collaboration within Italy mean that they were thereby prevented from too excessive or apparent a collaboration in international affairs? What, if anything, did Italy expect of the Holy See in relation to foreign interests and, similarly, what did the Holy See expect of Italy?

The other level concerns the relationship between the Italian Government and the national branches of the Catholic Church in those countries with which Italy had active dealings. How did the Lateran Agreements influence those national Catholics in their attitude toward Italy and toward Italian aims? Did this help or hinder the furtherance of Italian interests? What was the relationship of Catholics to other groups with whom Italy had active dealings within those countries? Did the national Catholics seek to enlist Italian assistance for their own particular projects?

The difficulty inherent in these two levels of analysis is that they are not mutually exclusive. In all matters of faith and morals, the Pope, according to the dogma of the 1870 Vatican Council, is infallible when he speaks *ex cathedra*. His jurisdiction also extends to 'all matters which appertain to the discipline and the law of the Church throughout all the world'.[7] In local political matters, on the other hand, the national hierarchies normally act on their own initiative and at their own discretion. Political initiatives of these national hierarchies, therefore, did not necessarily represent the policy of the Holy See, as was the case when the strong support of Cardinal Seredi, the Prince-Primate of Hungary, and of the Hungarian hierarchy for the restoration of the young Habsburg heir, the Archduke Otto, to his throne was viewed with indifference by the Pope. It was also the case over the differences that existed between the Spanish hierarchy and the Vatican over the appropriate reaction to the establishment of the second Spanish Republic in 1931. In the interests of Church discipline, however, the Pope did have the authority to enforce political conformity to Vatican policy should he deem it to be necessary. One such situation arose after Pius XI had condemned Charles Maurras and his monarchist newspaper, *Action Française*, in 1926. The continuing support of much of the French hierarchy for that institution occasioned severe disciplinary measures from Rome, including a request to Cardinal Louis Billot for the return of his cardinal's hat for showing sympathy to Maurras after the condemnation.[8]

Instrumental in the implementation of the policies of the Holy See were the Apostolic Nuncios, the accredited representatives of the Pope to the secular states. Not only did the nuncios fulfil a political role and responsibility in conducting diplomatic negotiations with the State governments but they were also the ecclesiastical representatives of the Pope to the national hierarchies.[9] The national primates of the Church held entirely honorary titles with no special jurisdiction, national primacies being attached to particular sees.[10]

To the Italian Government, the relationship between the Vatican and the national hierarchies was not always very clear. As the Pope, as Bishop of Rome, was also the Primate of Italy, such divergences did not arise in Italy itself. However, Mussolini frequently expected that the Pope would exercise his authority over other national hierarchies more than the Pontiff was, in fact, usually willing to do. At the least, Mussolini was prepared to hold the Pope accountable for statements and acts of national hierarchies which were hostile to Mussolini and Italian interests and in return to put direct pressure on the Italian Church. Thus, a final consideration of this study must deal with the way in which the international relationships of Italy and the Holy See were to influence the domestic position of the Church within Italy.

Mussolini and the Roman Question

Mussolini's religious policy arose entirely out of considerations of political expediency. When interviewed in 1934, he claimed that the *Conciliazione* had been an operation designed 'to counteract politically the weapons in the hands of our adversaries'.[11] Raised in the anti-clerical and irreligious tradition of radical socialism, Mussolini had taken little heed of the sensibilities of the Church in pre-war days. In 1908, he had dismissed priests as 'black microbes who are as fatal to mankind as tuberculosis germs', and one of his literary ventures at that time had been a scurrilous novel entitled *The Cardinal's Mistress*. According to Binchy, he was 'a connoisseur of blasphemy'.[12]

During the war, even after he had left the Socialist party, Mussolini continued to attack the Vatican, accusing it of being an agent of the Central Powers and, in early 1920, he preached against the 'rival Vaticans' of Rome and Moscow

> We are the heretics of both religions. We have torn to pieces all the revealed truths, we have spat upon all the dogmas, rejected all the paradises, scoffed at all the charlatans – red, white and black – who market miraculous drugs to give happiness to mankind.[13]

Only as the character of Fascism changed in 1920 and 1921 and as subsidies flowed in from the conservative land-owners in return for the anti-socialist services rendered by the blackshirt *squadristi* did Mussolini revise his attitude to the Church. Realizing the potential support for Fascism from the traditional institutions of Italian society, Mussolini spoke, in his first speech to the Chamber of Deputies on 21 June 1921, of the necessity for a future reconciliation between Church and State:

> I affirm here that the Latin and imperial tradition of Rome is represented by Catholicism.... I think and affirm that the only universal idea that today exists in Rome, is that which shines from the Vatican.... I thus think that, if the Vatican definitely renounces its temporal claims – and I believe that it is already on this road – Italy, profane or laic, ought to furnish the Vatican with material aid, the material facilities for schools, churches, hospitals and so forth which a secular power has at its disposal. Because the development of Catholicism in the world ... is of both interest and pride for us who are Italians....[14]

This speech was significant not only because it represented such a radical change from Mussolini's own past views but also because it increased the number of Italian politicians who were prepared to endorse a settlement of the Roman Question. Between 1870 and the First World War, because of the strength of anti-clerical sentiment, there had been few Italians prepared to consider a settlement with the Vatican, even had the Vatican been receptive. In the post-war period, there had initially been only two political parties which were prepared to work for a settlement.

One was the small but influential Nationalist Party, which had been founded as the Italian Nationalist Association in 1910 and whose programme had promoted social stability at home and self-assertion abroad. The Nationalists recognized the importance of the Church as an institution providing order and stability within Italy and sought a reconciliation so that Italian society might be better integrated and so that the Church might serve as an agency of this integration and as a pillar of the Italian State. At the same time, the Nationalists recognized the Church as an important traditional element of Italian life and, in particular, as a vehicle of past Italian greatness. Just as the Nationalists were interested in the traditions of classical Rome so, too, did they visualize the possibility of modern Italy taking unto itself the extensive world-wide influence of the Roman Catholic Church and using Catholicism as a vehicle for the expansion of Italian power and Italian influence. To the Nationalists, the Church was an essential *instrumentum regni*.

The other party was the *Partito Popolare Italiano*, which had been founded in 1919 by the priest Don Luigi Sturzo and which had enjoyed considerable success in the elections of that year. The *Popolari*, which encompassed a broad spectrum of Catholic opinion, represented the first specifically Catholic political party to be formed in Italy and, as such, sought to promote the interests of the Church. Yet the members of the party, which operated independently of the Vatican, were not always unanimous on the importance of an immediate settlement of the Roman Question. The existence of the *Popolari* was tolerated but not encouraged by the Holy See.

Certain other Italian politicians, such as former Prime Ministers Orlando and Nitti, bore goodwill to the Holy See but had found the obstacles to a reconciliation to be too great.[15]

Mussolini's speech of June 1921 created difficulties for him with the anti-clerical and Masonic element within the Fascist movement,[16] but it did attract the support of members of the Nationalist Party[17] and of the right-wing of the *Popolari*, many of whom were to come over to Fascism in 1923. It also caught the attention of the Holy See at the beginning of the pontificate of Pius XI with the result that, once Mussolini had become Prime Minister, as the first holder of that office publicly committed to resolving the Roman Question, he was immediately approached by a 'high emissary' from the Vatican inquiring about the possibility of a settlement.[18] The general agreement to work toward a settlement was then confirmed in a secret meeting between Mussolini and Pietro Cardinal Gasparri in January 1923.[19]

Once he had opened this direct channel to the Vatican, Mussolini also made deliberate concessions to the Italian Catholic community, such as the introduction of religious education in the elementary schools, the hanging of the crucifix in classrooms, legal parity for Catholic private schools, and so forth. In doing this, Mussolini outflanked the *Popolari* by showing that Fascism could adequately provide for the needs of the Italian Catholics, and with continuing Vatican support for Mussolini, Don Sturzo resigned from the secretaryship of the *Popolari* in 1923. It was not, however, until the resolution of the Matteotti crisis in 1925, that any concrete move was made by the Government to resolve the Roman Question. Mussolini had been, no doubt, impressed by the way in which the Vatican had openly disapproved of the anti-Fascist Aventine Secession and by the way in which the Pope had held aloof from all polemics associated with the 1924 crisis.[20] In his new programme for the abolition of Italian liberal democracy, Mussolini now sought the support of the Church for his institutional changes.

What is significant in the negotiations leading up to the Lateran Agreements is that they were conducted for Mussolini by former Nationalists and *Popolari* and not by Fascists. It was Alfredo Rocco, the Minister of Justice and a former Nationalist, who appointed a commission to review Italian ecclesiastical legislation on 6 January 1925. This commission, which was headed by Mattei-Gentili, a former *Popolari*, reported at the end of the year and this report eventually formed the basis for the Italian Concordat of 1929.[21] In March 1925, a plan was put forward for a revision of the Law of Guarantees, the statute of the Italian Parliament under which Church–State relations had been regulated since 1871. This plan was produced by Senator Santucci, another ex-*Popolari*, acting, apparently, at the behest of the Holy See. The planned revision, generally accepted by the Italian Government in 1925[22] was to become the basis of the Lateran Treaty. As Margiotta Broglio has clearly demonstrated, the basic outlines of the settlement had been agreed upon in 1925 or early 1926, before the opening of secret official negotiations between Domenico Barone for Italy and Francesco Pacelli for the Holy See in the autumn of 1926.

It was from the Nationalist conception of the potential for a dynamic Italian foreign policy that Mussolini had developed his initial views on international relations.[23] In this connection, in his speech of June 1921, Mussolini had adopted the Nationalist view of the importance of the Church when he expressed his willingness to use Catholicism 'as one of our greatest national forces for the expansion of Italy in the world'.[24]

However, in spite of such early pronouncements, there is no evidence during the negotiations for a settlement between 1925 and 1929 that Mussolini ever intended the *Conciliazione* to be a vehicle for the expansion and extension of Italian influence abroad. He had, in fact, one clear objective in the negotiations: the definitive resolution of the Roman Question.[25] As the negotiations proceeded, it became clear that he was prepared to give way on the most contentious issue, that of recognizing the independence of Italian Catholic Action, *Azione Cattolica*, after he had first put a ban on the Catholic Boy Scouts.[26] As De Felice observes, Mussolini viewed the negotiations and the *Conciliazione* itself as representing a *sistemazione* of the on-going relations between Church and State in the domestic sphere, not as an immutable legal contract;[27] the question of *Azione Cattolica* could, therefore, be left to another day.

Because Mussolini approached the *Conciliazione* as an immediate practical domestic problem, for which he was, in fact, prepared to sacrifice some parts of his 'totalitarian' ideology, he was perfectly able to separate the domestic importance of the Lateran Pacts from their international implications. He was not devoted either to the Catholic views of the importance of supporting Catholicism in all its forms and in all its tribulations, wherever they might be; nor (although sympathetic) was he devoted to the Nationalist concept of Italy as integral society, resting its influence on its traditional institutions. Mussolini does not appear to have expected that the settlement of the Roman Question would be a prelude to similar cooperation in international affairs. His religious policy, like Fascism itself, was 'not for export'. This meant that Mussolini was to be extremely suspicious of any attempts by ex-Nationalists, such as the publicists Roberto Forges Davazati in *La Tribuna* or F. Coppola in *Politica*, or by the Holy See itself to promote Italian support for the Catholic cause abroad. He was equally wary of capitalizing on profferred support from foreign Catholics lest he thereby be swept into conducting a foreign policy not of his own making.

'Anti-clerical to the depths of his soul',[28] Mussolini had no intention of having his foreign policy dictated by clerical interests. Nor, at a time when he was giving domestic politics precedence over foreign affairs, did he wish to confuse the issue by risking his greatest domestic triumph for questionable international gains. Mussolini's reluctance was also based on his personal and political assessment of Pius XI. In the negotiations for the *Conciliazione*, the Pope had proved himself a determined and formidable negotiator who, through his conception of the function of his pontificate, was actively working to extend the power and influence of the 'Kingship of Christ' in the world. Under Pius XI, the militancy of the Church in the 1920s made the Duce of Fascism hesitate.

Pius XI and the Modern World

Much of this militancy had come as a surprise to those who had followed the early career of the enigmatic Achille Ratti.[29] A scholar and sometime mountaineer from Lombardy, Ratti had served as Prefect of the Ambrosian Library in Milan until 1911, and as Prefect of the Vatican Library from 1914 to 1918. In 1918, he was made Apostolic Visitor to Poland and Lithuania, and then Nuncio in Poland before his appointment as Archbishop of Milan in 1921. From this position, he was elevated to the Papacy in the following year.

What had been remarkable about Ratti in the years of his earlier career was that, despite the conflicts that had raged within the Church over the Modernist controversy, he had occupied positions of considerable responsibility and yet managed to avoid giving any real indication of his position in this controversy. Similarly, during his early years in Milan, although a member of the local administration of the Church, he moved at the same time in those social circles of the Milanese upper bourgeoisie who were closest to the operation of the Italian Government. It would seem, in fact, that his reluctance to commit himself on the political and theological issues of his day had been the decisive factor in his emergence as a compromise candidate for the Papacy during the 1922 Conclave.

Once installed as Pope, however, Ratti was not only prepared to establish clear objectives for his pontificate and to set about their achievement in a deliberate and systematic way, but also to show a stubborn intransigence whenever he met any opposition. This strongwilled and, not infrequently, headstrong leadership of Pius XI stood in stark contrast to the enigmatic behaviour of the scholarly librarian of some years before. Binchy attributes Ratti's papal 'style' to his background as a scholar and an administrator and to his limited experience in both diplomatic and pastoral roles

In him a keen intellect, sharpened by constant research work,

was allied to an iron will, a formidable combination in all circumstances ... in many respects a difficult and exacting chief,
as hard on others as he was on himself. ... Nor did he ever
acquire that prudent scepticism about the value of statesmen's
assurances which comes only from long experience of their
ways [as a diplomat]; on the contrary, he was always willing to
credit them with his own limpid honesty and when, as frequently happened, he was deceived, his reaction was corre-
spondingly violent.[30]

Pius XI recognized the significance of his new pontificate in
this post-war era, when the European peoples were beset by the
doubts and uncertainties, both political and spiritual, engen-
dered by the conflagration of 1914–18. Ratti's experience in
Poland had shown him at first hand the sufferings of the peoples
in the post-war chaos. During the Russo-Polish War of 1920–1, he
had also learned how persistent the atheistic Russian Bolsheviks
could be in their determination to take advantage of the political
and spiritual vacuum in Europe. Pius XI was fully conscious of
his moral authority as Roman Pontiff at this critical moment in
European history and he recognized his duty to exercise this authority and that of his Church in these uncertain times.
    The key objectives of his pontificate were outlined in the ency-
clicals *Ubi arcano Dei* of 23 December 1922 and *Quas Primas* of 23
December 1925

In the first, the new Pope bluntly belittled the effectiveness of
any efforts by the lay world to bring about its own revival and
restoration after the tragic experiences of the war, declaring
that the Church alone could offer the guarantees for the longed-
for peace ...
    But *Quas primas* ... went even further, unravelling with
inexorable logic all the consequences of the thesis of the Kingship of Christ the Word incarnate. For the principality of the
Redeemer, according to the new Pope, includes not only
Catholics but all other men ... and not individuals alone but
also societies. Governments and rulers, therefore, as well as
individuals should be submissive to him. The thesis of the
Kingship of Christ further permitted Pius XI to emphasize his
struggle against the secession of the civil world from the
Church, attacking that 'pest of our age' which, in his view,

secularism represented. Humanity, in short, had no other possible choice but to submit anew to the Church and through it to
the Pope.[31]

As Carlo Falconi observes 'Not even Leo XIII had dared to
advance so frankly medieval a vision of the mission of the papacy
in the modern world.'[32]

What, then, did these objectives mean in practice? The policy
of Pius XI may be examined in its pastoral, diplomatic and
missionary contexts.

(a) The Pastoral Context

In his rejection of the possibility of the laity restoring peace to the
world, Pius XI was arguing that the laity, by emphasizing secularism and materialism, had permitted that decline in spiritual
values which was at the root of the contemporary hatred and
moral confusion. Attempts, such as those sparked off by President
Woodrow Wilson, to revise European political institutions and
preserve the peace through a League of Nations could never be
but partial solutions; for true peace, it was necessary to restore
man's spiritual and moral values, and this was the proper and
unique task of the Church.

Pius XI also believed that such a restoration was the direct
responsibility of the clergy. Quasi-independent Catholic political
parties could never be as effective as the non-political laymen's
association, Catholic Action, functioning as an 'apostolate of the
laity' under the direct guidance of the ecclesiastical authorities.
The Pope intended that spiritual values should be realized and
promoted in the educational, social and occupational lives of the
laity through those institutions affiliated with Catholic Action.
Those institutions, be they youth groups, men's and women's
organizations, trade unions, businessmen's associations, savings
banks or rural cooperatives, were to be deliberately and distinctly
apolitical. Only through the agency of Catholic Action could
Christian values be rooted deeply in modern society and, once
firmly established, branch out to bring more and more men into
this Kingship of Christ, the only true guarantee of world peace.

It was therefore essential to secure political protection through
concordats for the national branches of the Church, for Catholic
Action and for other lay associations as a preliminary to the
extension of this Kingship of Christ. Fundamental to this con-

cordatory policy of Pius XI was his willingness to work with any government that happened to be in power, whether it be a democracy or a dictatorship and to negotiate with that government, if possible, a concordat which would enumerate the rights and privileges of the Roman Catholic Church in that country. Pius XI believed that once the rights of the Church had been secured, the Church would then have a legal guarantee of protection as it set about making its spiritual influence felt in that society. In his dealings with the national hierarchies, the Pope found that he had the greatest difficulties where the bishops, such as those in France or, later, in Spain, had established positions in opposition to the government in power, thereby hampering papal negotiations with those governments.

If such a policy of negotiating concordats with existing governments were to be implemented, the first and most obvious priority for Pius XI was the resolution of the Roman Question. The Pope could hardly expect the national hierarchies to accept their governments if he were not prepared to do the same in Italy.

In the 1929 *Conciliazione* the Italian Concordat was the unique contribution of Pius XI. In 1918 and 1919, Benedict XV had been prepared for a settlement of the Roman Question along the lines of the eventual treaty. The failure to reach a settlement had been due to liberal and anti-clerical influences on the Italian Government, not the least of which had been that of King Victor Emmanuel.[33] By 1921, Cardinal Gasparri claimed that the Church was still waiting for the right Italian statesman with whom it could negotiate:

> There are no insuperable difficulties about the longed-for settlement of the Roman Question.... It is the particular men concerned that put us in a state of uncertainty.... We are still waiting for our man.[34]

That man would, of course, turn out to be Benito Mussolini, with whom the Vatican lost no time in making contact and opening negotiations once he had become Prime Minister.

As the Italian Government had set about its review of its ecclesiastical legislation in 1925 through the Mattei-Gentili Commission, it was the Pope in 1926 who had insisted that he could not accept unilateral Italian legislation and had opened the door for negotiations between Italy and the Holy See on the matter.

With the opening of these negotiations in the autumn of 1926, it was quickly agreed that there should not be just a settlement of the Roman Question, but also a regulation of the position of the Church in Italy along the lines of the recommendations of the Mattei-Gentili Commission, embodied in a concordat. The Italian Concordat was in keeping with the policy of Pius XI but it was also necessary because, with the institution of the Fascist dictatorship in 1925 and 1926, Mussolini had been seeking to establish his control over all aspects of Italian life. In the case of the Church, he had been smothering it with kind attention and Pius XI deemed it wise to use this particular time to secure a clear guarantee for the position of the Church for the future.[35] In particular, the Pope sought to preserve the independence of *Azione Cattolica* against encroachments from the Fascist party, the Fascist trade unions and the Fascist youth organizations. As the negotiations progressed, it became ever more evident that the guarantee of the continued independence of *Azione Cattolica*, as it was eventually granted in Article 43 of the Concordat, was the Pope's basic condition for reaching any settlement.[36] To the Pope, the Concordat was the fundamental unit of the *Conciliazione* and he intended it to be used as a basis for a possible future legal defence of the Church against the Fascist regime. The settlement, in fact, almost failed to be ratified because of papal insistence in 1929 on making the continued existence of the Lateran Treaty dependent on the terms of the Concordat being met – an interpretation which Mussolini refused to accept because it would have meant that the Roman Question had not been completely settled.[37]

(b) The Diplomatic Context

There was another consideration related both to the concordatory policy and to the settlement with Italy. During the nineteenth century, the Papacy had relied very strongly on Austria for international protection of its vital interests. Because of this, Vienna had been able to exercise a veto over the election of the Pope, this veto being last exercised against the candidacy of Cardinal Rampolla in 1903.[38] Under Napoleon III, France, too, had stood as a defender of the Papacy especially during the wars of Italian unification, when the Papacy was seeing its temporal powers eroded by the new Italian state. After the rise of anticlericalism during the Third Republic culminated in the Dreyfus affair and, by 1905, in the disestablishment of the French Church, the Papacy once again saw the Habsburg monarchy of Austria–Hungary as its sole temporal ally. The outbreak of the First World War forced the Holy See to adopt a position of neutrality, yet its sympathies for Austria–Hungary were well known and made the Papal peace note of 1917 suspect among the Entente Powers.

However, the collapse and disintegration of Austria–Hungary in 1918 meant that the Papacy would, in future, have to fend for itself. A concordatory policy became imperative in the sense that the Papacy, no longer able to rely on particular national governments, had to ground its support in its own institutions and in its own laity more than before. Yet, because of the demise of the Austro-Hungarian monarchy, concordats could be more easily negotiated since the Holy See was no longer committed to support a monarchical form of government. At the same time, the collapse of Austria–Hungary made the settlement of the Roman Question imperative as it seemed necessary to develop the friendship of Italy as a possible substitute for the lost 'alliance' with Austria–Hungary.

(c) The Missionary Context
The missionary policy of Pius XI was a corollary to these other policies. Once having secured or protected the rights of the Roman Catholic Church, it was then his intention that the Church should expand its influence and membership both within the European world and outside it. As Falconi remarks:

> ... the function of the concordatory policy was not so much to bring peace and defend the Church's rights, as to foster struggle and open rivalry, even if cautiously dissimulated, with the secular forces. In other words, with [Pius XI], the Church became an anti-State in every State...[39]

Of particular interest to Pius XI were the members of the Orthodox Churches of eastern Europe. The weakening of the Russian Orthodox Church as a result of the 1917 Revolution had had two possible results. One was that the Russian people might now be willing to accept the Roman Church and, to this end, negotiations with the Soviet Government were conducted between 1922 and 1927 for the right to send missionaries to

Russia.[40] The other was the recognition that the Russian Church had been the mainstay of the national churches of eastern Europe and a hope that these churches might now be prepared to accept the leadership of Rome. The proposed vehicle for such conversion was the Eastern rite of the Roman Catholic Church, which accepted the Slav Orthodox liturgy while recognizing the supremacy of the Pope. During the 1920s, a very active campaign was conducted by the Vatican in eastern Europe in an attempt to encourage branches of the Orthodox Church to convert to becoming Catholic Eastern rite, or Uniate, Churches.

By 1929, Pope Pius XI had proved himself to be a man of firm faith, with a clear conception of his duty in the modern world. Moreover, in his treatment of those French ecclesiastics who resisted his 1926 condemnation of the *Action Française* and, especially, in his brutal reduction of Cardinal Billot, he had demonstrated his iron determination to have his own way.

To Mussolini, the Pope was a very determined antagonist indeed and one who had to be handled with the greatest delicacy, which is one reason why the Duce kept dealings with the Holy See in his own hands and preferred to deal with the Pope through the Jesuit intermediary, Father Tacchi-Venturi, rather than through diplomatic channels. The Pope himself, ruling autocratically as he did, was also satisfied with this direct channel. At this very personal level, it was important for Mussolini to restrict the operation of the *Conciliazione* to domestic matters. To embark on any cooperation in foreign policy could well leave him vulnerable to manipulation by Pius XI, with little real benefit accruing to Italy. Whereas the pragmatic Mussolini could quite easily dissociate his domestic religious policy from his foreign policy, the doctrinaire Pope could never do this, with the result that he could be counted on to try to make Catholic nations serve Catholic ends if the opportunity arose.

2 Areas of Cooperation before 1929

Italian Definition of a Post-War Foreign Policy

From the time of the *Risorgimento*, Italy, frequently in cooperation with Britain, had sought to use Franco-German continental rivalry to its own advantage. Whether pursuing an expansionist or a quiescent foreign policy, Italy had sought to derive national advantage by making its support available to the highest foreign bidder. Such had been the case during the First World War when the Treaty of London represented the price of Italian assistance. Yet, by helping to defeat Germany and Austria–Hungary in the war, Italy had also helped to upset the European power balance, creating a situation where Italy was no longer of use to France and could be ignored when the peace settlement was being formulated. The only real counterweight to the French in 1919 was the United States of Woodrow Wilson but Italy's aspirations were so patently out of sympathy with Wilsonian idealism that it was impossible for the Italians to play the Americans against the French.

In 1918 France was in control of Europe and was determined to retain its hegemony into the limitless future. Germany, Russia and Austria–Hungary were in collapse and disintegration and the only real counterweights to French hegemony – the British and the Americans – were extra-European powers. During the 1920s, as France set about securing its continental control through alliances with Poland and the Little Entente, Italy was being thrust, and was thrusting itself, into the role of continental counterweight to France.

The disintegration of the Austro-Hungarian Empire had, *de facto*, conferred great power status on post-war Italy. Without the continued weight of this traditional enemy on its northern and eastern frontiers, the Italian kingdom had acquired greater freedom of manoeuvre. The post-war power vacuum on the

Danube and in the Balkans invited the exercise of the new-found Italian power and thereby brought Italy into direct contest with France. Franco-Italian hostility in the 1920s was thus inherent in the post-war configuration of European power. For Italy to have become a satiated power and to have been willing to stand by the European *status quo*, it would have had to be prepared to accept a secondary position in a French-dominated Europe.

This was as unwelcome a prospect for the Italians as it was for the British. The Locarno Agreement of 1925, therefore, represented an attempt to recreate a Franco-German balance, whereby the British and the Italians might oversee the diminution of French power. In theory, the Locarno era which followed should have allowed Italy to return to its role as a power-balancer, but such was not to be the case.

Under Locarno, Italy could have played the Germans against the French in the context of the League of Nations. Such a traditional policy had been the intention of Salvatore Contarini, Secretary-General of the Italian Foreign Ministry until 1926, but his policy had run aground on the shoals of German Foreign Minister Stresemann's dislike of the Italians and of Mussolini's preference for a different policy.

A certain natural coolness in Franco-Italian relations was aggravated by the existence of Fascism in Italy. Mussolini's desire to cut a dashing figure on the international stage could, in the 1920s, only be done at the expense of the French; Fascism thereby added an ideological dimension to the Franco-Italian conflict. Not only was France regarded as the decadent democracy to which Fascism was the antithesis but, after 1925 and much to Mussolini's annoyance, Paris served as the centre of activity for the Italian anti-Fascist exiles, the *fuorusciti*, In both ideological and diplomatic terms, France stood solidly athwart the path of Fascist Italy.[1]

For Mussolini, the alternative to playing the Germans against the French was to create an independent Italian sphere of influence such that Italy would become a European power in its own right and could thereby become the counterweight to the power of France. By a supreme act of will, the Italian nation should rise above its natural weaknesses to utilize the many opportunities presented in the uncertain state of the post-war settlement.

This Italian sphere of influence was to comprise the Balkan

peninsula and the eastern basin of the Mediterranean. Control of the Balkans could act as a counterweight to French hegemony in Europe and was also essential for control of the eastern Mediterranean. The ultimate purpose for securing this Italian sphere of influence was to guarantee access to a prospective Italian empire on the Red Sea and in north-east Africa. Just as the French sphere of influence in the western Mediterranean protected French power and access to its north African colonies, so this Italian sphere of influence would do the same for Italy.

Central to the domination of the Balkans was control over Yugoslavia and, if Mussolini could so manage his diplomacy that Yugoslavia would be isolated and amenable to Italian influence, then he could effectively dictate the course of events in that part of Europe. This drive by Mussolini to force Yugoslavia to accept a role subservient to Italian dictates was the one constant in Italian foreign policy between 1925 and 1935, and was pursued with dogged determination by the Duce personally throughout that period.

Mussolini's Balkan policy had three aspects. One was the development of Albania as an Italian satellite which could be used to put pressure on Belgrade; a second lay in the development of friendly relations with the other Balkan states to enable Italy to isolate Yugoslavia and, in particular, to prevent the formation of an anti-Italian bloc; the third aspect required that the other great powers stay out of the Balkans. The Germans had shown little interest in south-eastern Europe and, in the mid-twenties, the French need for Italian support under Locarno, coupled with the close Anglo-Italian relationship in the Mediterranean, was expected to keep the French and British from direct interference.

Few of Mussolini's aides agreed with him in this programme. The career diplomats of the Foreign Ministry felt that Italy was not capable of acting without British or French patronage and did not want to pose too direct a challenge to accepted diplomatic norms. Officials in the Colonial Ministry and others in the Italian imperial tradition felt that a policy of cooperation in the maintenance of the European *status quo* should be used to secure expansion to the non-European areas. Certain radical members of the Fascist party and others of the Italian irredentist tradition believed that all Italian energy should be directed north of the Alps in seeking to remake the map of central Europe, possibly in conjunction with the other diplomatic outcasts, the Germans and the

Russians. Conflict over Italian expansionist foreign policy had traditionally divided imperialists and irredentists within Italy, but Mussolini's conception of expansionist goals displayed a remarkable consistency in representing a synthesis of these differing expansionist orientations.

Mussolini, therefore, could direct his attention to Hungary or Albania, to Bulgaria or Turkey, to Palestine or Libya and to the Yemen or Abyssinia without losing consistency. Having defined his sphere of action, he sought to utilize such opportunities as presented themselves from time to time for the augmentation and furtherance of Italian power.

This definition of Italian expansionist goals of the 1920s did not allow for Italian involvement in the politics of the Danube basin or of central Europe. Although he used the Hungarians in his quest for Balkan hegemony, Mussolini tried to avoid making any commitment to Hungarian ambitions in the Danube basin. The Duce's great fear was that, by assisting the Hungarians, he might thereby help to reconstitute the power of Austria–Hungary to Italian disadvantage. For the same reason, Mussolini showed little interest in any attempt to improve Italian relations with Austria in the 1920s.

There was yet another reason for this studied Italian disinterest in the Danube basin. Where both Italy and Germany had been dissatisfied with the peace settlement and the consequent power indirectly vested in France, an Italo-German alliance for the revision of the peace treaties was a distinct future possibility. Gustav Stresemann, while German Foreign Minister, would not entertain any forward German policies on the Danube or in south-eastern Europe, but there was always the possibility that this would change, in which case Mussolini could find himself presented with a serious dilemma. On the one hand, German union with Austria in the *Anschluss* would limit Italian freedom of action yet, on the other hand, there was the possibility that Germany and Italy working together might well effect significant treaty revision to their mutual benefit. Since the *Anschluss* was the most important post-war issue in Austrian politics, the Italians thought the best policy was to remain neutral until German policies were clarified. In order, therefore, to maintain his alliance with Hungary and to keep his options open with Germany, Mussolini made no effort to seek an Italo-Austrian entente.

The Holy See and Post-War Europe

In the 1920s the Holy See was also dissatisfied with the outcome of the war and the peace settlement and, consequently, was in real sympathy with the basic assumptions underlying the direction of Italian foreign policy during the decade.

In all Europe on the eve of 1914, the one Catholic regime on which the Vatican could rely for protection and support had been the Habsburg dynasty of Austria–Hungary which, with its close association of Throne and Altar, had also been the traditional mainstay of central European Catholicism. In those Catholic countries with liberal constitutional regimes, on the other hand, anti-clericalism had been the great scourge of the Roman Catholic Church in the late nineteenth century. The unification of Italy in defiance of the temporal interests of the Papacy represented one outcome of this threat just as, in the same year that Italian troops occupied Rome, the liberal Third Republic replaced the philo-Catholic Second Empire in France. In spite of later efforts by Pope Leo XIII to encourage French Catholics to accept the Republic, anti-clericalism became an ideology in the Dreyfus affair and resulted in the separation of French Church and French State in 1905.

To the Holy See, the dissolution of the Austro-Hungarian Empire, victim to these forces of liberal nationalism, was one of the great calamities of the twentieth century. The collapse of the Habsburg dynasty in the war, however, coincided with a revised and patriotic clericalism in France and Italy as a result of the active assistance given by the clergy to men at war.[2] Benedict XV and Pius XI, recognizing this, had made overtures for the restoration of working relationships with both Italy and France. Talks with the Italians eventually led to the *Conciliazione*, while more immediate results had been achieved with France through the re-establishment of diplomatic relations between France and the Holy See in 1921. This was made possible by the right-wing post-war Chamber of Deputies, the first since 1871 to contain a majority of practising Catholics.[3] The approach of the Vatican to the Third Republic was one of appeasement, of working with the French Government of the day in the hope that certain confiscated property and terminated privileges might eventually be restored to the Church in France. While the French Left could still unite on the anti-clerical issue, this attitude of the Vatican found favour with the Centre and the Right. A major stumbling block to the acceptance of the Church by the Republic and of the Republic by the Church, however, had been the identification of many Catholics and, particularly, of many members of the French hierarchy with the monarchist *Action Française*. This newspaper, edited by the brilliant Charles Maurras, had maintained a consistent series of attacks on the Third Republic from its first appearance in print in 1908. Maurras advocated the doctrine of integral nationalism and called for the restoration of the French monarchy and of social order. To Maurras, the Church was an essential bulwark of this social order, and this had appealed to French Catholics. Pius XI was disturbed, however. He objected to the conception of the Church being subservient to the State; he was upset by evidence of the obvious appeal of the *Action Française* to middle-class youth and, perhaps above all, he was upset as he was in the process of seeking a *rapprochement* with the Third Republic. He was thus led, in the autumn of 1926, to issue a condemnation of Maurras and the *Action Française* and, in the following year, to place the paper and all the works of Maurras on the Index.

Until the French Separation Laws of 1905 closed the seminaries which trained foreign missionaries, much French prestige and influence in the Middle East, Africa and Asia had been based on the extensive number of missionary vocations occupied by French nationals. Prior to 1905, three-quarters of the Roman Catholic missionaries in the Near and Far East had been French, and France had traditionally been looked upon by the Vatican as the protector of Catholics in those areas, with its diplomatic representatives being entitled to liturgical honours at Catholic ceremonies in the Levant.[4]

The separation of Church and State brought all this to an end. France could no longer be seen as the protector of Catholicism and the liturgical honours were discontinued. Within France, the closing of seminaries and the expropriation of certain missionary orders meant that the number of French vocations both at home and in the mission field noticeably declined. After 1918, French missionary influence suffered a further blow when, at the request of the American bishops whose parishioners were providing most of the financial support, the Vatican moved the centre for training missionaries for work in the Far East from Lyons to Rome.[5] By

1928 it was reported that, whereas in 1905 there had been a total of 1358 French missionaries in Japan, Korea, Manchuria, China, Siam, India and Burma, in 1928 there were only 1132.[6]

In furthering Pius XI's appeasement of France and contemporaneous with the papal condemnation of the *Action Française*, Monsignor Maglione, the Nuncio in Paris, concluded an agreement with French Foreign Minister Aristide Briand in December 1926, for the restoration of liturgical honours in the Levant.[7] This concession was granted by the Vatican in apparent expectation that Briand would see that the favour was suitably returned. It has also been suggested that the Vatican wanted to augment the influence of France in the Levant at the expense of Britain who supported and favoured Eastern Orthodoxy and Zionism.[8]

Although the Vatican sought this domestic *rapprochement* with France in the 1920s, it was distinctly unenthusiastic about French foreign policy. In the eyes of the Vatican, true peace would occur in the world when all men subscribed to principles of Christian charity. To achieve true peace, therefore, it was necessary to effect a change in the hearts and souls of individual men. Excluded on Italian request from the 1919 peace conference, the Vatican had applied these standards to the peacemakers and to the peace settlement and found both to be wanting. In his encyclical *Ubi Arcano Dei* of 1922, Pius XI explained the weakness of the peace settlement, 'Peace was indeed signed by solemn pact between the belligerents, but it was written in public documents, not in the hearts of men; the spirit of war reigns there still, bringing ever-increasing harm to society.'[9] Neither the programme promoted by the French at Versailles nor that promoted by the Americans would guarantee lasting peace. The French pressure for European hegemony and a punitive peace was judged too harsh by the Vatican, who accurately predicted that it would enhance and not diminish German hostility. Such a repressive approach would generate a desire for revenge, not reconciliation.

Nor did the Papacy have much greater faith that the liberal League of Nations and the American peace plan provided a more adequate solution; one does not achieve lasting peace by legislating new institutions. The Vatican had little faith in the principle of national self-determination which had served as the justification for breaking the Austro-Hungarian monarchy into a series of secular national states at the end of the war. By recognizing the various conflictual nationalisms of central Europe, the international community had created an area of continuing international discord. The experience with Bela Kun's Communist regime in Hungary in 1919, moreover, showed that these successor states were ill-equipped to withstand the Bolshevik virus. Where, prior to 1918, the Catholic Church had had a pervasive influence in this area, offering substantial resistance to the spread of atheism, now Poland, Austria and, to a lesser extent, Hungary were the only Catholic states, facing the secular and anti-clerical Czechoslovakia[10] and the Orthodox Rumania and Yugoslavia.

The Vatican was extremely pessimistic about the durability of the Versailles Settlement and Pope Benedict XV had publicly addressed himself to this.[11] During the 1920s, Pius XI applauded any moves designed to show generosity toward Germany and criticized the persistence of small-minded legalism which harped on preserving the letter of the Versailles *status quo*. In this latter connection, the Vatican was totally out of sympathy with French insistence on maintaining continental hegemony, feeling that this only made a future conflict more certain. In particular, the Vatican disliked French support of the Little Entente which aggravated the central European conflict and prevented any real settlement with Austria and Hungary. At the same time Pius XI's conflict with Czech anti-clericalism in 1926[12] did not enhance his sympathies for that country. To the Pope, such conflict as existed in Europe in the 1920s was a result of French intransigence and, consequently, he was particularly sympathetic to Mussolini's opposition to French hegemony and to the Little Entente.

This general sympathy for the Italian position and policy was augmented by more specific objectives pursued in conjunction with Italian policy both by the Holy See and by the national hierarchies in the 1920s.

One of the prime goals of the Vatican after 1918 had been the restoration of the privileged position of central European Catholicism. One way of achieving this would have been through the reconstitution of the Austro-Hungarian Empire and the return of the Habsburgs to their throne. Although Pope Pius XI was less enthusiastic about this solution than were the church hierarchies of Austria and Hungary,[13] the possibility was never rejected. The ex-Empress Zita, widow of Karl, the last Emperor of Austria–Hungary, was still received with full honours at the Vatican and was accorded a seat of honour at important ceremonies in St

Peter's Basilica whenever she visited Rome.[14] Failing a restoration, however, any planned confederation of the Catholic states and provinces of eastern Europe – Poland, Hungary, Austria, Bavaria, Croatia, Italy – could expect to receive Papal sympathy. Only in this way could these states defend themselves and their faith against the incursions of Orthodoxy, liberalism, Bolshevism or Protestantism.

At the conclusion of the First World War, Eastern Orthodoxy seemed to be in a state of crisis for the persecution of the Russian Orthodox Church by the Bolsheviks after the 1917 Revolution meant that Eastern Orthodoxy had lost a great deal of its spiritual and political support. To a certain extent, the Church of England attempted to fill this void in the 1920s, showing a particular solicitude for the Orthodox churches of Rumania and Yugoslavia.[15] Given this crisis of Eastern Orthodoxy, the Holy See, under Popes Benedict XV and Pius XI, hoped that the Oriental Rite or Uniate Churches of the Roman communion might assist in bringing certain branches of Orthodoxy into this communion as a move toward the eventual reunification of Christendom under the Pope. In contrast to those Latin Rite Churches of the Roman communion which used Latin for the liturgy, and generally were found in western Europe and America, the Uniate Church represented those churches which had retained the liturgy of the various eastern branches of Christianity but which accepted the primacy of the Papacy. Prior to 1917, the Oriental Rite Churches had come under the authority of the Congregation of the *Propaganda Fide*, that congregation responsible for missionary work. In 1917, however, as a means of giving the Uniate Church greater prominence and encouraging a better understanding of its peculiarities, it was put under a congregation of its own, the Congregation for the Eastern Church (of which the Pope himself was to be the nominal Prefect). Moreover, in order to provide for the education of the Uniate clergy, for the instruction of the clergy of the Latin rite in Eastern rites and even for the education of students from non-Roman Catholic Eastern churches, a Pontifical Institute for Oriental Studies was also established in 1917, and was headed, during the 1920s, by the French Jesuit, Monsignor Michel d'Herbigny.[16]

As evidence of the interest of Pius XI in the work of the Uniate Church in the late 1920s, a new building was constructed in Rome to house the Pontifical Oriental Institute and, in an address at the beginning of 1927, the Pope 'made an eloquent reference to his desire for the re-attachment of the separated Eastern Churches to the See of Peter' and called for Roman Catholics to develop a new understanding of the point of view of their '"separated brethren" if any progress towards complete unity was to be made'.[17] This plea was repeated in the encyclical *Rerum Orientalium*, issued in September 1928, which served as the guiding directive for the Holy See in its dealings with the churches and the governments of eastern Europe.[18]

Of particular interest to Pius XI was the possibility of reviving Christianity in Russia after the Russian Revolution by attracting surviving members of Russian Orthodoxy into communion with Rome. As Rhodes expresses the Catholic view, 'Roman Catholicism would fill the spiritual vacuum created by the decay of the Orthodox Church. Here was a chance in a thousand years'.[19] Initially, the Holy See had sought negotiations with the Soviet Government for the admission of Catholic missionaries to Russia. D'Herbigny even indicated Catholic support for the schismatic Living Church Movement which had been fostered by the Bolsheviks in 1922 in an attempt to undermine continuing popular support for the Russian Orthodox Church. The negotiations between Rome and Moscow collapsed in 1927, however, and, in preparation for future missionary work, a Pontifical Russian Seminary, the 'Russicum', was created in 1929 as part of the Pontifical Oriental Institue for the instruction of Russian converts to Catholicism.[20]

Thus there were both general and specific areas of cooperation in foreign affairs between Italy and the Holy See in the years prior to the conclusion of the Lateran Agreements. There was a mutual interest in the welfare of Hungary, the international outcast of the 1920s. Both Italy and the Holy See had expansive goals in the Balkans and cooperated in some of their approaches to Rumania and Bulgaria and, in particular, to Albania. Finally, they were able to work together in their approaches to some of the littoral states and colonies of the eastern basin of the Mediterranean.

The Hungarian Relationship

The inauguration of Mussolini's Balkan policy through his alliance with Hungary in 1927 was a direct affront and challenge to the Little Entente and, as such, was warmly supported by the Holy See. Representatives of the Catholic Church in Hungary, however, were initially out of sympathy with Italian goals, promoting as they did the restoration of the Habsburgs.

The Italo-Hungarian alliance began with the agreement signed in April 1927 which publicly ended Hungary's self-imposed diplomatic isolation. It was developed through the winter of 1927–8, and culminated in secret meetings between Mussolini and Count Istvan Bethlen, the Hungarian Minister-President, in Milan in April 1928. In addition to providing mutual diplomatic support, the two countries agreed on the isolation of Yugoslavia, the rearmament of Hungary with the assistance of Italian money and matériel, and on the installation of a cooperative government in Austria which could share in their revisionist plans and aspirations.[21] This tie with Hungary brought Mussolini into contact in 1927 with a variety of subversive organizations which had been looking to Budapest for aid – the anti-Zogu Albanians,[22] the Bulgarian Internal Macedonian Revolutionary Organization,[23] the Croat Rights Party of Yugoslavia[24] and the Austrian *Heimwehr*.[25]

Although Mussolini's anti-Yugoslav campaign in the Balkans was largely dependent on and facilitated by this Italo-Hungarian entente, by the end of 1928 it had become apparent that Mussolini was not very interested in the actual revision of the Hungarian frontiers. He saw the Hungarians' immediate utility to him being in the form of an external pressure on the disintegrating Yugoslav state, in spite of the fact that he knew they were more interested in central European revision directed against Czechoslovakia than in Balkan revision directed against Yugoslavia.[26] It was Bethlen's intention that the Italo-Hungarian relationship should form the basis of an eventual Italo-Hungaro-German relationship and that Hungary should play a key role in central Europe as the bridge between the great revisionist and anti-Slav powers.[27] Mussolini, however, resisted this particular scheme[28] and did not develop the Italo-Hungarian relationship any further than necessary lest he be dragged into belligerence in central Europe and away from the Balkans.[29]

The 'Neo-Baroque' regime[30] of Count Bethlen, Minister-President since 1921, had ensured domestic stability in Hungary by the consolidation of political power in the hands of the traditional ruling classes and, at the same time, had developed

Hungary's industrial capacity in order to base this stability on economic prosperity. As the Hungarian Left had been discredited by the experience of Bela Kun's Communist regime in 1919, Bethlen's domestic task had been that of achieving a consensus among the factions of the Right.

Domestic opposition to his policies from within the Right had emerged over two main issues: the restoration of the monarchy and social reform. Since 1919 the throne of Hungary had been occupied by Admiral Miklos Horthy as Regent, while a number of people had argued for the restoration of a proper monarch to this throne. The largest and most evident of the monarchist groups was the Legitimists led by Count Albert Apponyi, who sought the restoration of the Habsburgs as the legitimate rulers of the Austro-Hungarian monarchy. The Legitimist candidate was the oldest son of the Emperor Karl, the Archduke Otto, who reached the age of fifteen in November 1927. Otto's mother, the ex-Empress Zita, a woman of considerable influence and determination, worked closely with the Legitimists on her son's behalf. Representing the former high aristocracy of the Empire, the Legitimists were strongly supported by the hierarchy of the Catholic Church in their quest for the eventual coronation of Otto as the king of a restored Austria–Hungary.

Yet, the Legitimists were not particularly sensitive to Hungarian national aspirations, especially as they were felt by the Magyar landed gentry, who had played a secondary role to the German Austrians under the Habsburg monarchy. There were, consequently, other groups of monarchists who felt that a more 'Hungarian' monarch was appropriate and that the monarchy needed only to be restored in Hungary and not in Austria. These groups tended to support the candidacy of either the Archduke Joseph or the Archduke Albrecht, descendants of other branches of the Habsburg family,[31] in opposition to that of Otto.[32] The Archduke Joseph 'who had strong Magyar roots and sympathies' had been the Emperor Karl's designated lieutenant in Hungary in 1918[33] and was known to have considerable support within the Hungarian general staff and among circles close to the Regent Horthy.[34]

Bethlen had deliberately avoided taking a position on this complicated 'King question' and had studiously cultivated an enigmatic posture whenever the issue was raised. Not only were the monarchists themselves divided, but there were other groups who, equally strongly, were opposed to a restoration. The states of the Little Entente were one such group. Having achieved their full independence as a result of the break-up of the Austro-Hungarian Empire in 1918, they opposed anything which might bring about the restoration of that empire, especially as agitation in that direction would be certain to find a responsive chord in certain sectors of their own populations, such as the Croats or the Slovaks.

There was also strong domestic opposition to a restoration from the Right Radical movement which was staunchly loyal to Admiral Horthy and almost equally strongly anti-Habsburg. Fervent Hungarian nationalists, the Right Radicals tended to be of Swabian German origin and to consist of that socially mobile segment of the population which was well represented in the officer corps of the Hungarian army. The spokesman and most influential leader of the Right Radicals was General Julius Gömbös, who was particularly close to Horthy, having worked with him in instituting the White Terror of 1919.

A further factor causing Bethlen to avoid the 'King question' was that a restoration would involve a Catholic resurgence. This was particularly important since a majority of the Hungarian population were Catholic, being ruled by an essentially Calvinist minority.[35] Both Horthy and Bethlen themselves were Calvinists, as were many of the Right Radicals, and this Protestant minority stood to lose much of their power by a restoration.[36]

The other issue which Bethlen sought to avoid was that of social reform and, in this case, the pressure came from the Right Radicals against the interests of the landed gentry, the aristocrats and the industrialists. Bethlen incorporated members of all groups in his governments but avoided, as far as possible, taking any position on either of these two major questions.[37]

The entire Hungarian Right did agree, however, on the necessity for a revision of the peace treaties in Hungary's favour. Yet Hungary was disarmed, diplomatically isolated and surrounded by the determined hostility of the Little Entente, the common bond of which was resistance to Hungarian revision. Moreover, Bethlen, with his concern for economic development, had put great stock in the loans which had been negotiated through the League of Nations. Good relations with France, the patron of the Little Entente, were therefore necessary, as was also the case with Britain. Moreover, the stability of the regime was necessary to attract foreign investment, most notably from Britain and the United States.

For these reasons, with no major ally, Bethlen could not attempt any overt revisionist moves and had to wait on inter-national acceptance of the argument for the legitimacy of Hungarian revisionism. The 1927 *rapprochement* with Italy rescued Hungary from its isolation and helped to reduce Bethlen's dependence on French goodwill. As Mussolini was easily convinced of the value of subsidizing dissident groups, he could also help to share the cost of this intrigue with the Hungarians, to their mutual advantage. Consequently, from 1927, Hungarian policy became explicitly dynamic and expan-sionist.[38]

The Italian entente, however, was not universally popular in Hungary. Apart from the fact that bankers feared for anything which might affect foreign investment and the Left wanted closer ties with the Little Entente, both the Legitimists and the Right Radicals were suspicious of the value of close reliance on Italy.[39]

The Legitimists were hostile to Italy because their Catholicism did not permit them to accept any alliance with a country which continued to be at odds with the Papacy; moreover, Mussolini was not sympathetic to such a major Catholic cause as the Habs-burg restoration. The Legitimists, therefore, sought their foreign support in France from those statesmen who saw the restoration as offering the Austrians a viable alternative and an impediment to *Anschluss*.[40]

The Right Radicals, on the other hand, admired the domestic policy of Fascism, but disagreed with Mussolini's foreign policy. Because of their Swabian origin, they felt a natural affinity to Germany and were prepared to condone the *Anschluss* and seek the return of the Burgenland from Austria on the assumption that Germany could then assist Hungarian revisionism. While Gömbös, like Bethlen, thought in terms of a possible German-Hungarian-Italian revisionist axis, he disliked the idea of an ex-clusive relationship with either of these powers, lest Hungary thereby lose the considerable freedom of action it could have as a bridge between them.[41]

In their willingness to cut Hungary off from its imperial past, the Right Radicals opposed any ventures designed to restore the former imperial boundaries. Thus, they promoted the *Anschluss* and opposed attempts to foment Croat separatism in Yugoslavia, standing, rather, in defence of the Serbs and the Belgrade government. In this way, they opposed Mussolini's basic thrust in foreign policy.[42] Yet, they were prepared to accept assistance in rearmament from Italy and, in this connection, sought to secure Italian support of the Austrian *Heimwehr*, which had recently acquired the patronage of the Hungarian army.[43] It was thus through Hungary and the *Heimwehr* that Mussolini was first brought into Austrian politics.

The *Heimwehr*, whose common bond was an aggressive anti-Marxism, originated as a series of provincial leagues for the defence of bourgeois interests. It emerged on the national scene in Austria as a more-or-less unified body after the Socialist riots of July 1927, and in 1928 sought funds abroad to enable it to exert pressure on the Austrian Government to take a firmer line in dealing with the Social Democrats. Although seeking help from Germany and Hungary, the *Heimwehr* was divided in its external orientation between those factions, mainly in Vienna, which aspired to bring about the *Anschluss* and those, mainly based in the Catholic countryside, who sought a restoration of the Austro-Hungarian monarchy.[44]

The Right Radicals, sympathetic to the anti-Marxist orientation of the *Heimwehr*, saw it as a possible bridge between Hungary and Germany should the *Anschluss* occur. In the context of the Italian entente, however, the army wanted to use the *Heimwehr* as the vehicle for smuggling arms from Italy to Hungary[45] and backed the *Heimwehr* with Bethlen, who tried to interest Mussolini in its support.

Bethlen's relationship with Mussolini, therefore, was always conducted with one eye on the Legitimists and another on Gömbös and the Right Radicals. If the latter could be convinced of the value to Hungary of the Italian entente and if Mussolini could be persuaded to supply arms and to subsidize the *Heimwehr*, then the German orientation of the Right Radicals could be considerably lessened in Italy's favour.

Rumania

During the 1920s, Italy and the Holy See had a common interest in extending their influence in the Balkans. They cooperated to varying degrees in different Balkan capitals.

In Rumania there was little collusion. Italo-Rumanian relations remained amicable throughout the 1920s[46] and the first
concordat with an Orthodox country was that concluded with
Rumania in 1927, although it was not ratified by the Rumanian
Government until 7 July 1929, owing to the need to secure Orthodox acquiescence to this delicate agreement. Through the Rumanian Concordat, the territories received from Hungary after 1918
were placed under Rumanian dioceses, so that the ecclesiastical
boundaries were brought into line with the political. In return for
this, the position of the Catholic Church in Rumania was regulated and its practice of both the Latin and the Eastern rites was
recognized.[47] When the Rumanian Orthodox Patriarch sent Orthodox students to the Pontifical Oriental Institute in 1928, this
was a good sign that the *rapprochement* between the Roman and the
Rumanian churches was developing positively.[48]

Albania

In Albania, on the other hand, there was much more evidence of
collusion between Italy and the Holy See. The starting point for
Mussolini's Balkan policy lay in Italian control over Albania.
From economic assistance to President Ahmed Zogu in 1925,
Italian involvement had expanded through the Pact of Tirana of
November 1926 into public Italian support of Zogu's regime.

Catholicism existed among only a small percentage of the Albanian population, the bulk of which was either Moslem or Greek
Orthodox. The Catholic stronghold in Albania was near Scutari
among the hill tribes of the north who had a history of independent behaviour. These tribes, in particular, disliked and distrusted Ahmed Zogu[49] and, in reaction to the 1926 Treaty of Tirana,
revolted against him with Yugoslav support under the leadership
of their priests.

Both Zogu and the Italians recognized the necessity of making
the former's regime acceptable to these northern Catholics. To
Zogu, this was a question of political survival and thus, following
the suppression of the 1926 revolt, he named a delegation to negotiate a concordat and made plans to visit the Pope during a proposed visit to Rome. The Italian motives, on the other hand, were
more complex and more extensive. In the first place, they had to
help Zogu remain in power and thus had to use their influence

with the Vatican to help secure Catholic loyalty to Zogu in
Albania. Beyond this, however, Baron Aloisi, the Italian Minister in Tirana, saw that Catholicism could serve as a useful
vehicle for Italian cultural penetration, especially if the Albanians could be encouraged to establish an autocephalous Orthodox church, freed from Greek influence, which might then be
brought into communion with the Church of Rome.[50] On 3
March 1927, in a series of recommendations to Mussolini on the
consolidation of Italian influence in Albania, Aloisi laid considerable stress on the development of a religious policy and outlined
the general guidelines for such a policy, to include bringing the
Scutari Catholics to a better acceptance of Zogu, possibly
through Italian subsidies to their clergy, promoting the conclusion of an Albanian concordat and the establishment of a
Uniate Church in Albania, and attempting to bring the Albanian
Orthodox closer to Italy.[51]

This policy was obviously accepted by Mussolini and became
the guiding directive for all subsequent Italian relations with
Catholicism in Albania. A few days after Aloisi's memorandum
was written, Dino Grandi, the Under-secretary at the Foreign
Ministry, met Father della Pietra, the Apostolic Delegate to
Albania, and Father Tacchi-Venturi, the Pope's personal envoy
to Mussolini, and announced that, if the clergy of Scutari could be
turned from their support of Yugoslavia, Italy would provide the
Church in Albania with financial assistance: 'the Italian Government is disposed to take account of the religious necessity of
Catholicism in Albania, of which it only desires to become the
natural protector'. That this proposal was received by della
Pietra in the presence of Tacchi-Venturi, the 'Pope's man', suggests that the Pope was more than willing to accept this Italian
patronage in Albania, for the chances of an independent Vatican
success in proselytizing were minimal.[52]

In September 1927, Zogu accepted further Italian conditions
for the creation of a protectorate, including a defensive alliance,
the transformation of Albania into a kingdom and the creation of
a ruling dynasty.[53] This agreement was sealed by the conclusion
of the defensive alliance in the second Treaty of Tirana in November 1927 and, in the following month negotiations were opened
for an Albanian concordat.[54] Although accepting Italian sponsorship of these negotiations in order to gain the loyalty of the Scutari
Catholics, Zogu tried to maintain his independence by turning

the negotiations against the Italians and insisting that no foreigners should be appointed bishops or archbishops in Albania, as had been the case in the recent appointment of an Italian as Bishop of Durazzo. The Vatican, however, would not accept this condition any more than it would accept divorce or civil marriage being included in the new Albanian Civil Code and the negotiations broke down in January 1928.[55]

Sola, Aloisi's successor in Tirana, followed and developed the religious policy. In the summer of 1928, the Albanian Synod of the Orthodox Church broke definitively from the Oecumenical Patriarch at Constantinople. This left the naming of an Albanian metropolitan as the only step remaining before an Albanian autocephalous Orthodox church was fully established. Sola followed these developments carefully, interpreting them all as a means of reuniting the Orthodox Albanians with Rome and, in order to hasten the naming of the metropolitan by King Zog (as Ahmed Zogu became on 1 September 1928) even suggested that Italy would like this move delayed for some months – a guarantee that Zog would act immediately in order to assert his independence.[56] The Albanian Orthodox Church was thus created on 11 February 1929 (the day of the signing of the Lateran Agreements), when Giovanni Vissarion was created Metropolitan of Tirana in a ceremony in which he was assisted by a Serb Orthodox bishop.[57] Sola was very satisfied with Vissarion who, although forced to cooperate temporarily with Serb Orthodoxy against the Greeks, had already expressed his intentions to Sola of falling in with Italian plans and eventually leading his Church to Rome.[58]

Bulgaria

Mussolini's ties with Bethlen's Hungary had led in 1927 to Italian subsidization of the Internal Macedonian Revolutionary Organization (IMRO). This was a terrorist organization, based in Bulgaria, pledged to free Macedonia from Yugoslav control. The Italian subsidy was designed to prevent a *rapprochement* between Yugoslavia and Bulgaria. However, while Italian interest in Bulgaria was initially limited to this secret subsidization of IMRO, the Vatican in the mid-1920s was making positive progress in this country. Relations with the Bulgarian Orthodox Church were being dealt with by the Apostolic Visitor to Bulgaria, Monsignor Angelo Roncalli (later Pope John XXIII) who, in 1926, was making considerable headway in discussing church union with Orthodox Archbishop Stephan and in securing the support and sympathy of the Bulgarian Government. Roncalli's work was complicated, however, by the opposition and attacks of some Bulgarian Orthodox clergy as well as by the activities of the French and Italians who saw opportunities for political advantage should Roncalli succeed in returning Bulgaria to Rome.[59]

The Maglione–Briand Agreement of 1926 restoring liturgical honours to France in the East, providing that the host government had no objection, posed a direct threat to Roncalli's work in Bulgaria. The French attempt to secure these honours could only annoy the Bulgarians and identify the Roman Catholic Church as the vehicle of a foreign power. Roncalli, accordingly, in March 1927 invited the Italians to protest at the granting of these privileges so that the Bulgarian Government could force the Holy See to suspend them in Bulgaria.[60] Although Italy did not immediately respond and, in fact, saw the advantage of having the Bulgarian people turn against the French,[61] a protest was eventually made through Tacchi-Venturi.[62]

Mussolini had begun to subsidize the terrorist IMRO during 1927[63] but a new possibility of Italo-Bulgarian *rapprochement* opened following a visit by King Boris to Italy in November of that year when he expressed an interest in marrying Princess Giovanna of Savoy, daughter of the King of Italy. Britain, France and Yugoslavia were united in their opposition to such a marriage[64] but Boris, by mid-December, had made up his mind to go ahead.[65]

The Italian Minister in Sofia gave the project his full support and it also acquired the tacit support of Monsignor Roncalli. Roncalli supported the marriage as a means of having a Catholic queen in Bulgaria and, possibly, of having some of the children raised as Catholics, although he accepted that the Church would probably have to concede that the heir of the throne would be raised as an Orthodox. Roncalli believed that the return of Bulgaria to Rome might be facilitated in this way. The more enthusiastic Roncalli showed himself over the marriage, however, the greater was the opposition of the Holy Synod of the Bulgarian Church and the Italians began to worry lest they lose out on this marriage over the religious issue.[66]

During the summer of 1928, the Yugoslavs took the initiative in an attempt to restore their relations with Bulgaria and a certain encouragement was simultaneously provided the Bulgarian Church by Serb Orthodoxy, presumably in resisting the entreaties of Rome.[67] Yugoslav pressure on Bulgaria intensified in September after IMRO had been particularly active, to the extent that Liapcev, the Bulgarian Prime Minister, accepted that the marriage and the subsequent tie with Italy was the only way of protecting Bulgarian independence against Yugoslavia. It was the Vatican which now stood in the way and Boris indicated that he would go ahead immediately with the marriage if the Vatican would give him special dispensation to raise the heir to the throne in the Orthodox Church.[68] Roncalli could only point out that no such dispensation was possible in advance but that, for the sake of good relations with Bulgaria, the Pope might make an exception and not protest after the fact.[69] As the Pope gave no evidence of a willingness to make this exception, it would appear that Roncalli was more optimistic than Pius XI of eventual success in returning Bulgaria to Rome.

The Eastern Mediterranean to 1927

In his quest to establish and secure Italy's status as a great power, Mussolini looked on the eastern basin of the Mediterranean as the 'link in a chain which reached to the Levant and the zone of the Red Sea',[70] where Italian power might ultimately be exercised without hindrance from others.

There were a number of components to Mussolini's Mediterranean strategy. The first consisted of Italian control of the Balkan peninsula. The second involved friendship with Great Britain, who was expected to acquiesce in Italian hegemony in the eastern Mediterranean just as it had acquiesced in French hegemony in the western basin of that sea. So long as there was no interference with British interests and shipping routes, Britain need have no cause for complaint. France, with its mandates in Syria and the Lebanon, its Balkan interests and colony of French Somaliland on the Red Sea, also had considerable interest and influence in the area. Mussolini intended to recognize French preponderance in the western Mediterranean in return for France granting Italy a free hand in the Balkans and the eastern Mediterranean.

Apart from such general diplomatic considerations, Italy also sought to exercise direct influence and control on the shores of the eastern Mediterranean and the Red Sea. Fundamental to all imperial calculations and policy in the 1920s was the problem of unrest in the Italian colonies of Libya and Somalia. Troops, money and prestige had been committed to Libya, which had been captured from the Turks in 1912, in an effort to subdue the Bedouin tribesmen, especially those of Cyrenaica who were organized and inspired by the politico-religious leadership of the Senussi. From 1923, the Italians had sought to pacify Libya by force, only to be confronted and frustrated by the guerrilla tactics of the Senussi under their capable leader, Omar el Muktar.[71] Both Italian prestige in the Middle East and Italian freedom of military manoeuvre were coming, by the late 1920s, to depend heavily on a settlement of this particular war[72] which was not concluded until 1932. Similarly, Governor DeVecchi of Somalia had been working since 1923 to pacify the tribes in that colony; he eventually achieved success in 1928.[73]

One of the institutions which had initially proved useful to the Italians in their overseas ventures was the Roman Catholic Church, especially in those provinces served by Italian missionary orders. Moreover, in the developing *rapprochement* between Italy and the Holy See in the late 1920s, the Vatican was quite prepared to encourage the Italian Government by giving it the impression that a resolution of the Roman Question would result in increased Italian influence and prestige in the mission field. Such could only be a superficial impression, however, limited to colonies of Catholics, mostly European, practising Latin rites in the East. The Vatican had been particularly sensitive to the emergent nationalism of Asia and Africa as a result of the First World War and had appreciated that the Roman Catholic Church must no longer be seen as a vehicle for European cultural influence if it were to retain its position in those continents. Consequently, in his Apostolic Letter, *Maximus Illus*, of November 1919, Pope Benedict XV had urged all missionary bishops to 'forward the movement for the building up of a native clergy'.[74] This was coupled with the institution of the Congregation of the Eastern Church in 1917, to encourage Catholics in the East to practise their religion in a form more compatible with the traditional culture. Pius XI followed Benedict's policy, sensing that the alternative to Oriental rites and a native clergy could well be the spread of Bolshevism in its most virulent anti-Christian and anti-European form.[75] There was, therefore, little chance of the Church serving the interests of Italian cultural influence after 1918 as it had served those of France in the days before the First World War.

Both 1926 amd 1927 were years of Italian concentration on extending its influence in the Balkans and on pacifying its colonies. As a consequence, Italy cooperated closely with Great Britain in the Red Sea and the eastern Mediterranean.[76] At the same time, the Italians were sensitive to the advantage which had been granted to France by the Holy See in December 1926, with the rèstoration of liturgical honours in the East, and protested to the Vatican in April 1927 that this gave the French an unfair advantage in the Middle East, and that it worked against the best interests of those Italian religious who were resident in Syria and the Lebanon and who would thereby be forced to accept the superiority of an alien national authority in religious matters.[77]

The awkward fact was that such an issue arose at the same time as definite moves were being made in Italy for a settlement of the Roman Question. The Vatican was fully aware that the promise of some cultural benefits in the Middle East for Italy would be an enticement to a satisfactory conclusion of these negotiations.[78] Although unable to renege on its promises to France, the Holy See and Church authorities did make other proposals to the Italians. In April 1927, the Procurator-General of the Consolata Mission in Rome offered to intervene at Alexandria in the selection of a successor to the Coptic *Abuna* of Ethiopia, so that the new *Abuna* would be sympathetic to Italian interests. Although the Italians appreciated such consideration, it was felt that such a move might be rather premature.[79] In October of that same year, the Vatican mooted the possible establishment of a large seminary at Asmara in Eritrea to train native priests for mission work in East Africa. Gasparini, then Governor of Eritrea, was most enthusiastic about the prospects which could be opened for Italian influence by developing such a body of Italian-trained priests[80] and Italy confirmed to the Vatican its definite interest in such a project.[81]

Such gestures by the Vatican were deemed to be entirely appropriate and were well received as some Italians fully expected to use Catholicism as one of the binding links in their intended sphere of influence. In 1926, Fascist spokesmen were referring openly to 'Italy's "imperial mission" and the links which connect it inexorably with the Catholic Church'.[82] On 22 February 1927, the Chancellor of the Order of the Holy Sepulchre, Monsignor Perrin, was advised by his Fascist correspondent, Commendatore Fontana, that

> It is to be noted how greatly H. E. Mussolini has at heart the prestige of Catholicism and Italy in Palestine; and how it is always the wish of the Duce to acquire greater influence through our joint institutions which have such historical and political importance.[83]

Bastianini, the Secretary-General of the *Fasci italiani all'estero*, was very concerned in 1926 about the prevalence of Masonry in the Italian community in Egypt and about how this movement would have to be weakened in the interest of Catholicism.[84] Moreover, the Fascist Government was giving a free passage to all Italian missionaries bound for the Middle East at this time.[85]

It was primarily in Palestine that the Italians intended to act as the spokesmen for Catholicism. Here, the way had already been well prepared for Mussolini by the Latin Patriarch of Jerusalem, Monsignor Aloysius Barlassina. Appointed Patriarch in 1918, with pastoral responsibilities for the Latin rite in Palestine, Transjordan and Cyprus, Barlassina had sought to make the Patriarchate virtually an Italian fief. Almost as soon as he arrived, he prohibited the teaching of French in the French schools of the Patriarchate while putting no such prohibition on Italian. He also deliberately saw that preference in high appointments was given to Italians. Moreover, places in his seminary could always be found for Italian students while there were frequently no vacancies for British or French students or, in violation of Vatican policy, for Arab students. Barlassina was known by his Italian friends as '*L'Italianissimo*' and was consequently an ideal proponent of influence for Fascist Italy.[86]

There were, however, problems associated with Italian support of Catholicism in the Holy Land. In the first place, Palestinian Catholics were a small, finite group, offering little basis for extensive Italian influence. Aware of this, Pedrazzi, the Italian Consul-General in Jerusalem, advised Mussolini on 19 May 1927 that Italy might be better served by transferring its interest and money to become the sponsor of Zionism in Palestine.[87]

Moreover, within Catholicism, due to Pius XI's promotion of native clergy and Oriental rites, priests of the Oriental Rite were being given preference over those – notably the Italians – of the Latin rite.[88] Such a conflict within the Church does much to account for the strong support given by Barlassina to the Italian interest and consequently to that of the Latin Rite. In spite of Pedrazzi's suggestions, however, Mussolini decided, at the end of 1927, to continue with his emphasis on Catholicism in Palestine,[89] while making limited approaches to the Zionists.[90]

The Eastern Mediterranean in 1928

The year of 1928 was one of considerable diplomatic success for Italy. Not only had its ties with Hungary and Albania given it a strong position in the Balkans but, by his Senate speech of 5 June, Mussolini had put Italy forward as the leader of the revisionist camp in Europe. The tribes of Somalia had also been pacified. This meant that Italy could develop a more active policy in the Mediterranean and Red Sea than it had previously been able to do.

This confidence was reflected in Mussolini's rejection of British tutelage in the eastern Mediterranean and the Red Sea during that year. In the winter of 1927–8, Italy had entered into direct negotiations with Ras Tafari, the ruler of Abyssinia, for the concession of a motor-road linking Eritrea and Italian Somaliland through Abyssinian territory. Ras Tafari had agreed to this concession on condition that Italy sign a treaty of friendship and arbitration with Abyssinia,[91] and such a treaty was concluded on 2 August 1928. Not only did this treaty work to the apparent disadvantage of the French who had posed as the traditional protector of Abyssinia[92] but, by being a direct negotiation between Rome and Addis Ababa, it also represented a distinct break from joint Anglo-Italian manoeuvres in dealing with the Abyssinians.

In a similar way, Italian negotiations with Greece and Turkey in 1928 represented an independent Italian bid to become the chief arbiter of the chronic conflict of the eastern Mediterranean. Responding to a Turkish initiative of February 1928,[93] Mussolini had, by April, secured both Greek and Turkish agreement to the conclusion of three pacts to secure an Italo-Turko-Greek entente. Although the Italo-Turk pact was signed on 30 May and the

Italo-Greek pact on 23 September, the Turko-Greek pact was not realized until 1930 and was made particularly difficult to achieve because of changes in the Greek Government. The most important development from this initiative, however, was the close ties which had developed between Italy and Turkey by the end of 1928 and which effectively established Italy, without British assistance, as the dominant power of the eastern Mediterranean.[94]

Since relations between the Holy See and Turkey and Greece had not been easy, there was little chance for the Vatican to benefit from these Italian initiatives. Relations with Greece had been aggravated early in 1929 by the breakaway of the Albanian Orthodox Church from ties with Greece[95] and in Turkey the Government had prevented the opening of foreign schools and other institutions, which meant that Catholic missionary work in that country had been particularly difficult. In February 1928, the Apostolic Delegate to Turkey, Monsignor Rotta, had a secret meeting with the Turkish Foreign Minister, Roussdi Bey, to seek a clarification of relations between the Vatican and Turkey. As Rotta was strongly supported by France in this mission, the Italians also gave their support. Little, however, came of the meeting.[96] With the conclusion of the Lateran Agreements, Rotta immediately sought out the Italian Ambassador at Ankara and asked him to use his good offices to help restore normal relations between the Vatican and Turkey.[97] The Ambassador did raise the matter with Roussdi Bey, only to be told that reactionary Moslem elements in the Turkish Council of Ministers were opposed to any dealings with other religions and thus nothing could be done.[98] As further cooperation with the Vatican would be unproductive, the Italians quickly allowed the question to lapse.

The Italian Government continued to promote Catholic interests and Catholic rights in the Middle East in 1928. The Italian financial contribution to the missionary work of the Church had increased remarkably in 1927[99] and, early in 1928, Federzoni, the Minister of Colonies, allowed for an allocation of 7,500,000 lire in the public works budget for Libya for the construction of churches, arguing that such an expenditure

> is indispensable to assure spiritual assistance in our colonies and constitutes besides a necessary moral affirmation of the dominant race which reunites itself, in North Africa, to the tra-

dition of the church of St. Augustine.[100]

Coupled with this financial assistance went a deliberate Italian attempt to act as the spokesman for Catholic rights in the Levant. Although Italy had supported Vatican approaches to the Turkish Government in February 1928,[101] it was in Palestine that the Italians were most active. In April, Prince Umberto of Piedmont, the Crown Prince of Italy, made an Easter pilgrimage to the Holy Land in a gesture designed to show Italian 'determination to defend the Catholic rights over the Holy Places and . . . that in the Orient, Italy intends to defend not only her prestige but also the Latin and Catholic traditions'.[102] The Italians very carefully weighed up the impression which this visit made in the Levant.[103] Some months later, Mussolini protested to Britain that Catholic rights were not being protected in Palestine and that the British authorities were not sufficiently controlling the Arab opposition to Catholicism.[104] Although Britain was prepared to reassure Italy over incidents connected with the visit of the Prince of Piedmont, it did not intend to accept Italy as the spokesman for Catholic interests and indicated as much in its reply of 4 December.[105] Yet the Italians were quick to reply, claiming indeed that their interests were concerned with the Italian religious community in Palestine and that, alternatively, they would challenge the British authority before the Mandates Commission of the League of Nations.[106]

The Vatican was made rather uncomfortable by these Italian attentions and, although pleased by the Palestine visit of the Prince of Piedmont, reassured the British in April of its satisfaction with the functioning of the Palestine mandate, indicating that 'the last thing it would care to see would be any interference on the part of the Italian Government'.[107] While Monsignor Barlassina arranged for the conferring of the Grand Cross of the Order of the Holy Sepulchre on Mussolini on 11 February 1929 (the day of the signing of the Lateran Agreements),[108] the Holy See was embarrassed by the Latin Patriarch and, in this same month, extended the jurisdiction of the Delegate Apostolic in Egypt to cover Palestine, Transjordan and Cyprus, thereby bringing Barlassina under local diplomatic control.[109]

Nevertheless, informal external cooperation between Italy and the Holy See helped to create a climate for the domestic settlement of the Roman Question and, in August 1928, in line with

Italian requests, the Archdiocese of Rhodes was re-established to cover the Italian Dodecanese Islands off the coast of Turkey, which had formerly been under the ecclesiastical authority of the Archbishop of Malta.[110]

3 Areas of Conflict before 1929

There were two aspects of Italian foreign policy in the 1920s that the Holy See could neither ignore nor condone, touching as they did on questions of vital importance to the Church. These concerned Italy's unsatisfactory relationships with Yugoslavia and with Austria. The Holy See found that any condition of hostility between nations with large Catholic populations, such as these, was politically intolerable as it was always in danger of being forced to take a political position. The situation with these neighbouring powers was further complicated by the territories and populations which Italy had acquired from Yugoslavia and Austria as a result of the peace settlement and which the Fascist Government was attempting to Italianize against the wishes of their Catholic populations.

Negotiations with the French

By the autumn of 1927, Italy had surrounded Yugoslavia in a manner which, by exercising pressure from a number of points, could make it respond to Italian influence. The Belgrade Government, however, neutralized the effect of this Italian diplomacy by calling in an outside patron and, in November 1927, produced the Franco-Yugoslav alliance as a direct challenge to Mussolini's ambitions. Mussolini had correctly calculated that France was reluctant to come into direct conflict with one of its Locarno guarantors and Paris had no doubt resisted Belgrade's entreaties for an alliance as long as possible. It was not, in fact, Mussolini's moves in the Balkans so much as his sending of warships to Tangiers (to enforce an Italian claim to participation in the control of that city) which had prompted the French eventually to conclude the treaty with Yugoslavia. By this treaty, the French wanted to warn Mussolini away from Yugoslavia, and to warn it not to engage in diplomatic hostilities. The Franco-Yugoslav Pact was followed by attempts on the part of both France and Yugoslavia to open negotiations with Italy.

Mussolini, too, was prepared for negotiations as he was actually building his sphere of influence in order to force France to come to terms with him and to recognize Italian preponderance in the Balkans and the eastern Mediterranean. As De Felice remarks: 'Mussolini was making anti-French policy to reach an agreement with France'.[1]

In December 1927, Mussolini had shown his willingness to recognize a predominant French influence in the western Mediterranean by his willingness to accept Italian inclusion in the Tangiers statute, thereby rejecting the possibility of keeping the Tangiers question open as a means of interfering with French control in Morocco or elsewhere in the western Mediterranean.[2] He was also prepared to settle the question of the Italians in Tunis and the frontiers of Libya but, in return, he sought from France ' a free hand in the Balkans and in the Eastern Mediterranean such that Italian political and economic expansion will not be faced with either direct or indirect French barriers'.[3] On 30 January 1928, Mussolini had set out these conditions to the French Ambassador, Beaumarchais,[4] who returned with Briand's reaction on 19 March. Briand showed himself willing to develop a treaty of friendship and arbitration and to settle the questions of Tunis and the Libyan frontiers, as well as the Tangiers issue, where the negotiations were virtually completed. No mention was made at this meeting or subsequently by the French of the question of Italian influence in the Balkans or the eastern Mediterranean.[5]

Not all members of the Italian Government were as willing to reach an agreement at this time as was Mussolini. The leading officials of the Italian Foreign Ministry such as Dino Grandi, the Under-Secretary, and Raffaele Guariglia, the Director of the Office for Europe and the Levant, believed that the settlement with France which would be in Italy's best interest would be one in which Italy would agree to support the *status quo* in the Balkans in return for generous colonial concessions from France.

According to his memoirs, Guariglia was not happy with the direction which the negotiations were taking in 1928, for he felt that

peripheral issues were being discussed while the crucial question
of relations with Yugoslavia was being ignored. Accordingly, in his
capacity as Director of the Office for Europe and the Levant, he
set about torpedoing the discussions.[6] As the Foreign Ministry
was required to submit proposals for the Italian position in the
negotiations, so Guariglia's office submitted a proposal for the
southward extension of Libya which they knew France would
reject. This proposal, which aimed at extending Libya southward
across the Sahara so that it would take in much of French Equa-
torial Africa, including Lake Chad, was ultimately designed to be
linked with the cession to Italy of the Cameroons as a mandate
and, thereby, to give Italy a complete slice of Africa from the
Mediterranean to the Gulf of Guinea.[7]

This proposal, which had earlier formed the basis of Italian colonial claims during the First World War,[8] was presented to the
French in April[9] but remained without a reply until eight months
later when the French note virtually ignored it.[10] Mussolini was
unable to convince the French to pay for a guarantee of French
North Africa yet, at the same time, he was turning down
approaches from Syrian nationalists for material aid against the
French authorities in the mandate.[11] With the Italian control of
Cyrenaica still precarious by the end of 1928, Mussolini did not
want to give the French any excuse for direct interference in that
colony.

The Problem of Relations with Yugoslavia

Yugoslavia represented the most difficult foreign issue in relations between Italy and the Holy See at this time. Opinions
within the Fascist party and Government were very much divided
on the proper policy to be followed in dealings with Yugoslavia.
Originally, the Italian Foreign Ministry, under Contarini, had
sought Italo-Yugoslav *rapprochement*, with the 1924 Pact of Rome
representing the fruit of this policy. Contarini wanted Italy to
play its role in the pacification of Europe and to seek concessions
in the colonial sphere. This represented the 'imperialist' view of
Italian foreign policy.

Opposed to this view had traditionally been the 'irredentist',
that opinion which had argued prior to 1918 for the reunification
of the South Tyrol and Venezia Giulia to Italy and which had

promoted the expansion of Italian power in central Europe and the Balkans. The 'irredentists' had largely been responsible for Italian intervention in the First World War on the side of the entente powers and for encouraging D'Annunzio in his 1919 occupation of Fiume.

When the Nationalists joined the Fascist party in 1923, both these traditional views acquired their eloquent advocates within the government and the voice of the irredentists was augmented by a very serious and determined element among the Fascists themselves. The Fascism which had evolved at the end of the First World War in Venezia Giulia (the north-eastern portion of Italy, consisting of the five provinces of Gorizia, Pola, Trieste, Fiume and Zara) had been particularly virulent, compounded as it was with an element of racism, contrasting the Italians with the Slavs of the area and thriving as it had on the example of Gabriele D'Annunzio's capture of Fiume in 1919. Within the Fascist party and government these 'Julian' Fascists were to represent a determined group who maintained a continuous pressure on Mussolini for the satisfaction of their interests.

While Mussolini was consolidating his control of Italy, he had made little attempt to shape the direction of foreign policy, giving Contarini and the officials of the Foreign Ministry pretty much a free hand. After 1925, however, Mussolini began to intervene directly in the Balkans, particularly in Albania, provoking Contarini's resignation in 1926. Because of the continuing opposition of Foreign Ministry officials to an active Balkan policy, Mussolini conducted much of this policy on his own initiative and through his own agents. The Foreign Ministry was not only unsympathetic but also at times unaware of the real nature of Italian policy in the Balkans.[12] In spite of this, Mussolini did receive considerable public support for his policy from the Julian Fascists and from the irredentist ex-Nationalist press, such as Forges Davanzati's *La Tribuna*.[13]

Closely tied to foreign policy toward Yugoslavia, and of particular interest to the Julian Fascists, was the domestic policy of denationalizing the Slovenes and Croats of Venezia Giulia. As Italy had sought *rapprochement* with Yugoslavia in 1924, little attention had been paid to a domestic policy of Italianization. As Mussolini initiated his own Balkan policy, however, he gave his approval in the summer of 1927 to the forced cultural assimilation of the Slavs of Venezia Giulia. The resulting hostility of their fellow Slovenes and Croats within Yugoslavia guaranteed that any subsequent Italo-Yugoslav *rapprochement* would become virtually impossible.[14]

These same Slovenes and Croats were also Catholics and, in Venezia Giulia, it was the parish priests who objected most strongly to requirements that religious instruction be given in Italian when their parishioners did not even understand the language. The priests thus came to lead the opposition to the Italianization programme within Italy itself and, in Yugoslavia, it was Catholic Croatia and Slovenia rather than Orthodox Serbia which were most hostile to any concessions to Italy.

Relations between Italy and the Holy See in their dealings with Yugoslavia were, therefore, extremely delicate and, although the Church had provided Italy with certain assistance in preventing Catholic opposition to the ratification of the 1924 Italo-Yugoslav Pact,[15] further cooperation was deemed virtually impossible after the accelerated Italianization programme of 1927. It was the eruption of the domestic crisis of 1928, however, which altered a number of perspectives.

Yugoslavia: The Constitutional Question

The Kingdom of the Serbs, Croats and Slovenes, conceived in 1918 as a union of the South Slav peoples and upheld by the United States at the Paris Peace Conference as a living example of the virtues of national self-determination, was marred from the outset by inherent flaws in its constitutional and political complexion. Although the Serbs and the Croats (the dominant nationalities of the new state) shared a common language, they had radically different conceptions of the constitution of the new state. As Serbia had enjoyed national independence since the late nineteenth century, Serb political leaders wanted the new kingdom to be a unitary state under Serb direction, a 'greater Serbia'. The Croats, on the other hand, had only acquired their independence from the Austro-Hungarian Monarchy in 1918, and, having chafed under the external direction of Budapest, did not want to substitute one centralization for another. They, therefore, argued that the new state should be organized on federal lines. The Serb leaders, however, did not intend to compromise, with the result that the new kingdom had been established on 1 December 1918 as a 'greater

Serbia' and, despite the strong objections of the Croats, a centralist constitution had been adopted in 1921.[16]

The most influential leader of the Croats during the 1920s was Stephen Radic, the leader of the Croat Peasant Party, who responded to the arrogance of the Serbs in control of the central government by a determined policy of non-cooperation. Only in 1925, at the urging of King Alexander, did Radic accept the constitution and enter the government for a short period. By 1928 he had again returned to the opposition when, on 20 June, he was shot and fatally wounded during a session of the *Skupstina*. The shooting and, particularly, the eventual death of Radic on 8 August served to bring the simmering Serb-Croat conflict to the boil.

Within Croatia, there were five political parties. Three of them sought their support among the peasantry and had advocated a programme of social and land reform. Although seeking concessions from Belgrade, they had not really considered separation from Yugoslavia as they had also been united in their hatred and fear of Italy. The fourth party advocated a federal Yugoslavia, but it was the fifth party, the Croat Rights Party, which initially took issue with all the others in advocating Croat separatism. Representing the Croat upper and middle classes, the Rights Party looked back to their participation in the Hungarian portion of the Austro-Hungarian Empire, when they had been united in advocating a reform of the empire along trialist lines, as opposed to the Yugoslav ideas of the Serbs and other Slav radicals. The Rights Party nourished an implacable hatred of both the Serbs and of any kind of social reform and, in the 1920s, looked to separation from Yugoslavia and, if possible, a return to Hungary.[17] Always a small party on the right-wing of the Croat opposition, the Rights Party benefited from the defection of Radic when he joined the Government in 1925 and the Rights Party at that time had sought to take the leadership of the Croat opposition. The leader of the party in Zagreb, the capital of Croatia, was Ante Pavelic, while Gustav Percec ran the party newspaper.[18]

Although the Rights Party maintained close contact with the Hungarian Government, it was not until June 1927, after the conclusion of the Italo-Hungarian Agreement and presumably at Hungarian insistence, that they made initial contact with Italy.[19] The Italians were interested but reserved in their dealings with these Croat separatists in 1927, retaining contacts more to please the Hungarians than out of any disruptive intent.[20] Mussolini's original intention had been that of isolating Yugoslavia so that its politics could pose no threat to Italy. Domestic Yugoslav conflict was, of course, beneficial in weakening the Belgrade Government but, because of the Italian programmes in Venezia Giulia, it could be extremely unwise politically for Italy to be involved in direct encouragement of these conflicts. A separate Croat state, unless under the direct control of Italy, could pose a real threat to Italian domestic interests by rallying and supporting the Croats in Italy; nor was Mussolini interested in a separate Croatia united with Hungary for the same reasons.

After the shooting of Radic, all the leaders of the Croat political parties came together in opposition to Belgrade and now looked to either Italy, Hungary or Britain for support of a separatist movement.[21] At the end of July, Galli, the new Italian Minister in Belgrade, sent Mussolini a long despatch, in which he argued that the Croats were bent on separation, that Radic, still lying wounded, was prepared to countenance an independent Croatia with Italian support, that the alternative could be a Croat reunion with Austria and even the reconstitution of Austria–Hungary, and that Italy should act positively so that, should Radic die, the Croat movement would continue to be oriented toward Italy. A reconstituted Austria-Hungary would certainly not be to the Italian interest nor would a reassertion of Serb dominance within Yugoslavia.[22] With the death of Radic on 8 August, continuing Italian contact was established and maintained with the Croat leaders[23] and, in mid-September, Mussolini advised his diplomatic corps to give all possible support to the Croat cause.[24]

At the same time, Mussolini sought to make quite clear his attitude toward any reconstitution of Austria-Hungary and to the restoration of the Habsburgs. He suspected that Hungary might encourage the Croats in such an effort behind his back[25] and that the *Heimwehr* might be party to such a plan.[26] As the *Heimwehr* were planning a major demonstration in Weiner Neustadt in October 1928, Mussolini, in an interview with an Hungarian journalist, published early in October, declared

that any idea of restoring the Habsburgs would signify a mortal danger for the revision of the Treaty of Trianon and that

the destiny of the Bourbons, of the Orleans, and of the Napo-
leons also awaited the recently dethroned dynasties.[27]

Taking his cue from Mussolini's interview, Bethlen echoed this
anti-Habsburg note in speeches delivered a week later[28] and, by
referring to the Hungarian claim against Austria for the Burgenland, stirred Austro-Hungarian animosity. In so doing, Bethlen
was reassuring Gömbös and the Right Radicals who were upset
by Hungarian ties with the Croats. Subsequently, Bethlen and
Mussolini developed parallel contacts with the Croats.[29] Yet
Mussolini, being much more cautious than the Hungarian,
expressed strong reservations that the time was ripe for any overt
Italian action in support of the Croat movement.[30]

The latter half of 1928 had seen increased tension between
France and Italy, partly over further evidence of French sympathy for the Italian *fuorusciti*, which enraged Mussolini,[31] but
primarily over the domestic political crisis of Yugoslavia. Only on
21 December did Beaumarchais return the French reaction to the
proposals of 19 April. This proposal allowed for a new arrangement on Tunis and a Franco-Italian treaty of friendship and arbitration, but it only provided for the cession of the oasis of Tummo
on the Libyan frontier to satisfy Italian claims under the Treaty of
London.[32]

Mussolini's initial reaction to these proposals was quite favourable, indicating to the British Ambassador, Sir Ronald Graham,
on 7 February that 'his own impressions with regard to the
French proposals were distinctly satisfactory' but indicating that
they could not really be considered in isolation from the Yugoslavian situation, the solution for which one would have to wait;[33]
it was in terms of the degree of French support for King Alexander that Mussolini would judge the true worth of the French proposals. The Yugoslav crisis was to be the test of French
compliance with Mussolini's request for a free hand.

King Alexander visited Paris in November[34] where he was,
apparently, urged to institute a royal dictatorship and was
granted a loan for military supplies to be acquired from Czechoslovakia.[35] On 4 January, Alexander accordingly suspended the
Yugoslav Constitution in an attempt to restore order and internal
cohesion to his country. A man of undoubted political honesty,
courage and conviction, Alexander sought through this dictatorship to remodel his kingdom in such a way that the national in-

terest would prevail over sectional interests. To this end, he sought to redefine internal political boundaries, reorganize the constitution and civil service and provide truly national institutions for his divided country. Symptomatic of the theme of his programme was the change of the official name of the state in 1929 from the Kingdom of the Serbs, Croats and Slovenes to the Kingdom of Yugoslavia.[36]

Although Alexander sincerely sought to rise above sectional interests, he was never able to convey this sincerity to the Croats. General Zivkovic, the former Head of the Palace Guard, was made Prime Minister but, with the exception of the Slovene priest, Father Korosec, the Cabinet was entirely Serb, leading the Croats to interpret the royal rule as a more effective means of imposing Serb rule on the other nationalities.[37]

Confronted by this new determination of the King, the Croat leaders viewed their prospects pessimistically.[38] Pavelic broke with his gradualist allies when, on 7 January, he converted his political movement into the terrorist organization, the *Ustasa*, to be modelled on IMRO and sworn to conduct a 'Holy War' against the Serbs by all available means.[39] With increasing repression in Croatia, many of the opposition leaders left Yugoslavia at the end of January[40] and, by the end of February, it was reported that the internal opposition had been broken by the dictatorship.[41]

Yugoslavia: The Religious Question

Underlying and closely related to this Serbo-Croat political struggle was the religious question of Yugoslavia. In pre-war Serbia, the Orthodox Church, to which the majority of the population belonged, had been the State Church and, as such, had received its due rights and privileges. With the addition of the Roman Catholic Croats and Slovenes in 1918, however, the Orthodox Church found itself confronted by an almost equal number of Roman Catholics and in a minority when all the religious denominations of Yugoslavia were considered.[42] King Alexander, himself an Orthodox Serb, realized that, if the Croats and Slovenes were to accept the Yugoslav Constitution, some concordatory arrangement with the Vatican would be necessary to guarantee certain rights to the Catholic Church. Thus, negotiations for the concordat had been opened in 1925, only to founder on the strong opposition of the Orthodox hierarchy.[43]

The major issues in the negotiation, in addition to the usual questions of Church rights and property, had concerned the use of the Old Slavonic language for the litany, on which the Vatican was reluctant to make concessions, and the disposal of the Institute of St Jerome of the Slavs in Rome which had been reclaimed by the Yugoslav Legation after the 1924 Italo-Yugoslav Agreement, in spite of the fact that the Vatican also had its own claims on the building.[44] The greatest concern of the Orthodox clergy, however, was the proselytizing activity of the Catholic Church in Yugoslavia and this was what had really forced the breakdown of negotiations.[45]

The Vatican and the Yugoslav Catholic hierarchy stood aside from the political conflicts between Serbs and Croats in the 1920s. Because of its eventual interest in a concordat and because a political position could only complicate its missionary goals, throughout the 1920s the Vatican maintained correct relations with the legal government of Yugoslavia. Moreover, while the Croats were in conflict with Belgrade, the Catholic Slovenes, whose fellows within Italy were being persecuted by the Italians, sought the support of the Serbs against the Italians. Father Korosec, the leader of the Slovenes, participated in the national government in opposition to the Croats. The position of the Church, therefore, was a delicate one and could potentially become more delicate should open hostilities erupt between Italy and Yugoslavia.

After Radic's death, King Alexander had appointed Father Korosec as Prime Minister in an attempt to prevent the Serb-Croat conflict being defined on religious lines.[46] In spite of the hopes of the Croat leaders that the Vatican would allow the Croat clergy to act according to their political conscience,[47] there was no evidence of this occurring. In fact, it was suspected in November 1928 that Father Korosec had been in close touch with Monsignor d'Herbigny of the Pontifical Oriental Institute in a supposed attempt, under French influence, to suffocate the Croat movement.[48]

The impasse with Austria

In a similar way, the Holy See had sought to remain aloof from

Italian policy toward Austria, complicated as it was by Italian denationalization programmes in the South Tyrol, which had been acquired by Italy from Austria in 1919.

Prior to 1929, Italian hostility to Austria had been returned in kind as Austrian relations with Italy had been cool and, whenever the issue of the South Tyrol was activated, veered to the frigid. The one policy on which most politically-conscious Austrians did agree was hostility to Italy, which gave the Italians little opportunity of moving toward a *rapprochement*, even had they wanted one. The reason for this situation was to be found both in Austrian domestic politics and in the matrix of international relations.

The divisive issue was the South Tyrol, with its large proportion of German-speaking inhabitants. Although the policy of assimilating these minority groups pre-dated the March on Rome, it had been continued with fresh gusto by the Fascist Government.[49] The Italian persecution of the German-speaking minority created considerable sympathy among their fellow-countrymen north of the Brenner Pass, for whom hostility to Italy was one of the few national rallying cries left to the truncated post-war Austria.

In addition to this common concern, each of the major Austrian political groupings had other reasons for being anti-Italian. To the Social Democrats, Fascist Italy was anathema on ideological grounds and, if Austria were to look anywhere for external support, it was felt that the natural direction should be toward the liberal democracies: Czechoslovakia, France and, above all, Weimar Germany. The Social Democrats, throughout the 1920s, were strong supporters of the forbidden *Anschluss*.

Whereas the Social Democrats supported the *Anschluss* for anti-national ends, the Pan-German movement was strictly nationalist in orientation and, because of this, was particularly offended by the treatment of the Germans in the South Tyrol. Any *rapprochement* with Italy could weaken their arguments in favour of the *Anschluss*.

The clerical Christian Social Party, which formed the backbone of the Austrian Government throughout the 1920s, was hostile to the state which had kept the Pope a prisoner in the Vatican since 1870. In the South Tyrol question, the party was particularly concerned about Italian attempts to prevent German children being given religious instruction in their own language. Although the Christian Social Party, of all the Austrian parties, was least attracted by the *Anschluss*, few of its members saw an Italian tie as a viable alternative and quite a number favoured a Habsburg restoration.

Father Ignaz Seipel, the dominant figure in the Austrian Government since 1922, was fully aware of this italophobia and yet, in devising his intricate foreign policy, appreciated that a weakened Austria, dependent on international financial assistance, could not afford to cultivate the permanent enmity of Italy or any of the other great powers. This being so, the *Anschluss*, to Seipel, was completely out of the question, at least for the present, because of the potential wrath of France. Seipel showed particular interest, however, in relations with Catholic Bavaria[50] and was suspected in some circles of working for a reunion of all Catholic Germans, possibly under a new Austrian monarchy.[51] Yet, because of strong domestic feelings on union with Germany, Seipel could not cultivate cordial ties with other nations any more than he could move toward the *Anschluss*. Long under pressure to make a public condemnation of Italian policy in the South Tyrol, Seipel resisted until the winter of 1927–8 and, on 27 February 1928, much against his better judgement, finally spoke out. The result was the immediate withdrawal of the Italian Minister, and Seipel's eventual capitulation on 5 June, when he promised that Austria would not in future interfere in internal Italian matters.[52] While engaged in his delicate balancing act, Seipel was thus incapable of responding to Italian overtures had there been any.

By the end of 1928, Mussolini had shown no interest in a *rapprochement* with Austria. Having just declared himself in favour of treaty revision, he could not afford to appear sympathetic to the one country where revision would work against the Italian interest, whether it be in the South Tyrol or in the *Anschluss* with democratic Weimar Germany. To Mussolini, any commitment to Austria implied a commitment to the maintenance of the European *status quo*.

Apart from this general consideration, there were more specific factors involved. Mussolini disliked and distrusted Seipel, especially after Seipel's attack of February 1928, and had no interest in dealings with Austria while he remained in office.[53] The South Tyrol was a delicate issue within Italy and any concessions in this area, which would be the *sine qua non* for a *rapprochement* with

Austria, would meet strong opposition from both members of the Fascist party and from the ranks of the irredentist former members of the Italian Nationalist movement.

At the same time Mussolini was not particularly interested in the *Heimwehr*, although this group had posed more of a dilemma for him. On the one hand, he approved of their right-wing anti-Socialist orientation and appreciated that a quasi-Fascist regime in Austria could be of benefit to Italy. He also saw the value of obtaining a foot-hold in Austrian domestic politics, particularly if by doing so, he could consolidate his entente with Hungary. For these reasons, he had agreed in August 1928 to Bethlen's request to provide arms to the *Heimwehr*.[54]

On the other hand, the incompetence and disinterest of the *Heimwehr* in failing to collect these arms once they had been offered had greatly annoyed Mussolini and the political un-reliability of that group, when they failed to control the attacks of their followers on Italian policy in the South Tyrol, did not en-courage renewed interest on Mussolini's part.[55] Moreover, Seipel, as he became progressively more disillusioned with the functioning of constitutional democracy in Austria was giving greater support to the *Heimwehr*[56] and thus decreasing its value to Mussolini.

The Italian Foreign Ministry was rather more interested in Austria than was Mussolini. Italian support for Austrian inde-pendence could, it was believed, go a long way to ensuring both Italian security and European stability and could serve as a sign of good faith to Britain and France that Italian 'revisionism' was a responsible policy. Auriti, the Minister in Vienna, and Ricciardi, the Consul-General in Innsbruck, were the prime movers at the end of 1928 in trying to interest Mussolini in widen-ing certain cracks which were appearing in the solid wall of Austrian hostility. They reported that the *Heimwehr* had recently renounced their interest in the South Tyrol and Auriti recom-mended that Italy should follow up this pledge.[57] At the end of December, Auriti reported Seipel's views that he was prepared to give pledges on the South Tyrol in return for Italian support for a renewal of the Austrian loan, due for renegotiation in 1929,[58] and Ricciardi reported a few days later that Seipel had asked the leaders of various irredentist groups, including the *Heimwehr*, to decrease their agitation on the South Tyrol question.[59]

Although Mussolini liked Ricciardi's idea that Italian support for the Austrian loan should be used to extract concessions from Austria,[60] he did not approve of the encouragement which Auriti was giving to Seipel and, on 5 February, Grandi ordered Auriti to refrain from any further conciliatory gestures, pointing out that the time was not opportune.[61] Nor was Mussolini any more interested in following up the *Heimwehr* initiatives, as, on 16 February, he indicated to his Minister in Paris that, should Britain be in agreement, he was quite prepared to support the French plan for the internal disarmament of Austria.[62]

While the Vatican was concerned about the long-term future of Catholicism in Danubian Europe, with Austria under Seipel, Pius XI had had no cause for complaint. Although uneasy about the strength of the anti-clerical Austrian Socialists and about the demands for *Anschluss* with liberal Germany, the Pope saw some hope in Seipel's cryptic relationship with the Austrian monarchists. The Pope was also satisfied with the stability of Bethlen's regime to such an extent that he was prepared to invest the monies he obtained from the 1929 settlement with Italy in Hungarian railways.[63] The institution of the Regency in Hungary held out hope of an eventual restoration. Moreover, the clergy of central Europe were particularly active in favour of this restoration. On the tenth anniversary of the establishment of the Austrian Republic, the Papal Nuncio, Monsignor Sibylla, was reported as having studiously refused to utter the word 'republic' in a speech given in honour of that occasion.[64] Cardinal Seredi, whose appointment as Prince Primate of Hungary was claimed to have been a result of his Legitimist views in 1928,[65] campaigned actively for the Hungarian Legitimists[66] and members of the Austrian hierarchy were found to be supporting those branches of the *Heimwehr* which advocated a restoration.[67]

4 Changing Perspectives in 1929

Although the conclusion of the Lateran Agreements on 11 February 1929 was interpreted noisily in the Italian press as representing a great victory for Italy over France, especially in terms of international influence and prestige, such a claim was shown, within the year, to have little substance. It was, instead, in terms of relations with Yugoslavia and Austria that the Lateran Agreements had their most marked effect on the international position of both Italy and the Holy See.

France, Italy and the Overseas Missions

In seeking reconciliation between France and Italy, Pius XI faced a dilemma. Although both the French and Italian political Right recognized the advantage of restoring privileges to the Church, such was not the case with the Centre and Left. The result was that any *rapprochement* with the Vatican had to be justified in terms of national advantage to acquire at least the support of the Centre if not of the anti-clericals of either the Fascist or the democratic Left. Such appeals to national interest invariably augmented the conflict between France and Italy who then sought to use their increased influence with the Vatican to further their own position at the expense of the other. And yet, in order to acquire positive advantages for the Church in these countries, the Vatican had to condone these justifications in terms of the national advantage.

The French separation of Church and State had worked to the advantage of Italy in the mission field. Not only did Italy no longer have to contend with recognized French pre-eminence in the Near and Far East, but the weakening French missionary thrust meant that Italian missionary orders were able to take over mission fields formerly operated by the French. Such was the case in Egypt where the Italians were instrumental in establishing in the 1920s a new Franciscan college for native priests.[1] Such was also the case in China, Siam and India, where the Italian Salesians took over missions formerly run by the French.[2] Even in the French mandate of Syria, the Alexandretta mission was run by the Italian Carmelite order which had been established there shortly after 1905.[3] Therefore when liturgical honours were restored to the French in 1926 this did not please the Italians.

In March 1927, Grandi had protested to the Vatican, through the agency of Father Tacchi-Venturi, that Italy could not accept this decision by the Holy See which upset the *status quo* in the Levant in favour of France and he pointed out the difficult position in which this placed Italian missionaries throughout the Middle East.[4] Italy then moved to oppose French ecclesiastical privileges by trying to bring Spain into a joint protest[5] and, in the following year, sought to get Britain to join in opposition to these privileges.[6]

Even so, these French privileges did not hamper the growing warmth in the relationship between Italy and the Holy See in 1927 and 1928, a warmth which was reflected in increased Italian contribution to and participation in this missionary work of the Church.[7]

In its dealings with France, the Vatican was playing a subtle game, both by granting concessions to the French and then by using the pending settlement of the Roman Question to encourage the French to grant concessions in return. Eventually, in October 1928, the new French budget appeared with Articles 70 and 71 containing provisions for restoring certain properties to the clerical *associations diocésaines* and for providing certain support and privileges for French missionary societies. In supporting these articles against the strong criticism of the anti-clerical Left, both Premier Poincaré and Foreign Minister Briand stressed the decline in French foreign prestige as a result of its failure to support missionary activities. A *rapprochement* with the Church would, therefore, be very much in the national interest.[8] In fact, the French made much of this proposed concession to the Vatican just as the negotiations over the Roman Question were reaching a conclusion in January 1929. One observer felt that France was at last moving to restore its position with the Vatican which had recently been slipping very much in favour of Italy.[9]

The conclusion of the Lateran Agreements could have represented a major stumbling block on the path to *rapprochement*
between Paris and the Holy See, especially as the French had
been defining such a *rapprochement* in terms of enhancing French
Catholic influence abroad. Now the Italians had obviously
brought about a major diplomatic and ecclesiastical coup which,
both directly and indirectly, would react, it was believed, to the
disadvantage of France. The French press, especially that of the
Left, accepted the situation with particularly bad grace, claiming
that the Lateran Agreements represented 'the alliance of the two
Romes against the France of 1789'.[10]

The Quai d'Orsay was also visibly distressed about the implications of the agreements. It expressed its concern for French
prestige and for the future of French religious missions in the
East[11] as well as its disappointment that the agreements were not
being registered with the League of Nations, thereby becoming
part of that international *status quo* which the French were pledged
to uphold. The fact that the Lateran Agreements required no international guarantee was particularly galling to Paris.[12]

Within the French Church, there was also considerable apprehension about the significance of the agreements. Although the
hierarchy seemed to accept the new situation relatively quickly,
Catholic laymen raised many questions about the debt which the
Vatican would now owe to Italy.[13] Under the circumstances, the
French clergy took particular pains to show themselves to be good
Frenchmen, with the result that some deliberately discriminated
against the Italian community resident in France by not now
allowing religious instruction to be given in Italian.[14]

In spite of, or perhaps because of these disappointments, the
French Government persisted with their legislation on Church
property and missions, which was introduced to the Chamber of
Deputies early in March 1929 and received the approval of the
Chamber with a sizeable majority on 29 March.[15]

French misgivings about the political intent of the Lateran
Agreements were encouraged and enhanced by the behaviour of
the Italian press and the Italian clergy. The Italian press
responded with alacrity to the charges made by the French press,
pointing out that the existence of the Roman Question and of the
division between Italy and the Holy See had always worked to the
advantage of France who would naturally be very sorry to see this
dispute resolved. Other organs pointed out how the Vatican had

now at last achieved its freedom from French tutelage, which was particularly important since French Catholics always conceived of themselves as Frenchmen first and Catholics second. Even the anti-clerical Roberto Farinacci could argue that

> The universality of the Church will help Italy, making her acquire greater prestige in the world. Her name, joined with that of the Bishop of God, will pass the Alps and the oceans, symbol of wonderful accord between the pre-eminent forces of Christian civilization.[16]

The anti-French tone of the Italian press was echoed by the Italian clergy, perhaps most notably by the Archbishop of Turin, Cardinal Gamba, who, during an official *Te Deum* in his cathedral on 17 February announced that 'Now Italy is truly the eldest daughter of the Church', a reference to the title which had traditionally been held by France.[17]

However, the most striking outcome of the Lateran Pacts in the Near and Middle East was the way in which the earlier co-operation between Italy and the Holy See came to a rather abrupt end in 1929.

It had been expected that the Italians would reap some of the benefit of the Lateran Agreements in the mission field[18] and, in fact, the Italian Government lost little time in testing the continuing willingness of the Holy See to grant liturgical honours to France in the Middle East. On 21 February Grandi instructed the Consul-General in Aleppo, Syria, to see that a solemn *Te Deum* was celebrated in the church of the Italian Carmelite Fathers in Alexandretta where the Italian Vice-Consul was to receive full honours.[19] At the same time, the Italians challenged French rights to speak for Catholicism with the British authorities in Egypt.[20] The Italians were soon made aware, however, that the Lateran Agreements had changed nothing in this respect when the Superior of the Carmelite Order refused to act without new instructions from the Apostolic Delegate in Beirut.[21] The retort of the Italian Government was to order the service to be held without permission to force the Vatican to accept a *fait accompli*.[22]

The French restoration of funds and property to certain missionary orders in the spring[23] was followed in July 1929 by an agreement between France and the Vatican on the procedure for making high ecclesiastical appointments in French colonies.[24] In the autumn, squabbling between France and Italy intensified over the appointment of the new Apostolic Delegate in Iraq, with each nation urging the candidacy of one of their countrymen on the Vatican.[25]

In the Red Sea area as well, the Italians sought to utilize Catholicism to assist in their imperial aspirations. Emilio De Bono, Under-Secretary of the Colonial Ministry until September 1929 and subsequently Minister of Colonies, planned to make Eritrea a secure base for Italian expansion by developing it as a Catholic colony in contrast to the Coptic Christianity of the Abyssinians. He intended to encourage the conversion of the Eritrean natives to Catholicism. The plan, viewed suspiciously by officials in the colony itself, received Mussolini's blessing in June 1929. In the autumn, Count De Vecchi, the Italian Ambassador to the Holy See, sounded Vatican officials on the matter, only to be received with cold indifference and to conclude that the time was quite inopportune for raising such a question.[26]

The time was indeed inopportune as the Vatican was most upset by the unseemly squabbling between the 'Latin Sisters' for imperial advantage and was determined to deny them the use of the Church for these ends.[27] Not only was the Pope committed to using native clergy and the Oriental Rites wherever possible in the mission work of the Church, but he also wanted to heal the rift between the two major Catholic European powers. Neither the French nor the Italians had proved to be of much help in areas where the Vatican really needed it: for example, in an attempt to normalize relations with Turkey, in February the Apostolic Delegate had sought to open negotiations, only to be rebuffed by the Turkish Council of Ministers in spite of close Italo-Turkish friendship.[28] Moreover, the Pope had been unable to get more than mild support from Mussolini in his campaign against Lord Strickland's anti-clericalism in Malta.

The Holy See, then, would negotiate directly with non-European powers and would not rely on the influence of the European imperialists. This was the policy which guided the Congregation of the *Propaganda Fide*, and the Secretary of that Congregation, Monsignor Marchetti-Selvaggiani, was accordingly despatched on a special mission to Abyssinia in November 1929. The Marchetti-Selvaggiani mission, representing a direct approach to Ras Tafari by the Vatican to secure his permission for Catholic missionaries to continue to work in Abyssinia,[29] was a clear rejection of French and Italian patronage. The Italians were most disturbed by this mission, especially as Marchetti-Selvaggiani had a reputation with De Vecchi as 'the most authoritative anti-Italian and anti-Fascist born in Italy'.[30]

This demonstration by the Vatican was followed in December by a statement by the Pope on missionary policy, in which he warned missionaries

> against the spirit of nationalism and said that in no way must nationalist propaganda be indulged in. Nationalism was the scourge of missions and missionaries must keep aloof from it, for its boasted advantages often proved to be a mere illusion.[31]

On 3 August 1930, the first native Ethiopian bishop was consecrated in Rome.[32] By this time, the Italian Government was already aware that it could no longer count on Italian missionaries to support the imperial presence in the colonies and, instead, could only look to the advantages of developing the common bonds of Catholicism where they existed between ruler and ruled.[33]

Albania

It was in Albania that the Lateran Agreements had their most immediate effect in the Balkans. The creation of the autocephalous church at the same time as the signing of the Lateran Agreements had led to a number of rumours in Albania. One rumour had it that the new church would soon join the Uniates and, when that happened, all the Albanian Moslems would also turn Catholic.[34] Another had it that the Moslems would turn Catholic after the new church came under the influence of the Greek Church and also that Zog was about to marry an Italian and turn Catholic himself.[35] It was true that Sola, the Italian Minister, in trying to help with the creation of a dynasty, had been promoting the idea of an Italian wife for Zog,[36] possibly the Princess Giovanna, but with the rumours of Zog's possible conversion to Catholicism, his Moslem subjects had become so infuriated that, by March, Zog and Sola had agreed that it would be best to drop the marriage question for a while.[37] Zog's relationship with Catholicism was becoming perhaps the most sensitive aspect of his Italian alliance.

It would appear in fact that cooperation between Italy and the Vatican had had a better chance of success in Albania before the Lateran Agreements than after, as the Albanian suspicion of their mutual collaboration reacted against the policies of both: for Italy in the marriage question and for the Holy See in the question of the Uniate Church at Elbassan.

Collusion between Italy and the Holy See did not become evident within Albania until 21 September 1929, when a branch of the Uniate Church was inaugurated at Elbassan, the inauguration being attended by an Italian representative and by a special envoy from the Pope.[38] The Albanian Government had been ready, however, and, on the same day, it promulgated a new law on religious communities, giving the king control over all appointments, finances and religious utterances.[39] The priest who had been instrumental in the establishment at Elbassan was expelled by the Albanian Government, only to be returned under the protection of the Italian Consul, which led Archbishop Vissarion, with the support of the king, to publish a proclamation against the Uniates on 7 October.[40] The new autocephalous church did not now intend to be swallowed by Rome.

Yugoslavia

In negotiating the Lateran Agreements, the Vatican had sought concessions from the Italian Government such as the Slav and German minorities in Italy might always be provided with priests fluent in their mother tongue, regardless of whether these priests were Italian citizens or not. Given the importance of these minorities to the Fascists, such a concession by Mussolini had proven to be impossible and the Vatican was forced to swallow the eventual proviso in the Concordat that all priests must be Italian citizens and have a working knowledge of Italian, but they would be allowed coadjutors who, in addition to speaking Italian, also had fluency in the language of the minorities.[41] The complete inability of the Holy See to secure any concession in the delicate question of the Slavic minorities was an indication to practised observers in the Balkans that henceforth, where questions of the relationship of Italy and the Vatican to Slav Orthodoxy arose, the Italian position, which allowed of no concession, would always dominate.

The Lateran Agreements, by demonstrating subservience in this area, made the Catholic Church appear, perhaps for the first time, as a cultural agency of the Italian Government. Where the Holy See had been making some headway in its earlier advances to the Balkan Orthodox churches, it now started to lose ground because of these suspicions.

Certainly, Mussolini expected Vatican loyalty and co-operation in their dealings in the Balkans. The only person who does not appear to have accepted this was Pius XI. It is true that he had lost his point in the Italian Concordat but in Venezia Giulia the majority of the priesthood remained in opposition to the Italianization programmes and at least two of the five bishops of Venezia Giulia, Sedej of Gorizia and Fogar of Trieste, were also active opponents.[42] Thus, in practice, the Church had not conceded very much and could retain a relatively ambivalent position in the area. Similarly, Pius XI believed he had retained his freedom of action in Yugoslavia where the Church deliberately and conscientiously continued to remain above politics.

After the Lateran Agreements, Mussolini expected to receive greater sympathy from the Croats and the Slovenes because of the new respect of the Italian Government for their church, if not for their nationality. They were expected to have less hostile feelings toward Italy, especially if the Serbo-Croatian conflict could be defined on religious lines.

Although France represented the most important external threat to the Italian Government in the Balkans, the main external threat to the Vatican was now proving to be Britain or, more particularly, the Church of England. During the First World War, many of the Serb Orthodox clergy had received their training in Britain under Anglican auspices and, as a result, a close link had been established between the two churches, with the Church of England taking a paternal interest in the fate of the Serbian Church, particularly in the quality of its ministry and in its ability to withstand the missionary appeal of Rome. Immediately after the conclusion of the Lateran Pacts, the Anglican Bishop of Gibraltar visited Yugoslavia, having stopped at Malta *en route*, while the Archbishop of Canterbury visited Greece.[43] This Anglican interest in Yugoslavia certainly conditioned the papal attitude to British sincerity at this time.

In the spring of 1929, Mussolini recognized that France was not allowing him a free hand and was actually working against

Italian influence in the Balkans. He thus sought to bring further pressure on France to disinterest itself in that area. In late March, Italy published secret Yugoslav war plans which had come into its possession[44] and, at his meeting with British Foreign Secretary, Sir Austen Chamberlain, in Florence on 2 April Mussolini advised the latter that 'an agreement with France would be easier if it were not for her action in Yugoslavia'.[45] As Mussolini had given earlier evidence that he was prepared to accept the French colonial proposals,[46] Chamberlain, being interested in consolidating an anti-German front, advised the French of Mussolini's continuing concern over Yugoslavia.

The outcome was that the French put pressure on Yugoslavia to reach some settlement with Italy, warning Belgrade not to expect French support in any war with Italy.[47] The Yugoslavs made approaches to Italy in April[48] and again in May.[49] They also withdrew their minister from Albania where he had been involved in trying to turn the Albanians against Italy[50] but, as reinsurance, they also made approaches to Germany for possible support should France drop them in favour of an Italian *rapprochement*.[51] To be able to cope effectively with their domestic problems the Yugoslavs needed external peace at almost any price.

Mussolini was in no hurry and the Yugoslav overtures went unanswered. It was becoming quite clear that France had no intention of giving Mussolini a free hand in the Balkans and, on 29 June 1929, Mussolini rejected all of the offers which had been made by France in the previous December.[52] This was the end of this phase of Franco-Italian discussions. Although they had started with some promise in 1929, Mussolini's condition of a free hand in the Balkans was obviously not being respected by France. Where Guariglia had proposed extensive colonial concessions, Mussolini had used these in the summer of 1929 as a means of raising his 'price' as a result of the French intervention in the Balkans.[53]

One of the most important circumstances in the termination of these negotiations had been the election of a Labour Government in Britain in June 1929 which had thrown the Franco-British entente into confusion,[54] and which had created a decisive weakening of the international position of France. Where the Conservatives had believed in a close entente with France, the Labour Government preferred European pacification through direct appeasement of Weimar Germany and closer extra-

European ties with the United States.[55] The French were thus left with the option of a direct settlement with Germany in 1929 or of seeking alternatives to the British partnership. As the Italians watched these developments, they felt that Italy might well profit from this sudden isolation of the French.[56]

In addition to breaking negotiations with France in June,[57] Mussolini had made an active commitment to the Croats by finally giving refuge and assistance to Pavelic and the *Ustasa*, Percec having been established in a camp at Janka Puzta in Hungary for some time.[58]

Hungary

Italian policy in central Europe and the Balkans reached an impasse in February 1929. King Alexander had used his dictatorial powers to consolidate the authority of the central government in Yugoslavia and to break the back of the Croat opposition.[59] At the same time, warnings from Hungary about the pro-German orientation of the Hungarian General Staff[60] had indicated a deterioration in the Italo-Hungarian entente. A reassessment of Italian policy was obviously called for. Yet, the coincidence of the conclusion of the Lateran Agreements with this impasse offered new dimensions and alternatives to Italy in central Europe, where Mussolini overnight found himself *persona grata* to central European Catholicism. The support of the Austrian Christian Socials and of the Hungarian Legitimists was now made available to the Italians and Italian support was even sought for a Habsburg restoration.

When the signing of the Lateran Agreements coincided with Mussolini's strong interest in central Europe, the Pope initially seemed to have hoped that the Duce might act as the sponsor of a Catholic confederation of central Europe. Although the Pope was restrained from openly voicing this, he did allow hints to leak out in March 1929 through such persons as the Hungarian Count Karatsonyi of Vatican interest in a 'non-political Catholic bloc', consisting of a customs union between Austria, Hungary and Poland.[61]

Mussolini was not interested in such a Catholic policy and did not himself take any initiative to utilize this Catholic support. His Foreign Ministry and some of his career diplomats, however, sensed the way in which Danubian Catholics could turn their governments toward Italy. For some time, Durini di Monza, the Italian Minister in Budapest, had seen the leadership of Catholic central Europe as providing a worthwhile goal for Italian foreign policy,[62] and even before the conclusion of the Lateran Agreements, he had taken the initiative in trying to win the support of the Hungarian Legitimists for Italy. In January 1929, Durini had pointed out to Mussolini that his anti-Habsburg interview of October 1928 had given considerable distress to those fervently monarchist circles who looked to Italy to support a revision of the peace treaty.[63] It was recommended that Bethlen, who always kept his views on the monarchy very much to himself, should now be asked to clarify those views privately to Mussolini and that Italian policy should be developed accordingly.[64] The Italian diplomats in Budapest were being particularly active in trying to change Mussolini's mind since, by 30 January, they had talked to the leaders of the Legitimists and put forward a proposal designed to allay certain of the Duce's fears of a reconstruction of the Austro-Hungarian Empire; namely, that the restoration should only take place in Hungary on condition that the Habsburgs themselves renounce the Austrian Imperial throne. The Legitimists were certain that the ex-Empress Zita could be convinced of the wisdom of this plan[65] and responded to these Italian overtures with enthusiasm once the conclusion of the Lateran Agreements had eliminated their previous uncertainties about looking to Italy for support.[66]

However, only when Mussolini learned of the pro-German orientation of the Hungarian General Staff on 19 February did he try to restore his position in Hungary. He immediately invited Bethlen to send Hungarian Air Force personnel to Italy for secret training[67] and also offered to mediate in the perennial problem of the optants between Hungary and Rumania. (The optants represented claims for compensation by those former residents of Rumania who had opted for Hungarian citizenship after 1919 and had had their property confiscated by the Rumanian Government.)[68] On 1 March he received Bethlen's agent to discuss a loan to Hungary[69] and it was confirmed that Grandi would visit Budapest at the beginning of May. At the same time, Mussolini sought to secure his position with the Hungarian monarchists. At the end of April, he seemingly endorsed the Archduke Joseph's candidacy by meeting with him in Rome, producing the desired effect on the

Hungarian General Staff who were thereafter reported to be very interested in purchasing arms from Italy.[70] At the end of May, on the other hand, Mussolini received the Legitimist leader, Count Apponyi, and although not displaying any great enthusiasm for the Count or his cause, Mussolini did reverse his stand of the previous October by telling him that the restoration

> was a concern of the Hungarian people who, in the fullness of their situation as an independent people, will resolve the problem according to their needs.[71]

This approach to the monarchists was only one of a number of ventures designed to undermine the influence of the Hungarian germanophiles and, when advised early in June that a Hungarian military mission would be visiting Italy to consider arms purchases, Guariglia commented that this represented the triumph of Italy over the pro-Germans of Hungary.[72]

Yet, in spite of these moves, the Italo-Hungarian relationship remained an uncomfortable one in the summer of 1929. In June, Bethlen, conscious of forthcoming reparation negotiations, visited Paris under the wary eye of the Italians.[73] Nor were the Italians pleased by reports in July of further collaboration between the Hungarian and the German armies.[74]

Austria

In Austria, Seipel himself had sought to capitalize on the February reconciliation between the Pope and the Duce. Looking for some way to improve relations with Italy, the Austrian Chancellor stressed to the British Minister on 12 February what a triumph the Lateran Agreements represented for Mussolini[75] and, a week later, Schuller, the economic expert of the Austrian Foreign Office (in a vain attempt to interest Auriti in an Italo-Austrian loan agreement) pointed out how the *Conciliazione*

> has improved [the Italian] position here in the eyes not only of the Christian Socials, but also of the pan-Germans and even of the Socialists, having given them a more exact notion of the force and capacity of our government.[76]

In addition to his hopes for an Italian-led Catholic *mitteleuropa*, Pope Pius XI was particularly interested in an Austro-Italian *rapprochement*, as the South Tyrol put him in an impossible dilemma after the conclusion of the Lateran Pacts. The persecution of Catholic Germans in the South Tyrol by the Italian Government had put the Pope in danger of having to become embroiled in a public controversy on this issue. In March 1928, Seipel had sent the Primate of Austria, Cardinal Piffl, to Rome to ask Pius XI to mediate between Italy and Austria, but the Pope had refused to act and sent an evasive reply which Seipel then felt bound to interpret in the most encouraging manner possible.[77] Moreover, in the negotiations for the Concordat itself, Pius failed to get Mussolini to offer any real guarantee of the religious rights of the non-Italian minorities.[78] The only hope, therefore, for an improvement of the situation now lay in a direct agreement between Vienna and Rome which the Vatican hoped to promote. Certainly the clergy of the South Tyrol, after the conclusion of the Lateran Agreements, were noted as having 'assumed an openly favourable attitude' to the Fascist regime in place of their previous hostility.[79]

To encourage this *rapprochement*, Cardinal Piffl attended a special meeting of the Austrian Catholic Association on 10 March, called for the sole purpose of celebrating the conclusion of the Lateran Agreements.[80] Since Piffl served as Seipel's political and ecclesiastical confidant[81] and as Mussolini was unwilling to have any dealings with Seipel himself, one wonders whether the Vatican's urgent need for an Italo-Austrian agreement may have been one of the considerations which led to Seipel's sudden resignation as Chancellor on 3 April 1929. Suffice it to say that, given Piffl's lead, the clergy would have been active in promoting the opportunity which now existed for a détente with Italy.

The resignation of Seipel appeared to remove one of the main obstacles to Italian negotiations with Austria. Three weeks after Seipel's resignation, Auriti, by way of a critique of Seipel's attitude to Italy, let Peter, the Secretary-General of the Austrian Foreign Ministry, know that it would be possible to improve relations with Italy if the new Chancellor, Steeruwitz, were to give a definite lead in attempting to portray Italy in a new light to Austrian public opinion. 'It was not so much the effect of the illness, which had to be cured, as its causes', suggested Auriti.[82] A month later, after Steeruwitz had given evidence of a willingness to control anti-Italian demonstrations, the Italians pointed out that Italian support for the Austrian loan was contingent on Austrian control of her irredentist groups.[83]

At the same time as these explorations were occurring with the Austrian Government, the Italians were also resuming discussions with the *Heimwehr*. In March, Bethlen had made arrangements for Italy to receive a *Heimwehr* agent for discussion[84] and, in mid-June, Pabst, *Heimwehr* Chief of Staff, visited Rome where he outlined the needs of the *Heimwehr* to the Italians.[85]

This double policy of negotiating with the Austrian Government and with the group which was planning to overthrow it, reflected a basic difference of opinion between Mussolini and his Foreign Ministry. Even with the resignation of Seipel, Mussolini was not enthusiastic about negotiations with the Austrian Government. At the same time, he was seriously worried about the state of his entente with Hungary, and he wanted, as a sign of good faith to Bethlen and the Hungarian General Staff, to give his support to the Austrian *Heimwehr*. Yet, against this, was the fact that the *Heimwehr* and the Hungarian General Staff were unreliable bodies which were as prepared to look to Germany as to Italy.[86] At the same time the reports of the *Heimwehr* leadership and prospects were not very encouraging.[87]

International events were making a *rapprochement* with the Austrian Government possible and politic. King Alexander's dictatorship had, for the time being, destroyed the chances of the Croat separatists within Yugoslavia and, with the shipment of French war material to that country,[88] Mussolini was being faced with the need to look to his defensive position in the Adriatic. In addition, the election of the British Labour Government in June 1929 created uncertainties for Italy's Mediterranean and European security. Might not the British Socialists try to support their Austrian brothers by condoning the *Anschluss*?

Added to these considerations were also the views of Grandi and the Foreign Ministry, who now believed firmly that Italy should divorce its Austrian policy from Hungarian patronage. Rather than trying to appease the Hungarians as Mussolini would do, Grandi sought an independent agreement with Austria which could be used in turn to keep the Hungarians in line with Italian policy. The Foreign Ministry had not been impressed by Pabst during his visit to Rome[89] and tried to convince Mussolini of the wisdom of ignoring the *Heimwehr* in favour of an agreement with Vienna.

Mussolini wavered during the summer. The initial overtures to Steeruwitz at the end of June did not produce the desired control of the irredentist activity[90] and on 23 July Ricciardi reported that the Steeruwitz Government was really so weak that it was unable to exercise this control anyway. Instead of prolonging the life of this government by agreeing to support its loan application, Ricciardi felt Mussolini would be better advised to await the course of events, especially with a *Heimwehr coup* being planned for the autumn.[91] It was presumably these considerations that led Mussolini on 10 August to agree to provide more arms and money to the *Heimwehr*.[92]

Yet, although negotiations with Steeruwitz were held in abeyance in September, the promised Italian subsidy to the *Heimwehr* was not paid either,[93] in spite of Hungarian pressure for clarification of the Italian position in the event of a *Heimwehr coup*.[94] Mussolini had reluctantly accepted the necessity of Grandi's argument and, in appointing the latter as Foreign Minister in the middle of September, he gave Grandi a free hand to negotiate an explicit *rapprochement* with the Austrian Government.

5 Crisis over Malta

The crisis over Malta, which flared up between the Holy See and Great Britain in 1929, serves as one of the best examples of Italian reluctance to alter its foreign policy priorities as a direct result of the *Conciliazione*. In 1928 and 1929, Britain was seemingly interfering with the influence of the Catholic Church both in the Balkans and in Malta. Pius XI found, however, that, while Mussolini was prepared to offer the Church a degree of support in Malta, he was never willing to allow this support to disrupt the continuance of amicable Anglo-Italian relations.

The British colony of Malta (consisting of the two small islands of Malta and Gozo and boasting the excellent natural harbour of Valetta) was, in the early twentieth century, an important station on the British imperial sea-lane. Yet, lying only fifty miles off the coast of Sicily, and with a sizeable proportion of its inhabitants speaking Italian as their first language, the ownership and disposition of Malta were naturally also of interest to the Italian Government.

Malta was one of the few places where British and Italian territory were virtually contiguous, and it was deemed to be completely vulnerable to air attack from Italy. The security of the islands, therefore, served as a reflection and gauge of the real degree of cordiality and mutual confidence which existed between Britain and Italy. The confidence was such that, by 1935, when hostilities were suddenly threatened between the two powers over Ethiopia, Malta was judged to be completely defenceless; no attempt had ever been made to provide anti-aircraft defences against a possible Italian attack.[1]

This mutual confidence was put to a severe test in 1929 when the conclusion of the Lateran Agreements suddenly put Mussolini under considerable pressure both from Italian public opinion and from the Holy See to bestir himself on behalf of the Italian interest in Malta. The provocations emanating from Malta, however, at no time justified to the Duce the sacrifice of British friendship and confidence.

The Holy See, on the other hand, was somewhat less concerned about the importance of good relations with Protestant Britain. This was particularly the case in the 1920s when the Church of England, in seeking a *rapprochement* with the Eastern Orthodox churches, was running directly counter to Pope Pius XI's own ambition to lead some branches of Orthodoxy to Rome.[2] As both Italian and Catholic interests were involved in the Maltese crisis, the Vatican, becoming directly involved in the dispute after the conclusion of the Lateran Agreements, hoped that Mussolini would demonstrate his new loyalty to the Catholic cause.

Maltese society had traditionally been dominated by the Roman Catholic Church. Under the Knights Hospitaler of St John of Jerusalem from the middle ages to the end of the eighteenth century and under the British Empire since 1813, the Church was the institution which gave substance, continuity and direction to the lives of the Maltese people. In the absence of organs of local government, the parish priest had played an important political role, using his influence with the local ecclesiastical hierarchy to represent the interests both of individuals and of the local community; the hierarchy, in turn, used its considerable influence with the governing power in support of the lower clergy. The Church, thus, traditionally served as temporal and spiritual patron to the Maltese people. In this fashion, rural Malta was a model of the clerical organic society whose basis had not been challenged until the introduction in 1921 of representative government.[3]

The religious and social unity of the countryside was, however, combined with a linguistic and cultural diversity in the towns. Although most of the people spoke Maltese, mainly a Semite language, the middle and upper classes had traditionally spoken Italian, the language of the courts and of the administration until the British occupation in 1798. Although English became the language of administration in the early nineteenth century,[4] the British Government had made no further attempt to alter the status of English or Maltese for many years. By the end of the nineteenth century, the administrative class spoke English, the commercial and professional classes spoke Italian, and the rest of the population spoke Maltese.

Within the British Empire, Malta had been ruled directly as a Crown Colony from 1813 to 1887, at which time a form of representative government had been introduced when the elected representatives had become a majority on the Executive Council. This provision for a measure of local autonomy had, however, been revoked in 1903 and it was not until 1919 that Malta had been promised full self-government 'in all matters of purely local concern',[5] a promise which had been embodied in a new constitution in 1921.

This constitution, establishing a diarchical form of government, reserved the language question, the provision of religious toleration, the civil list and matters related to imperial defence to the competence of the Imperial Government.[6] All other issues were to be dealt with by a Legislative Assembly of thirty-two elected members and a Senate of seventeen members, consisting of seven members elected at large and two members each chosen by the clergy, the nobility, the university, the Chamber of Commerce and the Trades Union Council.[7]

The earliest political group to seek mass support had been the 'anti-Reform' group organized in the 1880s by Dr Fortunato Mizzi. As part of its campaign for local self-government, this group had claimed that British attempts to replace the use of Italian by the use of English would destroy the local rights and culture of the Maltese. This argument was improved upon in subsequent years when it was claimed that the English language could serve as a useful vehicle for disseminating Protestant ideas and that the retention of Italian was the only safe means of protecting Maltese Catholicism. This thesis had had a telling effect on the Italian-speaking upper and middle classes who were concerned about their status, and on the lower clergy who saw it as their duty to protect their faith.[8]

Although Mizzi's ends had been avowedly political, his tactics, by linking language, religion and social order, had created a potent social ideology which was to unite the professional classes and the lower clergy in the political arena in the following years. When five political parties had come into existence under the 1921 constitution, two of them had been based on this particular ideology.[9] In 1924, these two parties entered a coalition government and eventually merged to become the Nationalist Party in 1926.[10]

This party represented, firstly, the interests of the Italian-speaking business and professional classes who provided the political leadership. Although they were united in their determination to defend the status of the Italian language in Malta, most were by now quite satisfied with British constitutional arrangements and remained loyal to the Imperial connection,[11] although there was one faction in the party which admired the dynamism of Fascist Italy and, under the leadership of Fortunato Mizzi's son Enrico, actively sought to promote Maltese *italianità* for irredentist purposes.[12]

The Nationalists also received active support from the lower clergy, thus obviating the need for a permanent party organization in the constituencies outside election times.[13] Many priests actively campaigned for the party, some sitting as members of the Assembly and one serving as Minister of Public Instruction.[14] The hierarchy at first disliked seeing the Church identified so actively with one political party and – to little avail – issued a pastoral letter in 1924 suggesting that the clergy should not stand as candidates in the election of that year.[15]

The political activity of the clergy had been intensified by the effective politics and the belligerent attitude of Sir Gerald Strickland, the Leader of the Opposition since 1921. Strickland, by means of increasingly violent attacks, had been countering the claim of the Nationalist Party for an increased use of the Italian language and its extension in the field of education. On the contrary, Strickland asserted that the language of the people, Maltese, should be raised to official status in the colony in place of Italian. The desperation of the clergy and Strickland's eventual political success in 1927 suggest that Strickland, by turning Maltese against Italians, had hit upon a potent popular issue.

Although himself a devout Roman Catholic, Strickland was not averse to charging those priestly backers of the Nationalist Party with clerical interference in politics.[16] He was even prepared to draw the Maltese hierarchy into the political arena with his charges that they were directing their clergy in this matter, thereby intensifying the bitterness of the Maltese political scene.

Strickland – elevated to the peerage as Lord Strickland in 1928 – loved a good political fight. He was the leader of the Constitutional Party, formed by the merger of two more of the original parties of 1921 and primarily representing the interests of property owners who wanted an extended use of the English language and customs.[17] Strickland's politics were those of the Empire, best exemplified in his own life and career. Of Maltese and English parentage, Strickland started his career as a lawyer and politician in Malta. In 1888, he became Chief Secretary to the Government and, from 1902 to 1920, served as Governor of the Leeward Islands, Tasmania, Western Australia and New South Wales, successively. In 1920, he returned to Malta, taking the leadership of the Constitutional Party in 1921. He owned a home in England, Sizergh Castle, and, from 1924 to 1927, also sat in the British House of Commons as MP for Lancaster.[18]

The most notable feature of Strickland's personality, as it was of his long public career, was that the man thrived on political conflict. He always had a clear sense of the nature and justice of his own cause, an instinct for recognizing and defining his political enemies, and a compulsion for political battle. Yet, the love of this battle did not always secure the intended advance of his causes, as '... the very ardency of his patriotism, both as an Englishman and as a Maltese, brought out a pugnacity of manner which went far to antagonize his would-be sympathizers and to obscure the merit of his argument'.[19]

One of the most important factors in Maltese politics in the 1920s, therefore, was this conflictual personality of Strickland's, which helped to develop and sustain the polarization of the island[20] to the discomfort of the British Colonial and Foreign Offices, who judged Strickland to be 'a difficult individual',[21] 'politically ... a disaster',[22] and 'very much of a crank'.[23]

During the nineteenth century, Britain had interfered little with the social and cultural organization of Malta. After the opening of the Suez Canal had made Malta an important naval base, however, certain Maltese such as Strickland had seen the advantage of having Malta integrated more fully into the British imperial system. This integration was to include the introduction of British representative political institutions, the elevation of the English language and Maltese at the expense of Italian and the economic development of Malta so that the native economy could complement that of the rest of the Empire. Although the Italian-speaking community supported (and eventually took the lead in making demands for representative institutions, albeit for different reasons, it bitterly opposed any attempts to downgrade the Italian language and was reluctant to acquiesce in any diversification of the economy for which native capital would be required.[24]

With the establishment of representative government in 1921, it became apparent that the two political groups wished to use it for different purposes. The Nationalists had sought self-government as a means of protecting the *status quo*, whereas Strickland's Constitutional Party wished to continue the integration of the Maltese society and economy with that of the British Empire and to raise the status of the Maltese language.

As a result of Strickland's campaign, the Nationalists and the clergy were so unsure of their position that on the day before the elections for the Legislature in August 1927 they circulated copies of an affidavit – later admitted to be a forgery – claiming that Strickland was a Freemason. In spite of this damaging accusation, Strickland's party, with the assistance of the fifth of the original parties, the trade union-based Labour Party, was able to obtain a majority of seats in the Legislative Assembly.[25] Strickland thereupon took office as the Head of the Maltese Ministry with a vengeance. After searching the home of his predecessor for stolen documents,[26] he launched an immediate attack on the Italian language by banning the use of Italian in all official notices in Malta.[27]

Strickland's election victory occurred at a particularly sensitive time for the government of Fascist Italy when Mussolini was initiating his anti-Yugoslav policy in the Balkans. This Italian offensive was anti-French in intent, but it was made possible only through the acquiescence of Great Britain. As there was considerable British sympathy for Yugoslavia, the Italian Government realized that British opposition at this crucial time could be detrimental to Italian policy. The election of the anti-Italian Strickland in August 1927 was thus unwelcome to leading officials of the Italian Foreign Ministry. Italian Mediterranean policy was of particular interest to those members of the Fascist Party and Government whose ultimate interest lay in Italian expansion into Africa. Yet, the question of tactics tended to divide these Italian colonialists. Where members of the Foreign Ministry, such as Grandi and Guariglia, favoured colonial expansion with the agreement and cooperation of the British, another faction, centring on Forges Davazati and *La Tribuna*, tended to be more pro-French and to favour Latin Catholic solidarity and expansion at the expense of British sensibilities.[28]

On the day after the election of Strickland, therefore, *La Tribuna* launched a press campaign against the man, calling him a vulgar anti-Fascist and suggesting that his government would be factious, violent, coarse and corrupt.[29] Fileti, the Italian Consul-General in Valetta, sought, on his own initiative, to reassure Strickland about Italian intentions[30] but, when Strickland banned the use of Italian in official notices, Fileti took it upon himself early in September to make a formal protest to the Acting Governor.[31] One may assume that Fileti believed that the attitude of *La Tribuna* on Maltese affairs was representative of official attitudes in Rome and thus that the Consul-General was rather surprised to receive firm instructions from Grandi on the following day, ordering him to make no more statements on the matter and to leave all dealings over Malta for direct negotiations between Rome and London.[32]

Grandi's attitude indicates that the Foreign Ministry feared that if Strickland did not show some restraint in his anti-Italian campaign, it might so inflame Italian public opinion that Mussolini might be forced to act against his better judgement to reply to this challenge to Italian honour. At the same time, Grandi appreciated that Italy had no real grounds for objecting to Strickland's behaviour and thus he asked Bordonaro, the Italian Ambassador in London, to suggest discreetly to British officials that Strickland's behaviour could do injury to Anglo-Italian relations if carried to extreme.[33] As a sign of goodwill to Britain, Fileti was replaced as Consul-General in Valetta early in November 1927.[34]

Yet, just as Grandi was seeking to contain a potentially difficult situation, the British Foreign Secretary found that he was also unable to act very effectively. Through communication with the Colonial Office, Chamberlain was advised that, because of the grant of internal self-government to the Maltese, Whitehall was in no position to comment on measures of a domestic nature which Strickland might take. Moreover, the attitude of certain segments of the Italian press seemed to convince Chamberlain that very possibly there was some justification for Strickland's behaviour.[35] By the beginning of 1928, therefore, it seemed there was little either the Italian or British Governments could do about the situation in Malta.

Although Chamberlain supported Mussolini's claim to participation in the international administration of Tangiers, relations between Italy and Britain lost much of their former warmth during the summer of 1928, particularly when Britain moved into closer cooperation with France.[36] The most striking evidence to the Italians of this new Anglo-French cooperation lay in the compromise plan for naval disarmament reached between London and Paris at the end of July 1928, in which Britain demonstrated a preference for the French position on disarmament over the Italian.[37] The British attitude to Italy seemed to be confirmed by the continuing refusal of the Foreign Office to exercise any control over Strickland when asked to do so by Bordonaro.[38]

Sensing a need to exercise some control over the Maltese situation in this deteriorating state of Anglo-Italian relations, Guariglia made a proposal in November. Believing that the continuing press campaign in Italy was the least effective way of protecting Italian interests in Malta, he sent a memorandum to Mussolini in which he recommended strict control of the press by the Foreign Ministry and the institution of a programme of cultural propaganda in Malta 'to draw sympathy to Italy'.[39] As Guariglia was to repeat this same memorandum to Grandi some months later, it would appear that Mussolini had not been interested in these proposals when they were first made. It would, in fact, appear that Mussolini was less concerned about the effects of the Italian press campaign on Strickland and on Anglo-Italian relations than were the Foreign Ministry officials, and that Mussolini was, in fact, prepared to retain a certain pressure on the British to force them away from too great a dependence on France in the Mediterranean.

Although considerations of national interest and foreign policy tempered the Italian official reaction to Strickland's anti-Italian campaign, such restraints did not operate on the Holy See when Strickland's diatribes were also directed against the clergy and the Maltese hierarchy. Being less concerned about its relationship with Britain, the Vatican had very good reason for standing firm against Strickland's anti-clericalism.

Strickland had defined his domestic opposition as clericalism and Italian Fascism and, as the Italian press were particularly sensitive to his campaign against the Italian language in Malta, he interpreted clerical opposition to his programmes as collusion between the Italian Pope and the Italian dictator. Certainly, by the spring of 1928, members of the Constitutional Party were convinced about the existence of this collusion.[40] In October 1927, Gasparri gave Governor Du Cane of Malta 'an assurance that the Holy See had in no way encouraged or even countenanced the participation of priests in Maltese politics' and that the policy of the Holy See would in no way be influenced by pro-Italian propaganda.[41] Although there appears to be no reason to doubt Gasparri's veracity or sincerity at that time, this is not to say that there was not a good deal of cooperation between Italy and the Holy See in terms of general policy in 1927 and 1928 and that there could have been some general basis for Strickland's suspicions.

In August 1928, for example, the Vatican, in response to a persistent Italian request, and in return for Italian restoration to the Knights of Malta of their ancient headquarters on Rhodes, reestablished the Archdiocese of Rhodes in the Dodecanese Islands and appointed an Italian Franciscan as archbishop.[42] Until that time, the Bishop of Malta had acted as titular Archbishop of Rhodes and thus, in compensation and so that this should not be interpreted as a slight on the beseiged Maltese hierarchy, the Holy See decreed that the Bishop of Malta should henceforth be styled the Archbishop Bishop of Malta. In this way he would retain the privileges of pallium and processional cross due to an archbishop.[43] Strickland suspected that this was a prelude to the See of Malta coming under an Italian diocese.[44]

Against this background of cordiality between Italy and the Holy See, Strickland's first budget was rejected by the Maltese Senate in 1928, with the two clerical votes being decisive.[45] The Head of the Maltese Ministry realized that this opposition of the clergy would prevent the implementation of his programmes and that his political survival, therefore, required a direct confrontation with the Church.

Strickland had frequently railed against 'the unclerical behaviour of "political priests"' and had sought, with little avail after 1924, to get the bishops to order their priests out of politics.[46] Now suspecting the existence of a plot to hamper his work,[47] he was determined to find an issue which would allow him to challenge the hierarchy and the Vatican with unconstitutional interference with the popularly elected government and, if necessary, to summon the Imperial authorities to his assistance. When such an issue appeared, however, the hierarchy, now thoroughly annoyed with Strickland, was equally prepared to call the Church Militant to its defence. As W. K. Hancock comments: 'The labouring mouse of Maltese self-government produced, one after another, the most awe-inspiring mountains.'[48]

In such circumstances, the necessary issue soon emerged. Father Carta, an Italian monk from Sardinia, was sent to Malta in 1928 by the Superior-General of the Franciscan Conventuals to investigate a disciplinary problem in the Order there. Carta found that a certain Father Micallef was one of the main trouble-makers and arranged for him to be transferred to Sicily. Micallef, however, himself Maltese, had been one of the few priests to support Strickland in 1927 and the latter interpreted Carta's action as a political decision on the part of the Vatican. He refused to allow Micallef to leave, claiming, in an argument de-signed to secure the sympathy of the British Government, that the Vatican did not have the authority to order a British subject to leave the British Empire.[49]

The Vatican was obviously sympathetic to the plight of the Maltese bishops, especially since Strickland (by challenging the position of the Church) had caused serious rifts to appear in Maltese society. Moreover, as the dispute developed, Strick-land's followers became ever more dangerously anti-clerical. The Vatican was determined to nip anti-clericalism – virtually unknown in the island before 1921 – in the bud and to curb Strick-land.

It also appeared to the Vatican that the British Government was about to play the game by Strickland's rules. When the Vatican in January 1929 protested to Britain about the Micallef affair, the British Minister in reply 'expressed the view of his government that "the intense participation of priests in politics" lay at the root of the trouble'.[50]

Thus, in the Vatican's eyes, the British Government was not at all adopting a position of neutrality in regard to Maltese domestic issues as it claimed to be obligated to do under the 1921 Consti-tution. Rather, it was endorsing Strickland's political argument and the British Government appeared to remain virtually unaware of the possibility that the clerical activity resulted from a fear of the consequences of Strickland's behaviour. If Britain proved unable to see this side of the case, the Vatican would have to join issue with it.

There was yet a third factor shaping the Vatican response over Malta. On 11 February 1929, the Lateran Pacts had been signed. Most of the Italian press, especially the organs of the Fascist party, interpreted the Pacts as a victory for Italy over France.[51] Pius XI, unwilling to allow the Lateran Pacts to become a bone of contention between two of the great Catholic powers,[52] was pleased to have an issue at hand whereby he could direct Italian imperial ambitions against the British rather than the French and thus, if necessary, was prepared to prolong and promote this crisis in which Italy and the Holy See had a common interest.

Less than a fortnight after the conclusion of the Lateran Agreements, the Vatican opened its counter-offensive against Strickland. On 23 February a note was written to Chilston, the British Minister to the Holy See, informing him of a series of 'propaganda lectures' given in the Governor's Palace in Malta by three visiting Anglican bishops, for which Strickland had suspended the sitting of the Legislature. Gasparri indicated that these facts were 'offensive to the convictions and sentiments of the large majority of Maltese who fervently profess the Catholic religion since they constitute a solemn and official favouring of the Anglican creed'. He concluded by expecting the British Government 'will effectively show their disapproval'.[53] The Anglican presence in Malta was doubly worrisome to the Vatican, as the Anglican Church was, at the same time, providing support to Yugoslavia's Serb Orthodox against Roman Catholic incursions in the Balkans and the Vatican was sensitive to the Archbishop of Canterbury's ominous presence in the Adriatic while convalescing that spring on a yacht.[54] The implication that Strickland's position had the support of this Anglican religious front no doubt concerned the Pope. The note of 23 February was followed, two days later, by a request that the British authorities should expel Father Micallef from Malta.[55]

It would seem that the note of 23 February was inspired by the Pope himself, as Lindsay, Permanent Under-Secretary of the Foreign Office, minuted that 'the Vatican diplomacy is not displaying its usual caution', suggesting that it was the truculent Pius XI rather than the experienced Gasparri who had been responsible. Further support is lent by the fact that the matter of the Anglican bishops had already been discussed by Mr Randall, the British Chargé d'Affaires, and Mgr Ottaviani, an Under-Secretary of State, some weeks earlier, presumably at that time to the satisfaction of the Secretariat of State.[56] In July, Chilton was informed that Gasparri had received a complaint from the Bishop of Gozo and, without thinking or asking, had sent off his note.[57] Yet Cardinal Gasparri, with his long diplomatic experience, was unlikely to make a move so calculated to raise British objection, while the Pope was quite capable of doing so.[58]

Both notes, of 23 and 25 February, were seen as making

'unjustifiable demands with regard to the internal administration of a British colony'[59] and led the British Government, on the one hand, to indicate that they had no authority to expel Micallef[60] and, on the other, to refuse to discuss the matter of the Anglican bishops with the Vatican.[61] At the same time, the Foreign Office supported the proposal of the Maltese Legislature[62] that the Vatican should appoint an Apostolic Visitor to Malta to

> investigate the whole question of the relations of the ecclesiastical authorities in Malta with the political government, having regard to the importance of avoiding friction in the future as a consequence of the intervention of Maltese priests in politics.[63]

This proposal was supported with some alacrity by the Holy See and, on 9 March, Monsignor Paschal Robinson, an Irish-born American, was named Apostolic Delegate to Malta,[64] to the apparent satisfaction of all parties to the dispute.[65]

Monsignor Robinson's mission lasted from 1 April to 2 June and he had amicable discussions with all parties in Malta. During conversations with Strickland, the latter presented the Apostolic Delegate with 'Notes for a Concordat',[66] which Strickland hoped would serve as a basis for subsequent regulation of the role of the Church in Malta.[67]

On Robinson's return to Rome, he submitted his report to the Pope, concluding that the troubles in Malta '... are the natural and inevitable result of the elections of August 1927 which put Lord Strickland into power as Prime Minister...' and '.... that there is every reason to doubt that there can be any peace and harmony in Malta as long as he remains in office'. Robinson reported that Strickland, for the 1927 elections, had hoped to obtain the political support of the clergy. When he had failed to do so, he then sought to break their power over the Maltese people by painting the clergy as agents of a foreign power. Where the Maltese were strongly loyal to the British Empire, Strickland launched his anti-Italian campaign and then, as many of the clergy were Italian, he sought to discredit them in the eyes of the Maltese by labelling them as being disloyal to the Empire. Since many of Strickland's followers were apparently unaware of this intent, especially when he claimed to be acting in the best interests of the Church, Robinson recommended that the Vatican should take a strong public position dissociating itself from

Strickland and that Britain should be urged to do the same.[68] Robinson also made some proposals for ecclesiastical reform in Malta, which the Vatican never saw fit to make public.[69]

It would seem that there had been two interpretations of the Robinson mission. The British had seen the mission as being designed to effect a settlement with the Vatican which could lead to a defined protection of the interests of the Church in Malta and, thereby, let the Church stand outside Maltese politics. Cardinal Gasparri had also expected to follow the traditional concordatory policy over Malta and this had been evident in the instructions which had been given to Robinson.[70] It had also been an arrangement which Strickland was prepared to accept.

And yet, the Pope does not seem to have intended it for this purpose at all. Rather, rejecting the British assertion that clerical interference in politics was at the root of the problem, he had seen the real purpose of Robinson's mission as being that of investigating, for the benefit of both Britain and the Vatican, the degree of Strickland's guilt, so that the British might be convinced of the need to dissociate themselves from the Maltese Prime Minister. The Pope certainly had no intention of allowing the Maltese hierarchy to withdraw from politics at such a crucial time and, accordingly, he sought to implement Robinson's recommendations regarding Strickland.

In June, Strickland went to London to discuss the Robinson negotiations and, on his return journey to Malta, he planned to visit Rome to continue discussions with the Vatican. The Foreign Office were agreeable to this, since Strickland did not have the authority to come to any final settlement[71] and they were unaware of just how sensitive the Vatican was over Strickland.

Much to the surprise of Strickland and the British Government, on the morning of Strickland's arrival in Rome, 5 July, Gasparri informed Chilton that Strickland was *persona non grata* at the Vatican and that neither he, Gasparri, nor any of his staff could see him, indicating that any negotiations should be conducted through normal diplomatic channels. He also handed Chilton a note, stating that a letter had been sent to the Bishops of Malta and Gozo containing instructions to inform the Maltese people of this new status of Strickland. The note concluded that

in view of the harm which Lord Strickland's activities occasion to the Imperial Government, the latter will no doubt adopt such measures as they may consider necessary to prevent such subversive activity, or at least to divorce their responsibility from that of Lord Strickland.

Not only were the Maltese people to be informed of the Pope's displeasure, but there was also a hint thrown out that the Italian Government might now take more than a passing interest in Malta, as Gasparri pointed out that 'he considered Lord Strickland was as great a danger to the British Empire as he was to the Catholic Church'.[72] This suggestion was explained to Chilton even more clearly by Robinson on 11 July, when he said that he felt Strickland, by his activities, was creating anti-British feeling in Malta which would, very possibly, give Mussolini his chance.[73]

The British Government, taken aback by this unexpected Vatican *démarche*, became even more determined to hold its perceived constitutional ground of supporting the popularly elected Head of the Maltese Ministry. It terminated the negotiations with the Vatican,[74] issued a strong note of protest against Vatican interference in the internal affairs of a British colony, and despatched Chilton on indefinite leave.[75]

On 19 July, Chilton had had a conversation with Robinson, who had confirmed that the Pope had given instructions to Gasparri to send 'the famous letter'. Robinson explained that

His Holiness is terribly worked up on the subject of Strickland personally, that he has been waiting in the hope that S. [sic] would mend his ways *vis-à-vis* the clergy, but that he lost patience... He has a way of bottling up things and not telling even his Secretary of State and immediate surroundings of his intentions.[76]

Relations between Britain and the Vatican remained in stalemate throughout the winter of 1929–30. Following the exchange of an inconsequential series of notes,[77] Gasparri suggested in December that negotiations might well begin again in the new year.[78] In January, however, nothing happened and on 31 January Chilton, on request, was given a copy of what was purported to be Robinson's report, although it only contained a list of Strickland's alleged crimes. There was no mention of negotiations.[79] Early in March, a promise by Strickland not to attack the clergy if the Vatican would order them to stay out of politics – important in view of the forthcoming Maltese elections – was rejected by Eugenio Cardinal Pacelli (later Pope Pius XII) Gasparri's replacement as Secretary of State.[80] A week later, Pacelli stated the Vatican position to Chilton: 'no negotiations for a Concordat were possible as long as Lord Strickland was in power. The Pope had said so quite definitely.'[81]

Following the conclusion of the Lateran Agreements, *La Tribuna* and certain other organs of the Italian press had continued their attacks on Strickland, to such an extent that, on 9 March, the Italian Consul-General in Malta protested to his Foreign Ministry that the press campaign was being counterproductive as it tended to give substance to Strickland's argument that an Italian plan was in effect to take over Malta.[82] Accordingly, Guariglia, in March, was prompted to send Grandi his earlier memorandum of November 1928, urging a programme of press control in Italy and cultural propaganda in Malta.[83]

On 2 April, Mussolini had a meeting with Sir Austen Chamberlain at Florence, during which Sir Austen sought to encourage Mussolini to improve relations with France.[84] As this meeting coincided with Robinson's departure for Malta, Mussolini seems to have been concerned about the effects of the violent Italian press campaign on the success of the Robinson mission[85] and, presumably in the euphoric mood produced by the Florence meeting, Mussolini approved Guariglia's proposal and ordered its execution.[86]

Yet, the implementation of this scheme later in the year differed rather markedly from what Guariglia had originally proposed and it would appear that the Anglo-Italian *rapprochement* set off by the Florence meeting foundered with the electoral defeat of the Conservative Government and the advent of Ramsay MacDonald's minority Labour Government to office in early June. It appears, in fact, that the election of the socialists to office in Britain caused Italy and the Vatican to reach a degree of agreement on the attitude which should now be taken to Britain and this cooperation was reflected in Mussolini's attitude to the Malta crisis.

While the advent of the British Labour Government was not expected to result in any great change in British relations with Italy, the ideological differences between Rome and London meant that any Italian advantages would now result more from a recognition of power relationships in Anglo-Italian relations than from mutual esteem and confidence.[87] Under these circumstances, Mussolini fell in more and more with the Vatican stance over Malta, seeking to gain additional levers for exerting pressure on the Labour Government.

In his memorandum Guariglia had recommended a tight control of the press by the Foreign Ministry, censoring all stories written on Malta and preparing a number of 'clearly objective' articles calculated to attract the interest of the Maltese people. During the remainder of 1929, however, the anti-Strickland press campaign was allowed to continue unabated.[88] Where, on the other hand, Guariglia's proposals for cultural penetration had been quite modest, including the purchase of the services of a Maltese newspaper, the sending of the occasional serious lecturer to Malta and the establishment in Malta of certain institutions for Italian cultural penetration, the programme as instituted went rather far beyond this. In 1929, Maltese branches of the *Milizia Fascista Italiana* and the *Combattenti Italiani* were opened, a Maltese–Italian dramatic society – *Goldoni e Giacosa* – was inaugurated and, in Rome, an historical journal, *Archivo storico di Malta*, was published for the first time. Between 1929 and 1932, new institutions and journals were added at the rate of four or five a year so that, by 1932, a considerable amount of time and money had been invested on Maltese *italianità*.[89]

After the Vatican had declared Strickland *persona non grata* in July, Mussolini interceded personally in the Maltese crisis. Early in August, he instructed Bordonaro to express the concern of the Italian Government over the anti-Italian hostility of Strickland.[90] Since Mussolini rarely intervened directly in the conduct of Mediterranean policy,[91] this would indicate that, in wanting to lend support to the Vatican, he did not feel that Grandi and Guariglia were sufficiently in sympathy with his policy. Moreover, Bordonaro's reply,[92] in which he carefully specified that he had not raised either the dispute between the Vatican and the Government of Malta or the matter of press campaigns in his conversation with Lindsay, would indicate that he well knew what had been on Mussolini's mind in sending his instructions.

Confronted with this modification of their plans, the Palazzo Chigi now sought to allay British suspicions and to warn them of the consequences of continuing to support Strickland. On 24 July Guariglia told Graham, the British Ambassador, that he admitted that the Vatican policy was a huge mistake, and then added 'but as for your Strickland he is perfectly impossible. He had succeeded in bringing to life in Malta an Italian party which never existed there before. I suppose we ought to be grateful to him, but we are not in the least!'[93]

While Graham was aware of the sympathy for the Vatican cause which the continuing press campaign was creating,[94] he did not believe 'that well instructed Italians want Malta' and advised Whitehall accordingly.[95]

In October, Victor Emmanuel III, sensing the public mood, made reference to Malta in a speech to the 34th Congress of the Dante Alighieri Society,[96] a wealthy and powerful organization designed to promote Italian language and literature both at home and abroad, yet an organization known to be anathema to the Church.[97] When Graham protested, Grandi replied that the speech had no official inspiration or countenance[98] and this was borne out by the fact that the Dante Alighieri Society did not become involved in Malta until 1931, by which time Italian collusion with the Vatican was long dead.[99]

The reason why the Pope had been unwilling to resume negotiations with the British Government became evident on 1 May 1930, when, in a joint pastoral, the Bishops of Malta and Gozo stated that any Maltese Catholics who voted for Strickland's party in the forthcoming elections would be committing a grave sin and would be denied the sacraments.[100] Pacelli, by his evasive reply to Chilton on the following day, confirmed that this pastoral was inspired by the Holy See.[101] The Pope had entered the fray against Strickland directly.

The reaction of the British Government was, first, to postpone the Maltese elections,[102] then to insist that the Vatican order the pastoral letter to be withdrawn before any negotiations over Malta should take place.[103] This the Vatican refused to do,[104] with the result that Britain reduced the status of its Vatican Legation by withdrawing the Minister.[105] When Pacelli suggested on 16 June that the pastoral might be withdrawn if Strickland first apologized to the Holy See,[106] the British Cabinet decided, two days later, to suspend the Maltese Constitution, while keeping the Strickland cabinet in office under the direct rule of the Governor as a gesture of defiance to the Vatican.[107] The Pope had overplayed his hand, with the result that Strickland was shown the full confidence of the British Government which had now taken a deliberate decision to retain him in office. The quarrel, from being one between Pius XI and Strickland, now became a direct issue between the Holy See and the British Government.

In these circumstances, Mussolini realized that the Vatican had gone too far. While permitting the cultural propaganda in Malta to continue, he now adopted the other part of Guariglia's programme, namely the muzzling of the press, urged on by Grandi who prophetically warned Mussolini upon hearing of the pastoral: 'This is just what may happen to us in a couple of years' time if we come to some disagreement with the Vatican.'[108] On 13 June, Graham, in reporting the reaction of the Italian press to the Maltese pastoral, noted the restrained tone and the lack of editorial comment in most of the papers and, perhaps most significantly, did not indicate that *La Tribuna* had commented on the affair in any way.[109] Mussolini's flirtation with the Vatican over Malta had come to an end.

Meanwhile, the Palazzo Chigi hastened to assure Britain of Italian disinterest in the Vatican's case. On 6 May Grandi told Graham that 'his experiences in dealing with the Vatican since the Concordat had almost destroyed his Faith' and added 'You do not know how lucky you are to have had a Henry VIII.'[110] Similarly, on 23 May, Bordonaro denied reports in London that Italy was supporting the Vatican over Malta.[111]

The Vatican waited for some evidence of Italian support and, when it was apparent that Mussolini was not prepared to jeopardize his relations with Britain on behalf of the Holy See, a disclaimer was finally issued. On 27 June Mgr Pizzardo, Under-Secretary of State and reputedly a confidant of Pius XI,[112] protested to Ogilvie-Forbes, the Chargé d'Affaires, 'that the Vatican's attitude was not animated by any pro-Italian feeling. Putting his hand to his throat, he said: "Do you think that we desire to tighten the grip of the Fascists on us?"'[113]

The impasse between Britain and the Holy See lasted until the beginning of 1931, when the British Government, on 4 February in a move to seek a solution to the constitutional crisis, appointed the Askwith Royal Commission to investigate the problems of Malta.[114] A month later, Strickland, still the Head of the Maltese Ministry, offered, in a speech to the House of Lords, to apologize to the Vatican.[115]

The appointment of the Royal Commission posed, however, a

very real threat to Italian interests in Malta, since, if the language question were to be raised and, more pertinently, if Italian cultural penetration were to become an object of concern, Italy could well find herself embroiled in an unwanted conflict with Britain. A complete dissociation of Italian policy from that of the Vatican could serve to allay British suspicions somewhat and one may assume that this was one of the divergent motivating factors in the Fascist attack on Italian Catholic Action and the ensuing conflict with the Vatican in the summer of 1931.

Grandi certainly intended to use this estrangement to convey Italian sympathy to the British Government. On 12 May, in the middle of the Catholic Action dispute, he assured Graham that 'as regards our [the British] controversy with the Vatican, Italian Government were in full sympathy with our point of view and hoped that we would not give way', adding that no responsible Italian wished to interfere in Malta. Because of the way that the Vatican were encouraging the press on this matter, he asked that Britain should go lightly on the Italian language issue.[116] A similar concern about the Italian language issue was expressed by the Italian Ambassador in London later in the summer.[117]

But, as Italy was trying to show its solidarity with Britain, one result of the Catholic Action dispute and of the crises in other Catholic countries in that same year (such as the proposal for a German–Austrian customs union and the abdication of the Spanish monarchy in favour of an anti-clerical republic) was that the Vatican took tentative steps toward *rapprochement* with Britain. In mid-April the Pope informed the British authorities through the Archbishop Bishop of Malta that peace proposals from Britain would be welcome[118] and that the episcopal ban against Strickland's party would be lifted if the latter made his proposed apology.[119] Moreover, the Archbishop markedly favoured the Royal Commission after his interview with the Pope.[120]

Although little came of these Vatican initiatives, they did facilitate the work of the Askwith Commission.. The defeat of the British Labour Party in the October elections was welcomed by the Holy See with the suggestion that a settlement of the Malta dispute was now possible.[121]

While Grandi had sought to reassure the British in the summer of 1931, Mussolini had been investigating other ways of influencing the Royal Commission and the British Government. On 20

May he wrote to Gabriele D'Annunzio and asked him to use his influence with certain English friends in defence of the Italian language in Malta.[122] While D'Annunzio initially responded favourably to the suggestion,[123] he never really got around to doing anything about it, finally indicating that he did not feel it was a matter to be rushed.[124] Instead, D'Annunzio, a lifelong anti-clerical, who had originally responded rather sourly to the conclusion of the Lateran Agreements,[125] became enthusiastic about Mussolini's conflict with the Vatican over Catholic Action and, on 16 July, wrote to the Duce, offering him encouragement and volunteering to assist in this dispute.[126] Such assistance, however, was not wanted and, as Mussolini turned down the poet's offer, he brought this particular exchange to an end.[127]

Another interesting move was taken in the summer of 1931 when Mussolini proved willing to enter discussions with Strickland in order to protect Italian interests in Malta. While the source of these discussions is not clear,[128] it appears that Guglielmo Marconi, acting for the Duce, had a series of conversations with Lord Strickland and his daughter, Mabel, in which Marconi attempted to ascertain 'the strength of the anti-Italian feeling in Malta and more particularly in the Constitutional Party', as well as 'the extent of the *French* [*sic*] influence in Malta'. While the outcome of these discussions is not known, Miss Strickland, when reporting them in September, felt that Mussolini was prepared to control Italian propaganda over Malta in return for Strickland's agreement to restrain anti-Italian propaganda among the Maltese in Tunis and France.[129] Miss Strickland 'appeared to be much less prejudiced against the Fascist Government' than previously,[130] thus suggesting that something satisfactory had been arranged.

While seeking to win over his potential opposition, Mussolini also increased the tempo of propaganda activities in the summer of 1931. Accordingly, the Dante Alighieri Society began to become involved in Malta, firstly under the cover of a branch of the Italian Naval League and, secondly, as the sponsor of the lavishly endowed Institute of Italian Culture, which was opened in February 1932.[131] This was coupled with an increase in the number of pro-Italian demonstrations in Malta late in 1931 and early in 1932.[132]

Although the Catholic Action dispute was settled in September 1931, and sealed by a visit from Mussolini to the Pope on 11 Feb-

ruary 1932, the report of the Maltese Royal Commission, issued
on that same day, brought the Maltese language issue to the fore
once again, much to Mussolini's chagrin. 'Trying to tread delica-
tely,' says Hancock, 'the Commission trod on a hornet's nest.'[133]
The Commission reported their belief that there was nothing fundamentally wrong with the 1921 Constitution and recommended
that the quarrel with the Vatican should be patched up, attribut-
ing its cause to the anti-clerical prejudices of Strickland and the
British Labour Government. The report suggested instead that
the real threat to Malta lay in the extension of Italian culture and
recommended that the use of Italian as an official language
should be phased out, starting with the elementary schools.[134]
The British Government, responding to the report and to warnings from Maltese officials about increasing Italian cultural penetration,[135] acted immediately and, on 2 March, announced that
the teaching of Italian was to be banned in all elementary
schools.[136]

A violent Italian public reaction ensued. The Italian Academy
and the Dante Alighieri Society passed resolutions of protest and
the press instigated a new anti-British campaign,[137] which
Graham interpreted as a spontaneous outburst of injured Italian
pride.[138] Sensing the public mood in April, Giunta, Under-
Secretary of the Office of the Presidency of the Council of Ministers, described by Graham as 'an impetuous firebrand, whose
xenophobia made him a dangerous counsellor',[139] made a fiery
pro-Italian speech in Malta[140] in an attempt to force Mussolini
into public intervention.

While Mussolini, in May, did approve the proposal of the
Dante Alighieri Society to sponsor throughout Italy a series of lectures on the history of the Italian language in Malta, he did so on
the understanding that these meetings would be designed to
underline 'the purely cultural and linguistic character of our agitation in regard to Malta'.[141] He did not, however, intend to be
pushed by his subordinates and Giunta, apparently as a result of
his Malta speech, was dismissed from office by Mussolini during
the summer.[142]

To Grandi had fallen the difficult task, when he was appointed
Foreign Minister in September 1929, of coordinating Italian relations with the British Labour Government but, during the term
of that Government, Grandi had had few tangible successes.
With the return of the British Conservative Party to office under

the 1931 National Government, Grandi's freedom of manoeuvre was reduced considerably as the British and French drew more closely together in the spring of 1932. Thus, although Grandi took care to disavow Giunta's April speech to Sir John Simon, the British Foreign Secretary,[143] the British offensive in Malta really signalled the failure of Grandi's general policy to the delight of those elements in the Fascist Party, who were now advocating an alliance with Hitler's rising star in a union of the 'have-not' powers against the 'haves'.[144] In a speech to the Chamber of Deputies on 6 May Grandi tried to square the circle by stating that the Fascist Government shared the sentiments of the Italian nation and hoped that Britain would keep this in mind, but he also gave public assurances that Italy considered Malta to be an internal British affair.[145] Grandi realized that his policy was doomed without some significant change in the British attitude and, early in June, he confided to Graham information about the growing strength of the extremists around Mussolini, suggesting that only colonial concessions to satisfy Italy's need for expansion would prevent an alliance with Hitler and an expansionist Germany.[146] The British refusal to side with Italy against France at the Lausanne Conference in June, however, added to Mussolini's loss of face over Malta, and finally brought about Grandi's resignation in July 1932.[147]

The resultant Cabinet shake-up was designed by Mussolini to bring the conflicting elements in Italy more directly under his control and, thereby, to give himself greater freedom of action in determining policy. This was felt to be necessary in view of the seriousness of the depression and the opportunities offered by the increasing polarization of European politics. By taking over the Foreign Ministry himself, Mussolini did not necessarily disavow Grandi and Guariglia and their preference for imperial expansion with the blessing of Britain and France. Nor did he disavow those party elements who wanted a revisionist partnership with the Nazis and support for the German position on disarmament. Rather, he kept both these strands of policy in operation while developing a third, in the autumn of 1932, when he sought to consolidate the Italian sphere of influence on the Danube and in the Balkans by fomenting the revolt of the Croats against the Belgrade Government.

Although the Vatican, on the strength of the Royal Commission report and of a full apology from Strickland,[148] was prepared to compose its differences with Britain in June 1932, the subsequent restoration of the Maltese constitution[149] and new elections brought the pro-Italian Nationalist Party to power. As Britain was taking the initiative against Italian ventures in Malta, Mussolini was faced with the choice of either supporting and encouraging the resistance of the new Nationalist Ministry in Malta or of using a benevolent policy to assist in securing British acquiescence to his ventures elsewhere. Given the strength of Britain in the Mediterranean and her obvious determination to bolster her position in Malta, the outcome of this decision was never really in doubt.

While the existing Italian schools and institutions in Malta continued extensive programmes among the Italian community and the Maltese,[150] Mussolini, on 14 October 1932, in response to mild British warnings, professed ignorance of this and gave assurances that 'no sane Italian cast an eye on Malta or desired to encourage an irredentist movement in that island'.[151] Moreover, with the European crisis occasioned by Hitler's accession to power in January 1933, Mussolini toned down the work of the Dante Alighieri Society by the withdrawal of financial support for their Maltese venture,[152] in order to guarantee British goodwill in the new crisis and to secure London's support for Mussolini's Four Power Pact.

With Strickland out of office, the Vatican conducted, from the middle of 1932, a policy of strict neutrality over Malta. On the one hand, it assured Britain that it was not 'interested in the slightest' in the Italian language dispute[153] and the Maltese clergy were ordered to behave accordingly.[154] It also refused to react to overtures from the Nationalist Ministry which itself was already in trouble with the British authorities.[155] On the other hand, when Britain, satisfied with the 'sincerity of the various professions of friendliness',[156] decided to reappoint a Minister to the Holy See in February 1933,[157] and try to enlist the Vatican in an anti-Italian policy, it met with little success. When the new British Minister asked for Vatican cooperation in replacing the Italian Jesuits in Malta by English Jesuits and in introducing new English religious orders into the island,[158] the Vatican, while quite rightly pointing out that, owing to the requirements of the British Empire, there were not enough English priests to go around,[159] did not display any great enthusiasm for the proposal or willingness to cooperate in the matter.[160] While prepared to restore good relations with Britain, the Papacy was still sufficiently Italian not to sympathize with the British policy in Malta.[161]

With the Nationalist Ministry seemingly undermining Imperial authority[162] and with warnings of the increasing Italian influence in Malta,[163] the British Government eventually decided, in July 1933, to restrict both the Italian penetration and the Nationalist Ministry.[164] Accordingly, Mussolini was approached by Graham on 26 July 1933, with a request for a voluntary restriction of Italian activities in Malta.[165] While agreeing to certain of the British requests, Mussolini indicated that he would have no objection if the British took what action was considered necessary in other areas.[166] This cooperation paid off, since Britain, being no more willing to have Malta upset her otherwise good relations with Italy, acted to close Italian schools while allowing the Institute of Italian Culture to continue in operation.[167]

The dismissal of the Nationalist Ministry in November 1933, and the suspension, once again, of the Maltese Constitution stirred Italian public reaction both in the press[168] and in the Chamber of Deputies.[169] But Mussolini again showed himself unwilling to make more than mild protest and in January 1934, he told Sir John Simon that 'Anglo-Italian relations in all great affairs were so good that he regretted what he called "this little cloud" arising between us.'[170] Throughout 1934, as Britain finally eliminated Italian as the language of the law and the university in Malta, Mussolini accepted all new restrictions on the Italian language without a murmur of protest.[171]

The history of Italian policy in Malta during this period indicates that, whereas the Vatican sought to enlist Mussolini's help in 1929 and, if possible, to trouble Anglo-Italian relations, the Duce, under considerable public pressure, was prepared to support the Vatican position but was not prepared to countenance any break with Britain. His support was withdrawn in 1930 when it really could have provoked a conflict with Britain and was never to be resumed. Mussolini's passivity when faced with a coordinated campaign on the part of the British Government in 1933 and 1934 to remove Italian as an official language of Malta suggests that he was never sufficiently interested in the fate of the island to allow it to become a touchstone of Anglo-Italian relations as the Vatican would have wished.

6 The Onset of the Depression, 1929–30

The onset of the worldwide economic depression following the Wall Street stock market crash of October 1929 had ramifications which were moral and spiritual as well as social and political. Not only was the matrix of international relationships disturbed by the social pressure of the unemployed, marked particularly by increased radicalism in Germany, but Western man was also suffering a crisis of confidence in his established political, social and religious institutions and values. Mussolini and the Pope were both highly sensitive to this state of affairs and both sought to respond to it.

Mussolini sought to demonstrate that Fascism and corporatism could offer a realistic *via media* between capitalism and communism. He was also intrigued by the diplomatic possibilities inherent in the economic collapse and, in the latter half of 1930, sought to turn the European crisis to Italian advantage. In so doing, the Italians found themselves in strange company for the Soviet Union was also seeking to take advantage of the crisis. At the end of 1930, these two proponents of radical and supposedly antithetical ideologies were to explore together the benefits they could derive from cooperation.

Mussolini's interest in cooperation with Moscow ran directly counter, however, to the anti-Communist campaign inaugurated by Pius XI in 1930. The Pope was concerned lest the Depression should make the alternative of Stalin's collectivist experiment in Russia, with its attendant atheism, an attractive model for distressed peoples, just as he also feared that the determined atheists of Moscow and the Comintern would attempt to use the social distress to further their own political ends. The Pope was, consequently, forced to begin a re-evaluation, at the end of 1930, of his relationship with Fascist Italy.

Grandi

By the summer of 1929, Mussolini had consolidated his power within Italy and, in his cabinet shuffle of 12 September 1929, in anticipation of the coming new phase in the history of the Fascist regime, he personally gave up a number of the ministries which he himself had occupied. In this new phase, foreign policy was to receive greater attention than previously and, to facilitate this, as well as to allow for ministerial representation at forthcoming international conferences, Mussolini entrusted the Foreign Ministry to the Under-Secretary, Dino Grandi, the obvious candidate for the post.

In 1929, the international situation was in a state of flux and future directions were by no means certain. The issue of reparations had been raised again in Germany with the Young Plan, which had elicited strong reaction from the German nationalist Right. The advent of the British Labour Government in June had presaged a changed British foreign policy. The Balkan situation with the imposition of Alexander's dictatorship, seemed to have stabilized for the time being, although developments in Austria were opening new opportunities for Italy.[1]

In turning over the Foreign Ministry to Grandi, Mussolini intended that Italy should pause to await developments in Yugoslavia and the Balkans and, in the meantime, that Grandi should work within the League of Nations, the Disarmament Conference and other such international gatherings, where possible in co-operation with Britain and France or, where feasible, in co-operation with revisionist Germany and Russia. Grandi's main directive was to have Italy act as a European balancer and mediator, thereby keeping open as many options as possible for future Italian exploitation. As Grandi believed that this was also the proper policy for Italy to follow, he began his work with some enthusiasm. Realizing that Mussolini only intended this policy to be temporary, Grandi hoped to be able to produce positive results in order to convince the Duce of its permanent value as an operative policy.

Rapprochement with Austria

Grandi's first success as Foreign Minister was in securing a *rapprochement* with Austria. The threat of a major anti-Socialist de-

monstration by the *Heimwehr* led to the resignation of the
Steeruwitz Government. It was replaced, on 26 September
by a government dedicated to the restoration of law and order
and headed by Johannes Schober, the Austrian Police President.

Schober 'was one of the chief representatives of the bureau-
cratic non-democratic tradition in the country', whose goal
was the depoliticization of Austrian life.[2] A forthright individual
of strong character, Schober was described by the British Minister
as being

> ... honest, plain and outspoken; his head is square and his
> body round ... his digestion is good, he says what he means
> and means what he says ... he now stands, a non-party man,
> square to the three winds [Socialist, *Bourgeois* and *Heimwehr*]
> that blow.[3]

Heading a Cabinet of 'experts', whose parliamentary support
rested on Schober's Pan-German following and on the Christian
Socials, Schober's immediate goal was to free himself from the dependence on parliamentary majorities which had bedevilled
Seipel by revising the constitution to give the President of the Republic greater authority.[4] In effect, this was to be a strong blow
against the Social Democratic Party and the independence of
'Red' Vienna.

While it was the *Heimwehr* agitation which had brought
Schober into power and while he spoke warmly of their support in
his first speech as Chancellor,[5] it soon became apparent that in
his attempt to depoliticize Austria he had no more intention of
being dictated to by them than by the Socialists.[6] In fact, by rising
above the need to be concerned about internal political restraints,
while at the same time securing the respect and confidence of all
parties,[7] he was to place himself in a position where he could take
a positive line in foreign affairs in the hope, particularly, of
improving Austria's economic and financial position.

The first necessity for achieving this end was a *rapprochement*
with Italy and Italian support for a new loan to Austria. Schober,
however, having Pan-German sympathies, did not intend to be
caught between Germany and Italy and thus was to couple his
rapprochement with Rome with a similar *rapprochement* with Berlin,
designed both to seek advantages for Austria and to satisfy his

Pan-German supporters. At the same time, he was to take a more positive stance in his dealings with Britain and France, being quite prepared to carry through the internal disarmament of the political armies of both Left and Right, as they wanted him to do, in return for their aid and assistance.

This radical change in Austrian foreign policy removed the remaining impediments to an Austro-Italian *rapprochement*. As a Pan-German himself, Schober was able to override the objections of that group to dealings with Italy. Auriti, the Italian Minister, lost no time in advising Schober that a clear statement by him on the matter of the South Tyrol would lead to an improvement in Austro-Italian relations[8] and, on 11 October, during their first full conversation, Schober not only informed Auriti that he was fully agreeable to controlling irredentist agitation but also that he would like to make his first foreign visit to Rome.[9] The Italians were delighted and assured Schober of their full support.[10]

This *rapprochement* with Schober, however, brought Grandi into conflict with the Hungarians. Not only did they disagree that the victory of Schober made the payment of the *Heimwehr* less necessary,[11] but they sent their own agent to Rome in an unsuccessful attempt to collect the money for the *Heimwehr*.[12] At the same time, the Hungarian General Staff delivered a deliberate snub to visiting Italian officers by not inviting them to meetings being held with visiting Germans.[13] Only when the *Heimwehr*, doubtless at Hungarian instigation, staged an anti-Italian demonstration on 11 October[14] did Grandi agree to pay them on condition that such demonstrations cease forthwith.[15]

From mid-October, the *rapprochement* with Schober moved slowly but steadily toward consummation. On 25 October, Schober agreed to act as quickly as he could in introducing his constitutional reform[16] and, during November, the satisfaction with Schober's evidence of goodwill[17] was such that, on 28 November, Grandi advised the Italian representative on the Reparations Committee that the Italian Government had officially decided to lift their objections to the Austrian loan.[18] On 8 December the Austrian constitutional amendments were approved by the National Council[19] and, five days later, Schober announced the loan agreement and made a public statement basing his foreign policy on a close friendship with Italy.[20]

There remained for Italy, however, the problem of the way in which the Austro-Italian relationship should be institutionalized.

The agreement to the loan was a card which could really only be played once and some other tie was necessary to maintain the relationship. It was for this reason that, on 26 October, Auriti had suggested the conclusion of a pact of friendship during Schober's visit to Rome.[21] Only on 11 January 1930, however, was Auriti authorized to begin negotiations for such a pact.[22]

A week before his departure for Rome, Schober asked Auriti whether Italy would entertain the possibility of selling arms to Austria. Mussolini, who had approached their meeting with little enthusiasm, now saw that Schober too might have revisionist ambitions and reacted most favourably to this suggestion.[23] During their conversations in Rome, Mussolini brought up this question with Schober who willingly accepted his offer of further discussions on the matter.[24]

Once Mussolini sensed that he and Schober might have some common interests after all, the Rome meeting was a great success in sealing the relationship between Italy and Austria. In addition to the signing of the Italo-Austrian Treaty of Friendship and Conciliation on 6 February, Mussolini gave Schober 'certain satisfying assurances' on the South Tyrol.[25] On 22 February Mussolini granted an amnesty to political prisoners 'of non-Italian origin' in that province,[26] and early in April, it was reported that he had permitted the appointment of a German-speaking cleric as Bishop of Brixen, one of the two dioceses making up the South Tyrol and the one with the largest German-speaking population.[27] Since the bishopric had deliberately been kept vacant for some time,[28] this represented a considerable concession on Mussolini's part, in spite of the fact that the incumbent Bishop Giesler took great pains to demonstrate his loyalty to Fascism and to Italy.[29]

The most significant result of the Rome meeting and of the Austro-Italian *rapprochement* was the settlement of the problem of the South Tyrol for a good many years. Both Austria and Italy substantially kept their parts in this bargain and, while issues did continue to arise in the South Tyrol, they no longer attracted the outside attention which had created such crises in the past.[30]

The resolution of this conflict between Austria and Italy was particularly gratifying to the Holy See. Less than a year after the conclusion of the Lateran Agreements, these two neighbouring Catholic powers had achieved a thorough settlement of the differences between them; no longer need the Pope fear pressure to choose between Catholics on either side of the Brenner Pass.

Stalemate with France

With Franco-Italian relations, on the other hand, Grandi was not as successful. One of the significant innovations in the foreign policy of Ramsay MacDonald's Labour Government was the emphasis on improved relations with Washington, which resulted in 1929 in the development of a joint Anglo-American position prior to the opening of the scheduled conference on naval disarmament in January 1930. As MacDonald was also very suspicious of the French,[31] it was felt in the Italian Foreign Ministry that Italy might well benefit from inviting France to preliminary Franco-Italian talks[32] and such an invitation was accordingly extended in mid-October 1929.[33] This new series of Franco-Italian talks took place in Paris, beginning on 19 November, when Manzoni, the Italian Ambassador, explained to French Foreign Minister Aristide Briand that Italy was prepared to disarm as much as possible so long as her maximum limit was equivalent to that of any other continental European power.[34] The French, however, found this Italian claim for parity to be unacceptable[35] and it was decided to continue discussions by examining the details rather than the general principles, in the hope that some basis of agreement might become apparent.[36] Where the issue of parity had become the central issue of the negotiations, matters were settled by Mussolini on 10 January 1930, when he intervened with explicit instructions to Grandi that Italy would never renounce parity with France at the naval conference.[37] The result was the failure of France and Italy to reach any agreement at the London Naval Conference.[38] No matter how much the officials of the Foreign Ministry wanted to negotiate a settlement with France, such was not the intent of Mussolini.

Adjusting to the Yugoslav Dictatorship

The institution of a royal dictatorship in Yugoslavia had guaranteed that internal dissension would not reappear in that country for some time. Yet the Croats remained the Italian hope. As Grandi emphasized in his report to the Council of Ministers on 5 November 1929 – obviously expressing Mussolini's foreign policy –

The Adriatic is no longer sufficient to defend from the Slav races our independence as a Mediterranean race. It occurs that beyond the Adriatic and on the shores of the Adriatic ... there is a chain of states which must be ... bridgeheads commanded by Italy.... We have made Albania, we must make Croatia.... Destiny wishes that the borders between the Occident and the Orient remain on the Sava.[39]

On 17 December, however, Grandi received a military report that Yugoslavia had been well strengthened during the year and gave no signs of disintegration. Using this as justification for a changed Italian policy, Grandi forwarded it to Mussolini[40] who, shortly thereafter, gave Grandi permission to open talks with the Yugoslavs, directing him to 'calm the spirits, but proceed slowly'.[41]

On 8 January 1930, Jeftic, the confidant of King Alexander and General Zivkovic, in Rome to attend the wedding of the Italian Crown Prince, had a long conversation with Grandi who showed himself willing to reach some agreement with Yugoslavia and explained that the main points at issue were the Franco-Yugoslav Pact and Albania.[42] That the Italians seemed to be serious was indicated by the improved attitude of the Italian press to Yugoslavia[43] and by Mussolini's reception of Rakic, the Yugoslav Minister, on 25 February when he repeated what Grandi had said and cordially hoped for improvement in Italo-Yugoslav relations.[44] Further soundings took place at Geneva on 12 May in discussions between Grandi and Yugoslav Foreign Minister Marinkovic, but as yet with little concrete result.[45]

The indeterminate state of Italo-Yugoslav relations worked to the detriment of the interests of the Holy See. The resolution of differences between Rome and Vienna in February 1930 had been warmly welcomed by the Vatican; in vain did it wait for a similar settlement between Rome and Belgrade. In the expectation that some settlement might be possible, the Holy See initially sought, under very trying circumstances, to remain aloof from the Italo-Yugoslav dispute.

Certainy the establishment of the Yugoslav dictatorship in the face of opposition from the Catholic Croats had put the Catholic Church in a most difficult position. If Belgrade suspected the Church of supporting the Croat or the Italian cause, it could well deny the Church many privileges; yet, if the Church was too cooperative with Belgrade, it stood to lose support in Croatia. The Catholic Church in Yugoslavia without a concordat was very much at the mercy of the whims of the Belgrade Government.

Late in 1929, King Alexander promulgated legislation designed to consolidate Yugoslavia as a unitary state. Among this legislation was a law of 4 December which provided for the creation of a single *Sokol* as a national youth organization where formerly there had been a *Sokol* in each region, with those of Croatia and Slovenia being under the close direction and control of the Catholic Church. The new *Sokol* would of necessity be secular and centrally directed. On 9 December a new Schools Act made religious education compulsory, but did not guarantee that Catholics would be educated by their priests. It also required private schools to come under the Ministry of Education and banned religious associations from all schools.[46] The reaction of the Church to this legislation was officially correct. A strong protest against the Schools Act was lodged by the Nuncio in Belgrade and, while the clergy in Slovenia and Croatia arranged for the property of their *Sokol* societies to be turned over to the Church before amalgamation, nevertheless the Yugoslav Catholic hierarchy gave no indication of any intention to turn their opposition to the legislation into any general demonstration against the government.[47]

This cautious behaviour was most disappointing to the Italians who now recognized the Catholic Church as the one internal institution which could keep alive the sense of Croat independence and thereby resist the growing power of Belgrade. Galli, however, had to report, late in 1929, that the Croat clergy, the Yugoslav hierarchy, the Nuncio and the Vatican had all given support to the centralizing work of the Serbs against the separatism of Croatia.[48] The patience of the Church seemed to bear fruit in January 1930 when the publication of new Yugoslav school regulations made concessions to the Catholic position, specifically in requiring that the religious curriculum be prepared in consultation with the religious authorities and requiring that teachers of religion first have the approval of their church.[49] While the new legislation was thus about to come into effect without equating the religious and national issues, this did not allow for deliberate Italian and Serb attempts to foment trouble.

On 22 January 1930, *La Tribuna* published a provocative article claiming that the Yugoslav Government was persecuting popular Catholic and Croat organizations. *Novosti*, a semi-official Belgrade newspaper rose to the challenge on 2 February, denying the charge of state anti-Catholicism and arguing

> that the protests ... of the Nuncio and Catholic clergy, whom it attacks strongly are unjustified and that a 'Catholic front' directed from abroad and in foreign interests (Mussolini is insinuated) has been set up to prevent the consolidation of the State.[50]

This press campaign brought into the open all the mutual suspicion which existed and, in spite of the public declaration of Monsignor Bauer, the Archbishop of Zagreb, that 'the Roman Catholic clergy cannot be divided into patriotic and non-patriotic groups, and that they are all united in their loyalty to the Holy Catholic Church and to Yugoslavia',[51] he was nevertheless called to Belgrade in February, by Dr Srskic, the Minister of Cults, 'who demanded that he make a public and full declaration of loyalty to the Karageorgevitch dynasty and of adhesion to the Belgrade regime, emphasizing especially that he is absolutely not under the influence of any foreign power'. The Archbishop refused, claiming that this would make him unfaithful to the Pope and, on returning to Zagreb, advised Croat leaders of his new opposition to Belgrade.[52]

The Italians were delighted by this turn of events and, now fearful lest the Vatican advise Bauer to behave differently, sought to determine the Papal reaction,[53] only learning that the Vatican had supported Bauer this far but would make no commitment on their future intentions.[54]

Mussolini and the Yugoslav Negotiations

Grandi's difficulty in developing his negotiations with either France or Yugoslavia was entirely due to the fact that as Foreign Minister he had very little scope for independent initiative. Not only did Mussolini insist on approving every new development of policy, but he continued to conduct his own policies through secret channels outside the purview of the Foreign Ministry. The relationship with Albania and the links with the Croats remained under Mussolini's direct control[55] as did the Hungarian relationship and contacts with the *Heimwehr*. Mussolini even had an agent in Vienna involved in promoting a Habsburg restoration[56] and perhaps most importantly, he insisted on controlling every detail of the relationship with Yugoslavia.[57]

Grandi was not inclined to question Mussolini's judgment on any of these or other matters and was to prove a faithful executor of the Duce's policies during his three-year tenure of the Foreign Ministry.[58] Nevertheless, he did try to avert what he considered the worst consequences of some of these policies. In the summer of 1930, he concurred with Guariglia's memorandum of 25 June, which warned that Mussolini might unwisely get Italy into a war with France over the Balkans and recommended that Franco-Italian relations should be 'chloroformed' pending the outcome of negotiations with Yugoslavia.[59] Occasionally one gets a glimpse of Grandi's frustration, as in his comment to Yugoslav Foreign Minister Marinkovic in September 1930 that his role as Foreign Minister of Italy was really only that of an 'ambassador for all countries'.[60]

From the summer of 1930, Mussolini intervened more openly in the conduct of Italian foreign policy. This was partly due to the international economic crisis which, with its attendant dislocation of industry and trade and the concomitant growth of unemployment, was creating political configurations which Mussolini deemed susceptible to Italian exploitation.

It was also due to a series of international events and developments in 1930 which augmented Italy's power and influence. One such event was the setting aside of the traditional animosity between Turkey and Greece in the conclusion of a convention between these powers in June. As Italy had helped to arrange this convention, she acquired extended influence in the eastern Mediterranean. Italian ties with Bulgaria, at the same time, were being strengthened by the decision of King Boris to marry the Italian Princess Giovanna.[61] A final decision on the wedding was only being delayed over Vatican concern about whether the children would be raised as Catholics.

As the Yugoslav Government was obviously willing to undertake substantial negotiations with Italy, Mussolini judged that Italy was in a strong bargaining position and, accordingly, on 14 July he presented Grandi with the Italian terms for a settlement with Yugoslavia. The terms represented Mussolini's attempt to secure by diplomatic negotiations what he had hitherto been unable to secure by external pressure and internal disruption: complete termination of the Franco-Yugoslav relationship and Yugoslav recognition of Italian predominance in Albania. Italy and Yugoslavia would either be close friends and allies or they would be enemies; Mussolini would accept no half measure. In other words, negotiations with Yugoslavia could only be brought to a successful conclusion if Yugoslavia were prepared to capitulate entirely to Mussolini's demands. Since the negotiators had no room to negotiate. the talks were doomed to failure without some marked change of fortune on one side or the other.[62]

The prospect of Grandi and the Foreign Ministry being able to negotiate a Yugoslav settlement did not appear to be helped by Mussolini's intention to bludgeon the Yugoslavs into an acceptance of his terms. The public show-trial of four captured Slovene terrorists at Trieste culminated at the beginning of September in their execution by the Italian authorities. This execution took place on 7 September, only two days before Grandi met Marinkovic at Geneva to present him with Mussolini's terms for an agreement.[63] This meeting now took place amid a storm of protest in the Yugoslav and, notably, the Slovene press and a surge of anti-Italian feeling throughout that country.[64]

Yet in spite of this strong popular feeling, Marinkovic and King Alexander wanted to follow up on the negotiations with Italy. Father Korosec, the political leader of Slovenia, when learning of this, resigned from his position in the government and put strong pressure on that government not to have dealings with Italy.[65] Marinkovic and the King, on the other hand, recognized how Italy's position and influence in the Balkans was being strengthened in the fall of 1930 and, more importantly, how French influence in Europe and the Balkans was being seriously undermined. King Alexander, in particular, was prepared to exchange his French alliance for one with Italy, provided he could overcome the objections of his government and his people to such a settlement.[66]

Germany and Austria

Italy's diplomatic position was further strengthened by developments in Germany and Austria in September. Prior to the death of Stresemann in October 1929, there had been virtually no diplomatic cooperation between Germany and Italy. This was due as much to the mutual antipathy between the German Foreign Ministry and the Fascist leadership[67] as it was to Stresemann's deliberate reluctance to become involved in Danubian or Balkan politics lest it arouse Anglo-French suspicions.[68] In fact, the main ties with Germany in this period appear to have been through the secret subsidies paid by the Fascists to German nationalist groups.[69]

The death of Stresemann and the increased radicalism associated with the advent of the Depression meant, however, that changes could be expected. The result of the German Reichstag elections of 14 September 1930 seemed to confirm this assumption when both radical parties, the Nazis and the Communists, showed striking gains in the number of their supporters. Germany was becoming restive again and this offered new opportunities for challenging the French position in Europe.

Austro-Italian relations had been especially marked by cordiality and trust in 1930. Schober continued his policy of 'fulfillment' immediately after his Rome visit of February 1930 with visits to Berlin, Paris and London, while the Italians looked on benignly, expressing concern only lest Schober should be drawn into any arrangements with France over Yugoslavia.[70] In fact, during his visit to Berlin, Schober agreed in principle to German Foreign Minister Curtius' proposal of a German–Austrian customs union[71] but the Italians unquestioningly accepted Schober's assurance that the road from Vienna to Berlin passed through Rome.[72] Schober also set about establishing an accord with Budapest,[73] although the Hungarians were less enthusiastic and a treaty of friendship was not concluded until January 1931.

The important development for Mussolini, however, was the changing orientation of the Austrian *Heimwehr*. At their meeting at Korneuberg in May 1930, the *Heimwehr* had pledged themselves to the replacement of parliamentary democracy in Austria by a non-democratic corporative state, in line with the Italian model.[74] At the beginning of July, Mussolini had received the young Prince Starhemberg who had sought the Duce's patronage for the *Heimwehr* movement and, on the strength of this promised patronage, was selected as national leader of the *Heimwehr* on 4 September. Not only did Italy remain on good terms with the Schober Government in 1930, but Mussolini was also encouraging the *Heimwehr* movement which was pledged to replace it.

In addition to his support of the Schober Government and of

the *Heimwehr*, there is also evidence that Mussolini, in the spring of 1930, had been encouraging the Legitimists in Austria and Hungary. To retain the support of these Legitimists, it had been useful to show some interest in the prospect of a restoration. The union of Austria and Hungary under the Habsburg monarchy could be an effective way of shutting out German influence on the Danube. Moreover, the Legitimist cause had a certain nuisance value for Mussolini in domestic Austrian and Hungarian politics. For these reasons, he had received Count Apponyi in May 1929 and had continued to show an interest in the Legitimist cause in 1929 and early in 1930.[75]

Mussolini's activities in this regard were probably conducted through Vittorio Mazzotti, his special agent in Vienna. Mazzotti, who would strongly advocate a Habsburg restoration to Mussolini in 1932,[76] was instrumental in the spring of 1930 in spreading propaganda in favour of this restoration.[77] At the same time, an approach was also made by Mussolini to the ex-Empress Zita, offering her 'a certain number of millions' if she would renounce the Archduke Otto's right to the Austrian Crown. While the context of this offer is not terribly clear, it appears to have been made in a friendly way for the purpose either of having Otto withdraw in favour of another Habsburg claimant or else of restricting Otto's claim to the Hungarian throne only. The ex-Empress is reported as having rejected the Italian offer.[78] In the summer of 1930, Mussolini was prepared to give Zita permission to set up a home in Italy, at Pianore.[79]

At the end of September, the prospect for augmenting Italian influence increased with the resignation of the Schober Government. The new government which took office on 30 September represented a Christian Social–*Heimwehr* coalition, with Vaugoin as Chancellor, Seipel as Minister of Foreign Affairs and Starhemberg as Minister of the Interior with one other *Heimwehr* member in the cabinet. It was the expectation of the Italians that the *Heimwehr*, once in power, would move directly to the consolidation of that power. They would either strengthen the authority of the central executive to exclude the future possibility of the Socialists coming to power or, if necessary, would seize complete power by *coup d'état*. For Italy, it was potentially an ideal arrangement, when the group they were subsidizing could soon be dominant in the Austrian Government.[80]

Yet, the confused goals of the Vaugoin government were

symptomatic of the increasing desperation of the period. Where Starhemberg and certain factions of the *Heimwehr* saw the need of instituting some sort of dictatorship, Seipel, the Christian Socials, and other elements in the *Heimwehr* felt the importance of moving to a restoration of the Habsburgs at this crucial moment. The *Heimwehr* was far from united and, in particular, was reluctant to vest any real centralized authority in their nominal leader, Prince Starhemberg.[81]

Where the Schober Government had been working toward closer relations between Germany and Austria, the results of the German Reichstag elections of mid-September, with the large increase in the vote for the nationalist right, increased the potential of a German move toward the *Anschluss*. To counter this, Seipel and others connected with the Vaugoin government felt this was the time to promote the alternative of a Habsburg restoration.

During the spring and early summer of 1930, there had been considerable activity in Austrian Legitimist circles.[82] Once the Vaugoin Government had been installed, certain Legitimist branches of the *Heimwehr*, under the leadership of the much-decorated General Ellison and with the encouragement of Seipel,[83] made plans to march on Vienna at some time between 20 and 30 October. By seizing Viennese public utilities, Ellison planned to force the government to place the Archduke Otto on the throne.[84] It was the Italians and the Hungarians who prevented the execution of Ellison's plan.

With the Nazi gains in the German elections and the entry of the *Heimwehr* into the Austrian Government, the Italians were much less interested in a restoration. Consequently, when the Hungarian Government, which also opposed a restoration at this time,[85] learned of Ellison's plot and informed the Italians, they together warned Vaugoin and his government. The Italians then advised both Seipel and the *Heimwehr* leaders that any attempted Legitimist *coup* would guarantee Czech intervention and would ruin the real opportunity of the Vaugoin Government to create a stronger executive with dictatorial authority in Austria.[86]

The Tide Turns

Mussolini had been excited and encouraged by the emergence of the radical Right in Germany and Austria in September. Both the

Nazis and the *Heimwehr* had sought to emulate the model of Italian Fascism and, on 27 October 1930, Mussolini, for the first time, declared that henceforth 'fascism' should be considered a universal principle and, therefore, an article for export. In doing this, Mussolini sought to demonstrate that fascism and corporatism could offer a realistic *via media* between capitalism and communism in these Depression years.[87] At the same time, he sought to rally the dissatisfied states of central Europe behind Italian leadership and to increase pressure on Yugoslavia and France with a loud assertion of Italy's loyalty to Hungary and of Italy's continuing support of treaty revision.[88]

In October 1930, Princess Giovanna and Boris of Bulgaria had relented, applied for and received a special dispensation from the Pope to marry on the condition that all their children be raised as Catholics. The wedding took place in the Papal Basilica of St Francis at Assisi on 25 October.[89]

This marriage both strengthened ties between Italy and Bulgaria[90] and promoted rumours of a Balkan revisionist bloc linking Turkey, Greece, Bulgaria and Hungary, much to the disquiet of the Yugoslavs.[91] Moreover, Mussolini's speech elicited soundings from Moscow about the possibility of Soviet Foreign Commissar Litvinov paying a visit to Rome.[92]

Mussolini's open challenge to France and Yugoslavia was not at all to the liking of Grandi and the Foreign Ministry; Guariglia judged Mussolini's speech of 27 October to have 'surpassed the bounds of good political sense'.[93] With this enormous pressure on Yugoslavia, Grandi was not optimistic about the prospect for any settlement, yet he sought to convince Mussolini in mid-November of the importance of making some conciliatory gesture to bring the negotiations to a conclusion.[94]

Mussolini did not, however, respond to the advice of his Foreign Minister and, by the end of the year, Italy had begun to lose a degree of her bargaining power. In Austria, the prospects for the *Heimwehr* and the Legitimist interest had been dashed by the Austrian electorate. In the general election of 9 November the Christian Social–*Heimwehr* coalition had only gained one additional seat, leading to the resignation of Vaugoin and the return of Schober to office as Foreign Minister at the beginning of December. Once again, Austrian foreign policy veered in the direction of Berlin.

In Yugoslavia, the king's willingness to conclude an agreement with Italy continued to be constrained by a number of factors. While Marinkovic was prepared to settle with Italy, he was not as willing as the king to accept Mussolini's conditions outright and, unlike the king, was inclined to spin out the negotiations. A second consideration was the strong Slovene antipathy to Italy and the general public revulsion against the September executions. A third was the seeming reluctance of the Italians to let the conversations with Yugoslavia develop at all and, by December, the Yugoslav king and government were becoming less interested in concluding any agreement.[95]

By the time that Grandi did resume his conversations with Marinkovic at Geneva on 22 January 1931, the opportunity for an agreement was slipping away. At this meeting, the Yugoslav Foreign Minister indicated that his country was prepared to conclude a pledge of reciprocal neutrality with Italy such that Yugoslavia would never use the Franco-Yugoslav Pact against Italy. Grandi felt this might be acceptable but he also required agreement on Albania. It was on this issue that these talks foundered as Yugoslavia would not accept the Italian right to defend the Albanian frontiers and would only go as far as a mutual guarantee of Albanian neutrality. The talks ended inconclusively.[96]

The Relationship with Moscow

The beginning of the Depression had made the Holy See markedly uneasy. Not only had the nations of Europe failed to come together in any real international reconciliation which could restore and protect the social equilibrium, but the Holy See itself, save through the Lateran Pacts, had not had very much success in restoring the influence of Catholicism in central Europe or the Balkans. The European peoples, faced with this major economic crisis, were judged to be particularly defenseless against the preachers of atheistic revolution and, from 1930, there was consequently a decisive shift in emphasis in the international outlook of the Holy See.

Prior to 1930, the Holy See had pursued an expansive diplomatic and ecclesiastical policy in seeking to extend the influence of Catholicism in the Balkans and eastern Europe. Starting in 1930, however, it revised its priorities and moved more and more onto the defensive against the expected expansion of Bolshevik radicalism. As the Depression worsened, Pius XI became ever more intensely committed to this new anti-Communist crusade.

Prior to 1929, relations between the Vatican and the Soviet Union had been cool but correct, as the Vatican had sought in vain to negotiate with Moscow for the introduction of Catholic missions into Russia. When Joseph Stalin's consolidation of power under the First Five Year Plan resulted in a renewed perse-cution of Russian Catholics in 1929, and when this was coupled with the onset of the Depression, the Pope dropped all attempts at conciliating Moscow in favour of an open attack on religious per-secution in Russia. The anti-Bolshevik campaign was launched with a solemn expiatory Mass for Russia and its persecuted Catholics in St Peter's on 19 March 1930.[97] This was followed by the creation of the special commission 'Pro Russia' on 9 April under the chairmanship of D'Herbigny 'to collect information regarding Russia and to consider and advise what steps can be taken for the restoration of religion in that country',[98] and by an active papal campaign in press and pulpit against the evils of Bol-shevism and all its works.

The Pope's campaign was justified by the Russian diplomatic outreach in 1930, when Litvinov sought to divide the forces of capitalism by organizing an anti-French bloc in Europe. This was the substance of his conversation with Grandi on 26 November when the Russians, encouraged by Mussolini's October speech, sought to link with the Italians and their client states in opposing any further extension of French hegemony. Litvinov intended that Germany, too, should be a member of this bloc.[99]

In October, Mussolini had attempted to challenge French hegemony in ideological terms by rallying the radical Right under the banner of a generic 'Fascism'. A month later, he had been confronted with the very different prospect of a union of the radicals of Right and Left against the democratic centre, a union which would necessitate the down-playing of ideological consi-derations. Mussolini was obviously intrigued by the possibility of countering French hegemony with a union of Italy, Germany and the Soviet Union and, early in 1931, sought, in cooperation with the Germans, to have Russia invited to attend meetings at Geneva on the Briand plan for European union.[100]

Yet, in so doing, Mussolini was offering the Soviets that bridge into Europe which Pius XI most feared. Ideology meant little to Mussolini and thus the Pope realized that he could not depend on

Italian Fascism to serve as a bulwark to Communist expansion. This obvious unreliability of the European Right to oppose the forces of the Left meant that the Vatican would have to develop its own policy for resisting Communism.

The important consideration now was that the Holy See felt an even greater need for reaching accommodation with non-Communist governments than had been felt before. Only by reaching some accommodation could the Vatican use its own influence within those nations to counter Communist influence and propaganda. It was more important than before to disregard the political complexion of the governments with which the Vatican had to deal in favour of some understanding, no matter how imperfect. This was to mean, in practice, that the Vatican would divorce itself from Italian tutelage whenever its own concerns took precedence over those of Mussolini. It would do this in Yugoslavia and in Malta and, indirectly, in Spain.

7 Conflict over Catholic Action, 1931–2

If Italian power and influence seemed to be in the ascendant in the latter half of 1930, the events of 1931, especially the German initiative on the Danube and the financial and economic collapse of central and eastern Europe, played very much into the hands of the French. It was, in fact, the French ability to survive the worst effects of the Depression which gave Paris the upper hand in the critical events of this year.

The anti-French and anti-Yugoslav bloc which Mussolini had envisaged in October and November 1930 had not really materialized and, when the Catholic Church sided with Yugoslavia against Italy in the early months of 1931, Mussolini took out his frustration in a direct attack on the position of the Church in Italy. The result of the 1931 conflict over Italian Catholic Action was that the Pope's independence in foreign policy was curtailed where Italy was concerned. The outlook of the Holy See became ever more defensive in resisting the perceived threat of Communism.

The collapse of Mussolini's initiatives of late 1930 meant that direction of Italian foreign policy returned to Grandi and the Foreign Ministry who were able, in the latter half of 1931, to resume talks for a settlement with France.

The Relationship with Berlin

The relative strength of Italy's international position in 1930 was soon undermined as the Depression created fundamental shifts in European society and politics. Some of the main differences between Grandi and Mussolini arose over the approach to be taken to Germany and the way in which Germany should be balanced against France for Italy's benefit. Mussolini was far more willing to trust the Germans in a revisionist partnership than was Grandi who put little faith in their reliability.

In January 1931, Grandi sought close collaboration with Germany in the disarmament discussions and at the League of Nations and he raised such possibilities with German Foreign Minister Curtius when they met at Geneva.[1] When, on 1 March 1931, France made concessions to secure a compromise on naval disarmament with Italy, the question deliberately left undefined and unresolved was that of land armaments – the area of greatest concern to the Germans.[2] Grandi was attempting to develop an Italo–German relationship which could be used to put pressure on the British and French and which could allow Italy to emerge as a relatively disinterested European power-balancer.

Yet Grandi's approach ran into difficulty with the sudden announcement on 21 March 1931 of the plan for a customs union between Germany and Austria. This plan represented the first overt German move onto the Danube and destroyed Grandi's carefully-managed equilibrium. The customs union, under discussion between Curtius and Schober since February 1930, was designed by Curtius to be a bold step toward the revision of the Treaty of Versailles. The plan had been accepted rather cautiously by Schober who hoped to emphasize not so much its exclusive Austro-German nature as its being the first step in a union which would eventually include a number of other states, including Italy, Hungary and Switzerland.[3]

Accepting Schober's interpretation, Mussolini initially saw the customs union as representing the nucleus of a Central European revisionist bloc and, as such, he gave it his full approval and blessing.[4] Grandi and Guariglia, however, disliking Mussolini's radical stance, and seeing the more sinister designs of Curtius behind the plan, set about to change Mussolini's mind, which they succeeded in doing by the beginning of May 'from white to black'.[5] Grandi's annoyance with the plan was that he felt it was too blatant a move toward the *Anschluss*. Since this was patently unacceptable to Italy, Rome was forced to side with Paris in opposition, thereby ruining any chance of Italy being able to balance German and French interests in central Europe.[6]

Yugoslavia and the Catholic Action Crisis

The Belgrade Government's suspicion of the Yugoslav Catholic hierarchy had continued into the summer of 1930[7] and seemed to be confirmed by the Eucharistic Congress in Zagreb in August which, contrary to the wishes of the clergy, was turned into a Croat, rather than a Yugoslav festival.[8] Suspicion of the Catholics was very much against the wishes of King Alexander, however, who seemed to understand the true feelings of the hierarchy and who had deliberately set about in 1930 to conciliate the Catholic bishops, to the point of receiving their blessings and attending service in their cathedrals. 'Zagreb', after all, 'was worth a mass.'[9]

The disaffection of the Catholic Slovenes after the Italian executions in September also prompted King Alexander to secure the support of his Catholic subjects by reaching a definitive settlement with their church. In October, the Yugoslav Government named a delegation to go to Rome to negotiate a concordat[10] and, at the end of the month, the Vatican announced that it was ready to receive this delegation.[11] In spite of these good intentions, however, the Yugoslav delegation never went to Rome, partly because of the opposition of certain members of the Yugoslav Government to such negotiations and partly because of the opposition of large numbers of the Croat clergy to any settlement with Belgrade.[12] A more open sign of the *rapprochement* between King and Archbishop was required to convince their followers and to pave the way for these negotiations. Accordingly, on 30 January 1931, Alexander conferred the Order of Karageorge on Archbishop Bauer in Zagreb and, on the same day, Bauer wrote a pastoral letter, to be circulated throughout Yugoslavia in February, calling on all Yugoslavs to pray for their Slav brethren being persecuted by the Italians in Venezia Giulia.[13] Such signs of mutual respect were designed to emphasize Catholic loyalty to Alexander and to Yugoslavia. Only by taking a deliberately anti-Italian position could Archbishop Bauer indicate the full loyalty of the Catholic Church to Yugoslavia.

While there is no direct evidence to suggest that Bauer's pastoral was authorized or inspired by the Vatican, there is circumstantial evidence which suggests that it represented a deliberate challenge by the Holy See to Italian policy. Certainly the Pope was aware of how sensitive Mussolini was to the Yugoslav situation and of how the Duce would hold the Vatican responsible for the behaviour of the Catholic Church in Yugoslavia. In September 1930, the Pope had made an appeal on behalf of the condemned Slovene terrorists.[14] This appeal had been ignored yet, only four days after the executions, Mussolini had asked the Vatican to control the anti-Italian tone of the Catholic newspapers in Slovenia and had received immediate compliance from the Vatican Secretary of State.[15] Archbishop Bauer would not, under these circumstances, have made such an extreme political statement without having obtained prior permission from Rome. It would appear that Pius XI, displeased by Italy's *rapprochement* with the Soviet Union in the previous November, had now decided to secure a concordat with Yugoslavia whether it accorded with Italian policy or not.

In pledging his loyalty to Yugoslavia, and thereby choosing sides in the Italo–Yugoslav dispute, Archbishop Bauer brought the wrath of the Italian Fascists on the Italian Church. Not only was there evident disappointment in the Italian Government that Bauer would not maintain his designated role as leader of the internal Croat opposition, but there was also anger as Bauer's pastoral served to encourage the clergy and the people of Venezia Giulia to continue and to increase their anti-government protests and demonstrations.[16]

The pastoral of the Archbishop of Zagreb seems to have been the incident which sparked off the Fascist attack on the Church in 1931, as the press attacks on the Church dated from the day after the pastoral was issued.[17] Initially, Mussolini expected the Pope to disavow the sentiments of the Archbishop[18] but, when the Vatican remained silent, the Duce was prepared to respond to the anti-clerical pressure from the Fascist Party and to seek to place a major restriction on the future activities of *Azione Cattolica*.

The Zagreb pastoral served to bring a number of issues to a head in the relationship between Church and State. Domestic relations since the Lateran Agreements had been marked by the increasing popularity and the expanded membership of those associations affiliated with *Azione Cattolica* and by their implicit and, at times, explicit competition with Fascist associations, especially those concerned with youth. Further, it appears that some branches of *Azione Cattolica* were becoming deliberately critical of Fascism and that the national organization of the movement was growing as a potential political opposition to the regime.[19]

At the same time, the violence of the Slavs of Venezia Giulia had been growing between 1929 and 1931 in opposition to the Italianization policies.[20] As the clergy of the area encouraged Slav resistance,[21] the pastoral of Archbishop Bauer was regarded as a direct interference in domestic Italian affairs. Mussolini might not expect the Vatican always to support Italian foreign policy but he could not tolerate direct interference with domestic policy.

In the 25 February 1931 issue of the *Berliner Tageblatt* an article appeared which was entitled 'The Vatican against Fascism' and which argued that, according to information from inside the Vatican, the Holy See had recently made a fundamental change in her foreign policy. In the past, the Holy See had supported particular individuals or political regimes as the best means of promoting the interests of the Church. The support of Seipel of Austria had, however, led to Seipel's defeat in the 1930 elections and the simultaneous withdrawal of 400,000 Catholics from the Church in Austria: 'The vote in Austria testified to the bankruptcy of the Christian Social–Fascist alliance and the result made an extraordinarily strong impression in the Vatican.' Similarly, the entente between Italy and the Holy See had not prevented Grandi from opening discussions for an entente with the Soviet Union. The conclusion of the article was that the Pope had recently decided to dissociate himself from the support of particular right-wing regimes. He had already dropped his support of Seipel, just as he had withdrawn his support from the Spanish monarchy and was also in the process of turning against Mussolini in Italy.[22]

What is important is that this interpretation of Vatican policy had been brought to the attention of Mussolini and a copy of this issue of the *Berliner Tageblatt*, marked with the Duce's characteristic blue pencil, is one of the few documents still remaining in Mussolini's file in Rome's Archivio Centrale dello Stato for the 2 March 1931 meeting of the Fascist Grand Council.[23] As it would seem logical that the 2 March meeting was one at which plans for the forthcoming attack on Italian Catholic Action were discussed,[24] this article could be said to have helped to inform Mussolini's thinking on his relationship with the Holy See. If he believed that the Vatican no longer felt obliged to support particular political regimes, then he could agree with his more anticlerical followers, who saw in Italian Catholic Action a dangerously independent institution.

On 8 April Mussolini forwarded his first demands to the Vatican for placing restraints on *Azione Cattolica* and restricting its sphere of activity. While a press campaign continued through the spring, little happened until the end of June when Mussolini, to force the issue, closed Catholic youth clubs and the Pope, at the same time, disbanded the national directorate of *Azione Cattolica*, placing the diocesan branches temporarily under the direct authority of the bishops.

The Pope, with this direct challenge to the focal institution of his pontificate as well as to a continuing Church influence in the education of youth, mounted a determined resistance both to secure his position in Italy and to demonstrate to the world his detachment from the Fascist regime. The climax of the Pope's campaign came on 5 July with the international publication of the encyclical *Non Abbiamo Bisogno*, a direct refutation of the Fascist claims for a monopoly on the education of youth.[25]

Yet, as De Felice convincingly argues, the encyclical was counter-productive; rather than rallying Italian Catholics in defence of their Church, it served more to rally the Fascists in opposition to these clerical claims. The result was a settlement on 2 September which, in any but the most long-range terms, must be regarded as a defeat for the Pope.[26] By the agreement of 2 September it was agreed that *Azione Cattolica* would, in future, have no separate national directorate and would operate under the direct control of the bishops. Nor would it develop any professional or occupational branches, and youth groups would restrict themselves to religious activities only.

Mussolini had, effectively, broken the will of Pius XI and extended Fascist control in Italy at the expense of the Church. In terms of foreign policy, what the events of 1931 demonstrated was that the Holy See could not remain indifferent to Italian foreign interests, especially those relating to Yugoslavia. In return for a continuing privileged position in Italy, the Pope was expected to adopt an unequivocal position in support of Italian foreign policy. The illusion of papal independence had been brought to an end.

The anti-Italian activities of the Slav clergy in Venezia Giulia had continued throughout the summer of 1931 and the ecclesiastical authorities had made little attempt to interfere,[27] the pressure being no doubt useful in the struggle with Mussolini. With the settlement of 2 September, however, the Vatican made a public show of capitulation in obtaining the resignation of Archbishop Sedej of Gorizia, one of the leaders of this Slav resistance. Sedej was finally pressed to resign his see in October and was replaced by an apostolic administrator, in sympathy with the Italianization laws.[28] At the same time, Bishop Fogar of Trieste, while remaining in office, underwent a noticeable decline in influence[29] and, throughout Venezia Giulia, the Church hierarchy thereafter supported Italian policy.[30]

The Habsburg Alternative

The crisis occasioned by the announcement of the German–Austrian customs union plan had been followed by financial chaos in central Europe. On 12 May the Austrian Kreditanstaldt had collapsed and this had been followed swiftly by the collapse of banks in Germany and, later, in Hungary. In the resultant atmosphere of chaos and crisis, it was necessary not only for Italy to help prevent the customs union but, more importantly, to propose some alternative solution to enable the central European states to regain a degree of economic viability. For the Italians, this was a particularly crucial problem since their two 'client' states, Austria and Hungary, were among the worst hit.

Yet, Italy really had very little with which to help her allies. While Grandi instructed Italian ambassadors to publicize an Italo–Austro–Hungarian economic arrangement as an alternative to the customs union and financial chaos,[31] the truth was that the Italian coffers themselves were none too reliable and that the Italians were really unable to help.[32] In fact, the only power with the funds to provide real assistance was France and it was to French benevolence that both Austria and Hungary were forced to turn in the summer of 1931.[33]

There was another card which the Italians could play in the central European crisis, however, and that was to hold out the possibility of a Habsburg restoration with Italian support. To both the Austrians and the Hungarians a restoration could now represent a real alternative to the customs union or the *Anschluss* and the possibility of such a restoration could at least encourage the necessary resolution to resist German blandishments. On 6 June, in order to consolidate his parliamentary position, Count Bethlen dissolved the Hungarian Parliament well ahead of its term and called for new elections at the end of the month.[34] In the middle of June, a rumour began to spread throughout Europe that the ex-Empress Zita had arranged for the engagement of the

Archduke Otto to the Princess Maria of Savoy, youngest daughter of the King of Italy, that the Pope had received Otto and given his blessing to the engagement and that Zita would formally announce the engagement on the day after the completion of the Hungarian elections.[35] It would appear that the rumour probably was disseminated by Mussolini's agent Mazzotti, with the intention of influencing the Hungarian election campaign.[36]

Since the end of 1930, Bethlen had cooled somewhat on his attachment to Italy[37] and the Duce was conceivably hoping, by this meddling in Hungarian politics, to encourage the Legitimists to keep Bethlen in line with Italy. The other presumed advantage to Mussolini was that this resurrection of the Habsburg issue would work against any French plan to create a Danubian union between Austria, Hungary and the Little Entente and thereby shut out the Italians. In fact, early in June, the Italian Minister had told the Czechoslovak Government of the approaching engagement, stressing that Italy would not support a restoration of the Habsburgs. As no other country had been informed in this way, it would appear that the Italians were deliberately encouraging the Czechs to be on their guard.[38] Grandi, when questioned by the British Ambassador, 'utterly excluded' the possibility of a Royalist coup in Hungary, saying it would have the support neither of Bethlen 'and responsible Hungarian authorities' nor of the Hungarian people.[39] With Bethlen's success in the June elections, nothing further was heard of the proposed royal marriage during that summer. By the end of July, the Papal Nuncio in Prague said that a restoration was no longer imminent, 'not this year at any rate'[40], and on 3 August Bethlen publicly announced 'that no discussions regarding the Kingship question were in progress with persons either in the country or elsewhere and that the attitude of the Government was unchanged.' By the end of July, in fact, the only remaining proponent of the restoration seemed to be the Hungarian Legitimist, Marquis Pallavicini, who was advocating the Austro–Hungarian customs union coupled with the restoration, still echoing Mussolini's schemes.[41]

The customs union crisis had served to damage the Italian entente with Schober who had not only promoted the customs union but, in order to save the Austrian economy, had also been forced to make concessions to the Socialists. As the Austrian relationship was in a state of flux in 1931, so, too, was the relationship with Hungary; on 19 August Bethlen suddenly resigned, having controlled the destiny of Hungary for the previous ten years.

Laval's Overtures of 1931

The reassertion of Germany in the summer of 1931 helped to resolve the stalemate in Franco–Italian relations as, with a restive government in Berlin, Italian assistance at last became important to French diplomacy. Grandi's conciliatory policy was to find in French Premier Pierre Laval, a willing collaborator. Becoming Premier for the first time in January 1931, Laval believed that the true course to European pacification lay through direct Franco–German *rapprochement*. Franco–German conflict had only left effective European power with Britain and Laval was always deeply suspicious of British intentions.[42] He was, however, hampered in making direct overtures by the nature of his parliamentary support which did not subscribe to the conciliation of Germany. Accordingly, Laval attempted to improve French relations in 1931 with both the Soviet Union and with Italy. While the Franco–Soviet *rapprochement*, the first since 1917, was concerned primarily with trade relations,[43] it was the Italian relationship which was of greater interest to Laval.

The first real sign of changed Franco–Italian relations occurred on 1 March 1931, when the conclusion was announced of a compromise agreement on naval disarmament between France and Italy,[44] a compromise made possible by French concessions on the question of naval parity.[45] This compromise was coupled with Grandi's speech to the Chamber of Deputies on 14 March when he repudiated 'sacred egoism as the mainspring of. Italian policy' and gave the impression 'that Italy is tending more and more to emerge from a narrow and isolated nationalism into the wider field of international collaboration in the cause of peace'.[46] Further, as the plan for a German–Austrian customs union was announced in mid-March, so Italy eventually stood with France in opposition to the plan,[47] which gave further evidence of the improving relationship between Rome and Paris.[48]

The French opposition to the plan for the customs union had, however, been responsible for the failure of the Kreditanstaldt, thereby bringing the full impact of the Depression to Germany and central Europe. In that summer, France was the one country whose currency remained strong and she sought to use her strength to offer Germany a loan in return for political pledges denying a future *Anschluss*. In doing so, Laval ran into considerable opposition from Britain and the United States who could ill afford to guarantee such a loan, and thus Laval sought to secure and consolidate his ties with Italy.

As Mussolini's condition of a free hand in the Balkans was not in the power of any French Premier to give at this time, Laval hoped that a sufficiently generous concession in other areas might serve the same purpose. Accordingly, during a series of meetings on the financial crisis in Paris and London in mid-July, Laval took Grandi aside to tell him of his firm intention to reach an accord with Italy and to suggest that, as part of a settlement, France would be prepared to consider concessions in Ethiopia. While Grandi was very impressed by Laval's directness and reported to Mussolini that Laval was 'the first Frenchman to whom I did not feel that instinctive dislike which always invades my spirit whenever I have contact with a Gaul', nevertheless, he handled Laval's proposal most carefully and, without comment, passed it on to the Duce for consideration.[49]

Failing any direct reply to the overtures through Grandi in July, the French sought to open negotiations through less official channels and thus Marquis Alberto Theodoli, the Italian Chairman of the Mandates Commission of the League of Nations, was approached in the fall by the French member of the Commission, Robert De Caix, with proposals for Franco–Italian negotiations. Having received authorization from Rome to proceed, particularly once Mussolini had satisfied himself in October that there was no real danger of a Franco–German agreement,[50] Theodoli continued his discussions during the winter of 1931–2 with De Caix, Berthelot and Laval himself. During these discussions the French offer was clearly set out of a free hand for Italy in Abyssinia, with French interests there protected, in return for Italian support of France in the League, opposition to the *Anschluss* and the settlement of Italian differences with Yugoslavia. Basically, it was to be an exchange of African colonies for Italian acceptance of the European *status quo*.[51]

This French offer opened the rift within the Italian Government over the proper direction of foreign policy. The imperialists of the Foreign Ministry, especially Guariglia, felt that Italy should accept the offer, join France in opposing German resurgence in the League of Nations and concentrate on colonial development.[52] · The more radical members of the Party and Government, however, such as Italo Balbo, saw Italy's real destiny as resting in opposition to France in central Europe where Italian Fascists and German Nazis might well work together. The French offer was thus interpreted as an attempt to buy off the Italians, a point of view which was in accordance with Mussolini's own interpretation. The Duce felt the French offer was an attempt to embroil Italy in an African adventure, thus preventing concentration on 'his great European policy and of putting all his weight on the decisive events which were rapidly reaching maturation'. It was out of this dispute over a Franco–Italian settlement that the internal reorganizations of the Italian government and foreign policy were to proceed in 1932.[53]

Loosening Ties with Albania

In Albania, the religious conflict over the Uniate Church at Elbassan in September 1929 had really been part of a continuing tension between Zog and his Italian protectors whereby Zog recognized the value of Italian support, but was under domestic pressure not to submit too much to the Italians.

The cooperation of the Italians with the Holy See in Albania was becoming most noticeable in the fields of health and education where, in the major cities of Albania, the Italian Government subsidized religious hospitals and a number of convent schools where instruction was carried out in the Italian language.[54] Not only did such cooperation irritate Zog and the Albanian Church, but it also bothered the Catholic Albanians of the north who were not particularly impressed by Italian sponsorship and were reported to have rejected donations for rebuilding one of their churches when they learned that the funds had come from Italy.[55] Catholicism was not proving a reliable guarantee of support for Italy. And yet, these Catholics on the Albanian–Yugoslav frontier were strategically important to Italy. This became particularly true after Zog's refusal to renew the 1926 Treaty of Tirana when it expired in November 1931. In cooperation with the Vatican, the Italian Government made a greater effort and sponsored a very successful tour of Italy by the Catholics of Scutari in the spring of 1932. When in Rome they were received by both the Pope and by Mussolini. With the growing independence of Zog, both Italy and the Holy See had greater need of one another's support in Albania.[56]

The Alexander–Mussolini Negotiations

As Laval believed in conciliating Mussolini and was not consequently a great supporter of the Little Entente, so the Yugoslavs in 1931 were forced onto their own resources in their dealings with Italy. It was under these circumstances that secret negotiations were developed between Mussolini and King Alexander.[57] Late in 1930, King Alexander had discovered that he shared the same interior decorator, Guido Malagola Cappi, with Mussolini. While no political discussions took place, Alexander first used Malagola to convey his attitude to Mussolini on a number of issues. Toward the end of February 1931, Malagola asked Alexander if he would be interested in a meeting with Mussolini. While the King was interested, discussions came to nothing during the summer of 1931 as Mussolini was unwilling to settle a date for such a meeting.

Late in November, when Mussolini was running into trouble with the refusal of Zog to renew the Treaty of Tirana, the Duce developed a new interest in negotiations with Yugoslavia. Italian security in Albania was in danger of being undermined and Italian military intervention might become necessary in the near future. Mussolini, accordingly, sent Alexander a draft agreement in January 1932, expecting Alexander to endorse a 'supreme' Italian interest in Albania. Alexander could not accept Italian 'supremacy' but was prepared to guarantee Albania neutrality as well as to offer Italy facilities in the Bay of Kotor and a permanent guarantee of peace if a treaty could be concluded. The real intentions of Alexander in the spring of 1932, according to Hoptner, were such that 'Not even his foreign minister Marinkovic knew anything of his ideas for strengthening Yugoslavia's ties with Italy, nor of his hope that Italy would supplant France as Yugoslavia's major ally.'[58] If an agreement with Italy could be worked out, Alexander was prepared to revise the Franco–Yugoslav Pact when it came up for renewal in December 1932.

The negotiations continued into April, when Alexander offered Mussolini a full guarantee of the supremacy of Italian commer-

1. At the signing of the Italian Concordat on 11 February 1929. Cardinal Gasparri and Signor Mussolini in the centre; Count Dino Grandi on the right (*The Times*)

2. Pope Pius XI (*Popperfoto*)

3. Benito Mussolini, with his son Romano in 1931 (*Popperfoto*)

4. Cardinal Eugenio Pacelli, Vatican Secretary of State, 1930–9
(*BBC Hulton Picture Library*)

5a. Count Dino Grandi (*BBC Hulton Picture Library*)

5b. King Alexander of Yugoslavia and Louis Barthou, French Foreign Minister, moments before their assassination in October 1934 (*BBC Hulton Picture Library*)

6a. Lord Strickland, Prime Minister of Malta (*Popperfoto*)

6b. Father Ignaz Seipel, Christian Social Leader and Chancellor of Austria in the 1920s (*Osterreichische Nationalbibliothek*)

7a. Count Stephen Bethlen, Prime Minister of Hungary, 1921–31 (*Popperfoto*)

7b. Englebert Dollfuss, Chancellor of Austria, 1932–4 (*Österreichische Nationalbibliothek*)

8a. King Zog of Albania (*Popperfoto*)

8b. Empress Zita and Archduke Otto of Austria–Hungary
(*BBC Hulton Picture Library*)

cial, financial and industrial interests in Albania, if not of military interests. It was not so much Alexander's refusal to accede to Mussolini's complete demands over Albania which ended the negotiations, but rather Alexander's too great willingness to accept Mussolini's conditions which would have required the Duce to share power on the Adriatic when, ultimately, he had no intention of doing so.

Mussolini was not interested in negotiations if there was any possibility of the disintegration of Yugoslavia. In March, he received a report advising of the restiveness of the Yugoslav opposition and of the decreasing interest of France in the fate of Yugoslavia.[59] As General Zivkovic resigned on 4 April and discontent with the royal dictatorship became more open,[60] so Mussolini prepared to resume his offensive against Yugoslavia and, in June, in answer to King Alexander, Mussolini sent him a message saying that, rather than continuing negotiations, 'I shall sit at my window and see what happens in Yugoslavia'. Thus rebuffed, Alexander was never again prepared to trust the Italian dictator.[61]

Caritate Christi

With the beginning of the Depression, the Holy See had curtailed its expansionist outlook of the 1920s in anticipation of having to contend with widespread social misery and political unrest. In the midst of the Depression, Pius XI sought to present some alternative theory of social organization to that offered by Moscow. As part of the celebration of the fortieth anniversary of the publication in 1891 of Pope Leo XIII's social encyclical *Rerum Novarum*, Pius XI issued the encyclical *Quadragesimo Anno* on 15 May 1931, amplifying the ideas of Leo XIII and supporting the conciliatory features of Catholic corporatism. Anti-clerical Fascists interpreted *Quadragesimo Anno* as also offering an alternative to Fascist corporatism.[62]

Yet the events of 1931 brought even this expansiveness to an end. The dispute with Mussolini over Catholic Action coupled with the extension of the Depression to central and eastern Europe in that year utterly sapped the Pope's combative spirit. On 11 February 1932, as evidence of the resolution of the domestic conflict between Italy and the Holy See, Mussolini paid

his long-awaited visit to Pius XI in the Vatican. According to
Mussolini's minutes, by the time of this meeting, the Pope had
adopted a completely defensive outlook on world affairs, arguing
to the Duce that the Roman Catholic Church must stand firm
against the encroachments of Protestants, Communists and
Jews.[63]

On 3 May 1932, Pius XI published his encyclical *Caritate
Christi*, 'On the Present Distress of the Human Race', in which he
sought to indicate the real dangers attendant upon the Depression:

> Profiting by so much economic distress and so much moral dis-
> order the enemies of all social order, be they called Commu-
> nists or by any other name, boldly set about breaking through
> every restraint. This is the most dreadful evil of our times, for
> they destroy every bond of law, human or divine; they engage
> openly and in secret in a relentless struggle against religion and
> against God Himself; they carry out the diabolical program of
> wresting from the hearts of all, even of children, all religious
> sentiment; for well they know that, when once belief in God has
> been taken from the heart of mankind, they will be entirely free
> to work out their will. Thus we see today, what was never
> before seen in history, the satanical banners of war against God
> and against religion brazenly unfurled to the winds in the midst
> of all peoples and in all parts of the earth.

The Pope then went on to offer the guiding standard for Catholics
at this moment of history

> For in this conflict, there is really question of the fundamental
> problem of the universe and of the most important decision
> proposed to man's free will. For God or against God: this once
> more is the alternative that shall decide the destinies of all
> mankind in politics, in finance, in morals, in the sciences and
> arts, in the State, in civil and domestic society.[64]

In the summer of 1932, the earlier calls of the Pope for a return of
Russia to the Church changed to expressions of the fear of Communist counter-attack through the misery of the Depression;
anti-Communism became his consistent theme. The emphasis
shifted to the defence of Catholicism against Communism and, by

1933, as the attention of the Holy See was focused more on Catholic countries, such as Dollfuss' Austria, the earlier interest in eastern expansion fell away completely.

The baptism by King Boris and Queen Giovanna of Bulgaria of their first child, a daughter, in the Orthodox faith early in 1933, in direct contravention of their 1930 agreement with the Pope meant a collapse of the earlier hopes that had been placed on this marriage and evoked a strong public protest from Pius XI – evidence in itself that Bulgaria deserved less consideration than heretofore. By the end of 1933, D'Herbigny had been replaced as the head of the Commission 'Pro Russia' and of the Pontifical Oriental Institute and both these institutions had fallen from favour. In 1934, Monsignor Roncalli, potentially the most successful of those prelates working for church union, was shifted from Bulgaria to become Apostolic Delegate to Turkey and Greece.[65]

8 The Spanish Catalyst

The crises of 1931 affecting the relationship between Italy and the Holy See can only be fully appreciated when examined against the background of contemporary events in Spain. The abdication of King Alfonso XIII and the establishment of the Spanish Republic in 1931 had an important catalytic effect on relations between Italy and the Holy See. The inaction of the Vatican on the occasion of the collapse of the Spanish monarchy convinced Mussolini that the Church would not use its influence to support any type of political regime, no matter how friendly that regime might be or how potentially damaging to the interests of the Church might be the alternative. Under such circumstances, the Fascist Government could not afford to be dependent on the support of the Italian Church and, therefore, Mussolini sought to force the Church in Italy and, particularly, *Azione Cattolica* into a position of greater dependence on the State. However, at the same time, the attempts of the Holy See to appease the Republican Government of Spain were to demonstrate to the Pope the complete unreliability of the anti-clerical and socialist Left and to confirm Pope Pius XI in his conviction that Bolshevism was the great peril of the modern world which would give no quarter and must be given none in any of its manifestations. At a time when Mussolini was sceptical of the value of the support of the Church, it was ironic that the Church, having burnt its fingers badly in Spain, came to appreciate the merit of its association with Fascism in the anti-Bolshevik crusade.

Since the seizure of Tunis by France in 1881, the western Mediterranean had been a French sphere of influence. Because of this, Spain had always recognized its diplomatic dependence on its northern neighbour, while Italy, since 1912, had evinced no more than a passing interest in the western Mediterranean, concentrating her colonial interests in the eastern Mediterranean and the

Red Sea. Only in such questions as the framing of the international statute for Tangiers in 1923 did Italy expect to be
involved as a western Mediterranean power. Relations between
Italy and Spain were normally very much contingent on the given
state of relations between Italy and France and therefore, as the
French had deliberately refused to include Italy in the discussion
over Tangiers, Mussolini sought to forge a cooperative alliance in
1923 with the new dictator of Spain, General Miguel Primo de
Rivera. The possibility of close cooperation between the two dictators was discussed during the Spanish royal visit to Italy in
November 1923, which took place only a month after the military
coup that had established the Spanish dictatorship. At the time of
this visit, Primo de Rivera was very enthusiastic about a draft
treaty for extensive cooperation which he had worked out with
Mussolini. The longer Primo was in office, however, the more he
came to appreciate Spanish dependence on French goodwill,
especially in the light of Spanish involvement in the Riff War in
Morocco. Consequently, during 1924, Primo became notably less
interested in the pact and the discussions eventually lapsed.[1]

With the conclusion of the Riff War, Spain sought to force
France to reopen the question of the status of Tangiers, and
Primo was willing to conclude a treaty of friendship and conciliation with Italy in August 1926, using Spanish influence to have
Italy included in the new discussions on Tangiers. As Britain also
supported Mussolini's claim for inclusion, Primo's move did not
really bring about much change in relations between Rome and
Madrid and these continued on a rather superficial level for the
duration of the decade.[2] Although there was a considerable show
on the part of Primo de Rivera of imitating Mussolini's dictatorship and while Mussolini continued to send advice to his Spanish
counterpart, personal relations between the two dictators
remained rather cool.[3] By 1929, Mussolini was particularly critical of the weakness and corruption of the Spanish Government.[4]
However, if there was no real community of interest between the
Spanish and Italian dictatorships, there was a certain ideological
affinity and Dino Grandi, as Foreign Minister in 1929, could
explain that the main importance of Primo de Rivera lay in his
role as a somewhat shaky bulwark against the extension of left-
wing influence in Europe.[5]

During the nineteenth century, the role of the Church in Spain
had undergone a dramatic change as a result of the extensive

expropriation of church property by the Liberals during the First Carlist War of the 1830s. The Liberal supporters of Queen Isabella II had expropriated the property to finance their war against the Carlist forces who had been backed by the Church. Before the Carlist War, the Church had been an institution of independent means and of independent political values. As a result of the Concordat of 1851, however, the Church had been forced into dependence on State funds and, therefore, into a position where necessity dictated that it should support the political values of the landed oligarchy which controlled the State.[6] Even under these circumstances, the Church did not remain passive and, consequently, the late nineteenth century witnessed a deliberate and successful policy of re-Catholicizing the Spanish upper- and middle-classes. The result was that the Church acquired a considerable amount of new wealth, some of which went on the upkeep of the secular clergy's ministry in the parishes, but the bulk of which was directed to the subsidization and extension of certain religious orders. Moreover, at this time, education came under the virtual domination of certain of these orders. The relationship between the monarchy, the ruling oligarchy and the Church hierarchy became, therefore, very much a symbiotic one, and the remarriage of the Spanish Throne and Altar was consummated anew in the early years of the twentieth century when the social order was challenged by the increasing radicalism of the proletariat. The protection of the monarchy and of the social order was seen anew as one of the main functions of the Spanish episcopate.[7]

While Primo de Rivera's dictatorship was designed to defend the monarchy against both the disorder of the Left and the corruption of the politicians, his old-fashioned populist nationalism was not particularly welcome to the Church. Seeing the monarchy as the symbol of the nation united, Primo identified the Church as one of the institutional pillars of the nation-state. The Church disliked both this subordination of its interest to that of the State and Primo's strong centralization, which forced the Church to abandon its policy of using the Catalan language in religious services. Ultimately, and perhaps most importantly, the hierarchy disapproved of Primo's attempt to co-opt the Socialist Party and its trade union to the support of his regime, making it the agency for the implementation of his labour policies to the exclusion of Catholic unions and labour groups.

The Spanish episcopate was, therefore, wary of what Primo de Rivera's populism might ultimately achieve in terms of social reforms and was quite content to see him go. It did not attempt to use any of its considerable influence with King Alfonso XIII to extend the life of the dictatorship.[8]

The basic concern of the Vatican was that Primo de Rivera's dictatorial regime, uninformed by any new social programme, represented a desperate attempt to paper over the deep fissures in Spanish society without effecting any more permanent degree of social cohesion. The dictatorship was a clear sign that the monarchy was in trouble but what was most distressing to the Holy See was the knowledge that the Church in Spain was as divided as the society it served. In its disunity, the Spanish Church was thus incapable of acting as a force for reconciliation and social cohesion.

The traditionalist element in the Church was led by the Primate, the Archbishop of Toledo, Pedro Cardinal Segura y Sáenz, who has been described as a 'good example of a thirteenth century churchman and a glaring anachronism in 1931, even in Spain'.[9] This element, drawing its support from the hierarchy and the bulk of the secular clergy, saw that the Church had to stand or fall with the existing social order and saw any talk of social reform as an attack not only on the oligarchy but also on Church rights and privileges.

Opposed to this position were the clerical social-Catholics and the anti-clerical liberal-Catholics. The social-Catholics believed that the Church should continue to play a dominant role in the life of the State but that it had a very real responsibility for social reform which it was not fulfilling. In representing this 'Christian democratic' point of view, social-Catholics were to be found more in the religious orders than in the secular clergy. Ángel Herrera Oria, the editor of the Jesuit-financed newspaper, *El Debate*, was the dominant figure in this camp. To the hierarchy, the preservation of the *status quo* was all-important, while to the social-Catholics the Church could only fill its mission by seeking to resolve the social question. Members of the latter group liked to refer to themselves as 'European' rather than 'Spanish' Catholics.[10]

A third position was that assumed by the liberal-Catholics who were devout but anti-clerical. Such men as Niceto Alcalá Zamora, believing that the Church should restrict its activity to problems of faith and morals, found themselves supporters of the republican movement by 1930 with the intention of negotiating the separation of Church and State within a republican framework.

By January 1930, realizing that he had lost the support both of the army and of his king, Primo de Rivera resigned. The experiment in dictatorship had been a patent failure, Primo having shown himself completely incapable of restoring a purified political life to the country. The real price for his failure, however, would have to be paid by Alfonso XIII, who had placed his confidence in Primo's experiment. With the dictatorship finished in 1930, it was generally recognized that it was only a matter of time before the king would follow his dictator into exile.[11]

As the question of the future of the monarchy was opened, so also was the question of the future role of the Church in Spain. As the Throne and the hierarchy had irretrievably committed themselves to one another, so that much of the criticism of the Bourbons was based on their clericalism and much of the criticism of the Church hierarchy rested on its close association with the monarchy,[12] it was certain that any republic established would be anti-clerical if not also anti-Catholic.

In the development of the Papacy's Spanish policy, the decisive figure was that of the Nuncio in Madrid, Monsignor Federico Tedeschini, and the policy of the Vatican in the early 1930s very much bears the mark of his personality and style. It clearly appears that Pope Pius XI was guided by Tedeschini's advice to accept policies for Spain which made anti-democratic friends of the Church, such as Mussolini, deeply suspicious. And yet, Pius did agree with Tedeschini that there was no real alternative to adopting a position in Spain whereby the Church would work with and within whatever political regime happened to be in existence at any given time.[13] In accepting this advice for Spain, Pius XI was adopting an approach which had been rejected in Italy when, in 1923, he had abandoned Don Luigi Sturzo and his *Partito Popolare* in favour of direct negotiations and, ultimately, a treaty and concordat with Fascism. In Italy, the Church had accepted a role as one of the apolitical institutions within the Fascist State; in Spain, to the contrary, the Church was prepared to do battle as one of the political interests in the State. While the Pope was not necessarily comfortable in sponsoring a new political movement, he was not inconsistent in doing so, as his main interest was in furthering the lay apostolate of Catholic Action and he would cooperate with any political regime or sponsor any political movement which would allow him to do this.

Yet, to those such as Mussolini, who looked at the world in political terms, the position of the Holy See in Spain appeared to be strikingly inconsistent with its position in Italy. Presumably, too, the fact that the Nuncio in Madrid had formerly been an ardent supporter of Sturzo and the *Popolari*[14] was not lost on Mussolini.

Before Pope Benedict XV appointed him to Madrid in 1921, Tedeschini had, indeed, been an ardent supporter of the *Popolari* and, until stopped by the advent of the dictatorship, had worked between 1921 and 1923 to create a similar Catholic political party in Spain.[15] In outlook very much a social-Catholic, Tedeschini had also taken up with relish his early assignment to develop the social component of Spanish Catholic Action (*Acción Católica*), in order, both to make a Catholic contribution to the social question and to develop *Acción Católica* as an institution which would stand above the warring Catholic political factions. By 1929, the Nuncio had acquitted himself with considerable finesse in this task.[16] His sympathies and affinities were obviously with the Spanish social-Catholics and he was a close personal friend of Ángel Herrera Oria,[17] while he was completely out of sympathy with Cardinal Segura whom he 'considered ... to be one of the main stumbling blocks to an efficient and aware national church'.[18]

Mgr Tedeschini was thus preparing in 1930 to protect the Church from the commitments of Segura and the hierarchy. While remaining on good terms with the hierarchy, the Nuncio was cultivating Catholic republican leaders, notably Alcalá Zamora, later to be president of the Republic.[19] It was, in fact, alleged that Tedeschini had even maintained contact with republican conspirators in prison.[20] In the divided state of Spanish Catholicism, the Papal Nuncio was playing a game designed, in the event of expected political turbulence, to give him control of Catholic policy in Spain.

The opening of the Spanish domestic crisis with Primo's resignation in January 1930, does not seem to have been of particular concern to Mussolini, for a report of 31 March 1930 on the weakness of the monarchy after the fall of Primo was filed with the marginal notation '*non importante*' once Mussolini had read it.[21] Of greater interest was any indication of a Franco-Spanish *rapproche-*

ment and consequently, following a visit by the French War Minister, Maginot, to Madrid in the winter of 1930–1, Grandi sought and received assurances from Madrid that this did not imply any change in the Italo-Spanish relationship.[22] In fact, it was only when Mussolini's thinking was drawn to questions of the relationship between Church and State in the spring of 1931 that the Spanish domestic crisis acquired a significance for him as an indicator of Vatican policy and of the ultimate political inconsistency and unreliability of the Holy See.

The article in the *Berliner Tageblatt* of 25 February 1931, which explained how the Vatican was withdrawing support from particular right-wing regimes and which helped to launch Mussolini's attack on Italian Catholic Action, described the relationship of the Vatican to the Spanish monarchy as being one of the touchstones of a changing Vatican policy. Thus informed in the spring of 1931, Mussolini could not but observe Vatican reaction to the course of events following the abdication of Alfonso XIII and the creation of the Republic on 14 April 1931.

With the establishment of the Spanish Republic, the political rift between the Vatican and the Spanish hierarchy soon became apparent. To the Vatican, it was necessary to reach some accommodation with the new government in order to defuse the anticipated anti-clericalism of the republicans and therefore Tedeschini entered immediately into negotiations.[23] The Holy See reserved its public judgement on the creation of the Republic[24] and, before the end of April, had extended it *de facto* recognition.[25] Tedeschini had seized the initiative in dealings with the Republic, had obtained a sympathetic hearing, especially from Alcalá Zamora and Miguel Maura (the two Catholics in the Cabinet) and had tried to pave the way for reasonable Church–State relations.[26] But, although Tedeschini and Alcalá Zamora were capable of reaching a working agreement, they both had to contend with their own extremists, none of whom really wanted an accommodation between Church and Republic. On 6 May Cardinal Segura broke his silence to issue a pastoral letter which was rather more offensive in tone than in content and in which the Cardinal praised Alfonso XIII and called on Spanish Catholics to stand by their ideals so that 'we shall have no right to lament when bitter reality shows us that we had victory in our hands, yet knew not how to fight like intrepid warriors prepared to succumb gloriously'.[27] In reaction to this pastoral, the anarchists instigated a series of church burnings throughout Spain five days later, which the Republican Government proved unable to control or prevent.[28]

The combination of these two events helped to undermine the position of the moderates in the Church and State. As the Left was triumphant in the June elections for the Constituent Cortes and prepared to inscribe radical anti-clerical articles in the new constitution, the Holy See made a final conciliatory move by sacrificing Cardinal Segura. On 1 October, on the eve of the debate on the religious articles by the Cortes, it was announced that Cardinal Segura had resigned as Archbishop of Toledo and Primate of Spain and that the Pope had accepted his resignation. It was hoped that this major conciliatory gesture would make the anti-clericalism of the Cortes less vindictive,[29] but such was not to be the case.

The creation of the Spanish Republic raised with the Italian Foreign Ministry the traditional question about Franco-Spanish relations and about the possibility of a democratic republican Spain moving closer to France and even possibly abandoning to France the Spanish interest in Morocco.[30] The official Italian position was, however, one of 'wait-and-see'.[31] It was really domestic issues in Spain which aroused more interest, as there was considerable press comment on the obvious passivity of the Church when confronted by events which could well produce a Communist Spain[32] and, most importantly, these domestic issues had a significant effect on Mussolini's thinking.

The Duce's personal interpretation of the significance of the creation of the Spanish Republic was set out in a document entitled 'Aphorisms' on 21 May 1931. In this document, he argued that the resignation of King Alfonso had created a political vacuum in Spain

A new regime is never born from the dismissal of a sovereign.

The Republic was entirely a negative creation

When a king abdicates, he ... must be replaced, either by another king, if one exists, or by a president. In the latter case, it is necessary, whether one wants to or not, to proclaim a republic.

Not only did the Republic lack any real substance, but it was also an anachronism in the twentieth century

> To make a parliamentary republic today is like using gas lamps when electric lighting is available.

The reason for Mussolini's apprehension was that such a political vacuum would be rapidly filled by the Left during these chaotic Depression years

> Kerensky did not bring Nicholas back. He prepared for Lenin. . . . Today, it is no longer a question of a republic or of a monarchy, but of communism or fascism.

What, to Mussolini, was most striking was the political naivety of the Spanish Church

> His Catholic Majesty of Spain had no defenders among the Catholics.

According to him the reason for this was that the Church had not concerned itself adequately with political instruction. Catholics had only been taught to make political decisions based on the attitude of any given group toward the Church. And yet, without any real political guidance, Catholics would reject the principle of authority in favour of the 'wonderful humbug' of democracy – promoted in Italy as much as in Spain. Consequently, because of an inadequate political education, Catholics had no idea where, at any given moment, their best interests might lie.[33]

From 1931, then, Mussolini was prepared to try to subvert the Spanish Republic lest it should ultimately come under Communist control. In seeking agencies for such subversion he would not work through the Church which he believed to be politically incapable of discerning a Bolshevik threat. In fact, he very much questioned how far one could now base any policies on an expectation of Church support.

The weakness of Tedeschini's position in Spain and of that of the Vatican in 1931 was that the Spanish Right was in complete disarray because of its former association with the monarchy. The Vatican had to rely, therefore, on the anti-clerical Catholic Alcalá Zamora within the Government for the protection of its interests in Spain. Alcalá Zamora was, however, no match for the surging tide of the Left and he was only able to offer his impotent resignation when the Cortes, in October 1931, gave approval to the notorious Article 26 of the new constitution. This not only made provisions for the financial separation of Church and State but also proclaimed that religious orders were 'not to engage in commerce, industry, or non-confessional teaching'.[34] The Pope was most upset by this frontal attack on the Church[35] which was continued into 1932 when certain provisions of the new constitution were enacted into law.

In Italy, the conflict with Mussolini had been resolved in September 1931 when the Pope had accepted restrictions on the activities of Italian Catholic Action. However this 'reconciliation' was ultimately gratifying to Pius XI, who barely restrained his enthusiasm for Fascism during his meeting with Mussolini on 11 February 1932. In fact, for Pope Pius, the critical events in Spain can only have convinced him of the wisdom of placing his faith in Italian Fascism at a time when, as he confided to Mussolini, 'there is a sorrowful triangle which augments Our grief: Mexico, a country totally absorbed by Masonry; Spain, where Bolshevism and Masonry work together, and Russia, which proceeds in its work of deChristianizing the people.'[36] The conclusion which the Pope was reaching on the basis of his Spanish experience seems to have been that it would, in future, be in the interest of the Church to stand by the authoritarian regimes lest, in the uncertain state of affairs in these Depression years, the Bolsheviks should gain further advantage from an apparent lack of resolution on the part of the Church. Yet, although there was to be a growing amount of cooperation with Fascism in the coming year,[37] it is significant that Spain was the one area where cooperation was not to be possible.

On 8 May 1932, the return to power of the French Left under Edouard Herriot opened the possibility of an anti-Italian bloc of France and Spain at a time when the growing strength of the German Nazis was threatening Italian influence in central Europe. These factors combined to help to explain Mussolini's decision to resume direct control of the Foreign Ministry in July 1932, and to initiate an offensive designed to secure the Italian position in central Europe. In doing so, Mussolini sought to protect his rear by neutralizing Spain either through subverting the Republic or through assuring it of his goodwill.

By the spring of 1932, the Fascist regime was offering encouragement and assistance to those groups of Spaniards which were plotting against the Republic. Initial contacts seem to have been between Spanish military and aeronautical circles and the Italian Air Minister, Italo Balbo. The chief military plotter was General Barrera who, in 1932, worked out a plan with the popular General Sanjurjo among others for a military rising to force the resignation of the left-wing Azaña Government.[38] In April or May 1932, Balbo was approached for Italian support and assistance for this rising[39] but, while arms and munitions were promised, the Sanjurjo rising aborted on 10 August before any Italian aid could be sent.[40]

Spanish suspicion of Italian involvement in the Sanjurjo rising brought expressions of concern from Madrid lest Rome become a centre for Spanish conspirators.[41] As part of the 1932 summer Cabinet shuffle, Raffaele Guariglia, who had effectively been the second man at the Foreign Ministry, was named Ambassador to Madrid, with instructions to create and maintain friendly relations with the Spanish Government, and in particular, to keep a close eye on Franco-Spanish relations.[42]

Guariglia had, however, barely arrived in Madrid before Herriot paid a formal visit to Spain in November. The Italians wrongly believed that, during this visit, Herriot had concluded a secret pact with Azaña for the transport of French troops through Spain and for French use of the Balearic Islands in time of war.[43] For this reason Italian hopes for any real Italo-Spanish *rapprochement* receded and Balbo continued to develop his contacts with the Spanish conspirators. In the winter of 1932–3, the monarchist politician Calvo Sotelo travelled to Rome from his Paris exile for discussions with Balbo.[44] Mussolini was indeed prepared to see Italy become a centre for anti-Republican Spaniards many of whom, ironically enough, had been attracted to Mussolini in the first place because of his good relations with the Vatican.[45]

Initial Vatican hopes that the anti-clerical provisions of the Spanish Constitution might have been somewhat tempered in their application[46] were not realized in 1932. In January, the Spanish Jesuit Order was dissolved and in October a draft law was introduced into the Cortes 'providing for the confiscation by the State of the properties of the religious congregations, forbidding them to teach and enabling them to be dissolved by decree of the Cortes.'[47]

By the beginning of 1933, the Pope was reported very much preoccupied with Spanish affairs.[48] His overwhelming preoccupation with Bolshevism in 1932 and the spring of 1933,[49] to the point of welcoming Hitler's accession to power as another anti-Bolshevik crusader,[50] was conditioned to no small extent by his apprehension over the increasing radicalism in Spain.

In May 1933 the Cortes passed the Law on Religious Confessions and Congregations and on 4 June, Pius XI finally spoke out, issuing his encyclical *Dilectissima Nobis* deploring the situation in Spain. While the Pope 'roundly condemned the attitude and conduct of the Republican Government towards the Catholic Church, and exhorted the faithful to use all legitimate means to obtain the repeal of a law so opposed to the rights of every citizen and so hostile to religion', he nevertheless took considerable pains in *Dilectissima Nobis* to point out that he was in no way criticizing the form of government in existence in Spain.[51] The Pope saw no alternative to the Church working within the framework of the Republic, especially now that a proper vehicle existed for expressing this Catholic interest.

What had been notably lacking in the first year of the Republic had been any real organization of a republican right-wing. The vocal right-wing positions had either been taken by enemies of the Republic or by rather ineffective members of the Right Republican Party from within the Government. There was an obvious need for a clearly right-wing party which would accept the Republic; it was the social-Catholics who eventually provided the leadership for such a movement.

Early in 1931 *El Debate* had accepted the existence of the Republic and Herrera had been instrumental in having a political movement created out of *Acción Católica*, designated *Acción Nacional*, as 'an organization for social defence' to seek wide support from all Catholics.[52] With the increasing volume of anti-clerical legislation, however, there was a need for a broader organization of the Republican Right to act in defence of the interests of the Church.

By 1932, *Acción Nacional* had changed its name to *Acción Popular* and had come under the presidency of José María Gil Robles y Quiñones, a former associate editor of *El Debate* and one of the protégés of Herrera. With the discrediting of the revolutionary Right in the Sanjurjo affair of August, Gil Robles reorganized his party on 22 October 1932 to give it a broader base and direction

and renamed it the Spanish Confederation of Autonomous Right-
ist Groups or CEDA (*Confederación Española de Dercehas Autónomas*).
In 1933 the CEDA put itself forward as the organized movement
of the Right and canvassed Catholic support in reaction,
particularly, to the Law on Religious Confessions and Congregations.

With elections called for November 1933, the CEDA sought
support from all branches of Catholicism in a campaign to defend
the Church and reverse the anti-clerical legislation. Just before
the election, Gil Robles and his party entered into an alliance
with the two monarchist parties, the Alfonsine *Renovación Española*
and the Carlist *Comunión Tradicionalista*, benefiting both from their
support and their funds. The result was that the CEDA emerged
from the elections as the largest single party in the Cortes and in a
position to control subsequent governments of Spain.

It was the intention of Gil Robles, once elected, to work within
the framework of the Republic, with a political strategy designed
to wean the Radicals from dependence on the Socialists. If a
Centre–Right Radical–CEDA coalition could be secured, the
position of the Church would, he felt, be relatively safe within the
Republic. Much to the annoyance of the Catholic monarchists
who had voted and paid for the CEDA, however, Gil Robles only
made his preference for this strategy clear after the elections.[53]
The monarchists had hoped that the CEDA would join them in
forcing new elections through non-cooperation and thereby pave
the way for a legal restoration.[54] While Gil Robles in December
1933 was explaining his republican strategies, the *Osservatore
Romano* and *El Debate* were simultaneously advising Spanish
Catholics to accommodate themselves to the Republic.[55]

The great tragedy of Gil Robles and the CEDA, however, was
that they were politically capable only of defending the Church
and reversing or delaying certain of the anti-clerical measures. In
terms of positive legislation, particularly that dealing with the
social question, they were blocked by their dependence on the
Catholic landed interests. The result was that the CEDA was
never able to counteract the polarization of Spanish society and it
consequently did little to allay left-wing fears of its imminent imposition of Fascism.[56]

The new Spanish Government, under the Radical Alejandro
Lerroux, but with the support of the CEDA, brought a good deal
of satisfaction to the Vatican by reversing the effects of the anti-

clerical legislation,[57] and in January 1934 Foreign Minister Pita Romero was named Special Ambassador to the Holy See, with the power to negotiate a concordat.[58] Pita Romero's visit to Rome for negotiations ultimately reached deadlock by the end of August 1934, however, over the issue of civil marriage and the considerable difficulty of dealing with anti-clerical provisions already written into the Constitution.[59] Moreover, given the difficulties which the Vatican was experiencing by this time with the German Concordat, it is not surprising that the Vatican was reluctant to conclude a concordat with a Spanish Government which did not even include the CEDA.[60] The entry of the CEDA into the Government at the end of 1934 did make prospects for a concordat appear brighter.[61]

The public stance of Gil Robles and the *Osservatore Romano* in favour of the Republic caused an open rift in the Spanish Catholic camp, both in Spain and among the Spanish exiles in Rome. The Monarchists were bitter about Gil Robles and about the part played by the Papal Nuncio in these developments. Sympathetic words for the monarchy in the *Illustrazione Vaticana* proved little compensation[62] and the Monarchists thereafter seemed bent on a violent solution.

A Catholic, right-wing Republic was most unwelcome to the Spanish Monarchists, as it could easily drain off valuable support. With a degree of increasing desperation in the spring of 1934, representatives of the *Renovación Española* and the *Comunión Tradicionalista* along with General Barrera sought out Balbo in order to seek guarantees of Italian assistance. To their satisfaction, they found Mussolini himself, having just announced his projected expansion into Africa, willing to receive them on 31 March 1934, to promise assistance in overthrowing the Republic and to provide an immediate gift of arms and money as evidence of good faith. On that same day, Balbo signed with the leaders of the two Monarchist parties an agreement planning for close Italo-Spanish cooperation in the event of a return of the monarchy, including the renunciation of the supposed secret Franco-Spanish pact.[63]

While the Spanish Left had been protesting against Gil Robles as a proto-Fascist, nothing was farther from the truth. It is true that Gil Robles had visited Austria's Chancellor Dollfuss in the spring of 1934,[64] but their common interest was more their social-Catholicism than their proto-Fascism. In fact, although Dollfuss' regime received the support of Mussolini, the Duce had no time for even a right-wing republic in Spain.

After the 1933 election victory of the CEDA brought a series of anarchist disturbances in Spain, Mussolini, pleased by the disturbances, observed to Baron Aloisi, his *chef de cabinet* in the Foreign Ministry, 'that the Spanish revolution serves us because it diminishes the strength of that country'.[65] Similarly, the promises to the Spanish Monarchists in March were also designed to encourage the polarization and, therefore, the weakening of Republican Spain, even though its Government was at the time in the control of the Right. This Spanish policy received Mussolini's personal attention in the spring of 1934 undoubtedly because of his own changed priorities. The Rome Protocols with Austria and Hungary of March 1934 represented the termination of his offensive in central Europe and his speech of 18 March marked the official opening of his East African programme.[66] Spain, thus, became a more important component in the development of Italian foreign policy after March 1934 than it had been before with the need now to secure the Italian rear in the event of a campaign in Abyssinia.

By the end of 1934, Italy and the Holy See were working at cross purposes in Spain. By subsidizing the Monarchist conspirators and bringing Carlist youths to Italy for military training,[67] Mussolini sought to encourage Spanish chaos. At the same time, the Vatican, through its support of Gil Robles and the CEDA was seeking to encourage the growth of a republican consensus in Spain, the Pope even going so far as to refuse an audience to Monarchists attending the marriage of Alfonso XIII's daughter in Rome in January 1935.[68]

The formation and subsequent election of the Popular Front in the Spanish elections of February 1936 effectively signalled the bankruptcy of this policy of reconciliation. It is significant that, at the end of 1935, the architect of this attempted reconciliation, Monsignor Tedeschini, had been created a cardinal and, in consequence, had submitted his resignation as Nuncio to Spain.[69] As the Vatican moved somewhat reluctantly to a position of opposition to the Republic in 1936, it finally came into line with Italian policy on this issue.

As it was a military conspiracy rather than a Monarchist conspiracy which eventually led to the Spanish rising of July 1936, the agreement of 31 March 1934 with Mussolini was never implemented. Such technical considerations were, however, of little moment as the Italians had waited for years for such an uprising. Mussolini sought only the advice of Antonio Goicoechea, leader of the *Renovación Española*, who had been present at the 1934 meeting, and then promptly answered the request from General Franco for Italian assistance in the 1936 rising.[70] Unlike the Vatican, Mussolini had no doubts about the right of the Spanish Republic to a continued existence.

9 The Quest for Four-Power Unity, 1932–3

The *rapprochement* between Italy and the Vatican of September 1931 was put to the test in the second half of 1932 when Mussolini resumed direct control of the conduct of Italian foreign policy and took a strong initiative in attempting to shape the pattern of international relations. This time, when the Italian challenge was once again flung at the Yugoslavs, the Holy See was unequivocally at the side of Mussolini.

Pius XI and European Polarization

To Pope Pius XI, the most notable feature of the Depression years was the increasing social radicalism of Europe. Where the full economic force of the Depression had hit central Europe in the summer of 1931, the year that followed produced a marked trend to political extremism. The most notable success was that of the German Nazis, demonstrated by their electoral achievements of 1932. The Austrian Nazis also showed increased support in the municipal elections in April 1932, and in Hungary the lack of success of the Government led by Bethlen's successor, Karolyi, brought demands from numerous quarters for the institution of a Right Radical Government in that country.[1] However, this extremism was not confined to the Right; the extreme Left, particularly in Germany, was also increasing its popular following. Throughout 1932 the Governments of Germany, Austria and Hungary struggled to contain this polarization and to defend their respective economies as best they could.

Social and economic stability in central Europe was necessary to prevent further polarization and, to this end, the Pope gave his support to all moves toward the cancellation of war debts and reparations in 1932,[2] just as he supported all moves toward political *detente* between the Western powers,[3] particularly France and Italy.[4] In looking at events in Germany, he was concerned by the increasing strength of the Nazis and the 'socialist' leanings of their programmes,[5] an attitude reflected in the views of the Bavarian hierarchy[6] who, in the summer of 1932, were considering a possible separation of Bavaria from Germany should the Nazis take power.[7]

The Pope was especially concerned because this social dislocation coincided with a new diplomatic outreach on the part of the Soviet Union. It appeared that, out of fear of Germany and concern about the political weakness of eastern Europe, states such as France and Italy were prepared in 1932 to invite the Soviet Union to participate in guaranteeing the European *status quo*. The states of central and western Europe had shown themselves totally incapable of achieving any significant degree of international reconciliation in the 1920s. Now, under pressure of the economic crisis, they were extending their international conflict by bringing the Soviet Union into their quarrels with one another, seemingly blind to the fact that the Soviet Union would only use the economic crisis to further its own revolutionary goals in Europe.

The return of Herriot and the French Left to office in May 1932 had upset the Pope who still remembered the pro-Soviet stance and the aggressive anti-clericalism of the 1924 Herriot Government. While the course of events in France showed that these latter fears were unjustified,[8] nevertheless this French Government was not one in which the Pope could place a great deal of confidence. As Herriot embarked on his policy of *rapprochement* with the Soviet Union in 1932, the reiterated theme of the reports of François Charles-Roux, the new French Ambassador to the Holy See, was that of Vatican warnings of the threat of Communism.[9] The Pope was concerned both that France should show itself flexible in disarmament negotiations to further Franco-German *rapprochement*[10] and, at the same time, that disarmament should not be taken too far lest it leave Europe wide open to the Bolsheviks.[11]

On the subject of disarmament, therefore, the Pope saw only two camps, Bolshevik and anti-Bolshevik, and on the eve of the resumption of the Disarmament Conference in October 1932, he expressed his strong belief that any disarmament by the non-Communist powers would only play into the hands of the Communists, thereby giving support to the German and Italian[12] arguments at the Conference. All his warnings to France were of little avail as a Franco-Soviet Non-Aggression Pact was signed on 29 November 1932.

In spite of ideological differences, relations between Italy and the Soviet Union were also close in 1932, and the Pope could only indicate his disapproval by rejecting Italian offers to mediate between the Vatican and the Soviet Union.[13] This had little effect, however, and relations between Rome and Moscow continued to be friendly throughout the year.[14]

This disagreement over the Soviet Union was the one exception to the close relations between Italy and the Holy See which followed Mussolini's visit to Pius XI in February 1932. In fact, in the latter half of 1932 and the first half of 1933, foreign observers were struck by the close support and cooperation in foreign affairs given to Italy by the Holy See.[15]

Mussolini Returns to the Foreign Ministry

Italy's international position in the spring of 1932 was none too secure, as it was apparent that a resurgent Germany now intended to continue to play a dominant role in the Danube basin. Where Guariglia and Grandi now sensed the need for a genuine accommodation with France,[16] Mussolini, together with others in the Italian Government, recognized in the revival of Germany the potential for new opportunities for Italy.

In order to avert a pro-German turn in Italian policy, Grandi sought, in vain, to warn the British and French of domestic developments in Italy and of the possible consequences of not making rapid concessions. The failure of Grandi's policy became apparent at the Lausanne Conference in July 1932. Not only did Britain and France come into alignment with one another on questions relating to disarmament,[17] but these two powers also reached agreement with Germany on the cancellation of reparations. Italy found herself excluded and completely isolated[18] and, before the month was out, Grandi had tendered his resignation as Foreign Minister.[19]

The resumption of the Foreign Ministry by Mussolini in July 1932 was a result of a new perception of international priorities occasioned by the reassertion of Germany. Mussolini's assessment was that Italy should take advantage of this situation by throwing her weight more firmly behind Germany in order to restore a Franco-German power balance which could then be exploited to Italy's advantage. The essence of Mussolini's policy was expressed to Baron Aloisi, his new *chef de cabinet*, on 4 October 1932: 'On the Rhine, we are against France, on the Danube with France'.[20] Mussolini intended to achieve this largely by playing on Franco-German hostility and supporting German claims to 'equality' at the Disarmament Conference, on the understanding that a rearmed Germany would provide a more effective counterweight to French influence in Europe.[21] A renewed Franco-German balance could then be combined with Italian influence to create a tripartite equilibrium or, including Britain, a four-power directorate of Europe. Such was the weight of Mussolini's message in his major speech of 23 October 1932 at Turin, foreshadowing the Four-Power Pact of 1933 when he proposed four-power collaboration for European peace and economic renewal.[22]

Another reason for Mussolini's return to directing Italian foreign policy was because Yugoslavia's domestic dissatisfaction with King Alexander's centralization policies in the spring of 1932[23] indicated that the time might be ripe for attempting to force the disintegration of that state.

The major thrusts of Italian policy in the autumn of 1932, then, consisted of attempting to secure Italian power in the Balkans by fomenting and developing the internal crisis of Yugoslavia and, on the Danube, by negotiating closer ties with Austria and Hungary. These moves which were essentially anti-German were balanced by Italian support for the German position at the Disarmament Conference. France could accommodate the increased Italian power either by dropping her support for Yugoslavia or by making colonial concessions to Italy. To facilitate the latter possibility, planning began in late 1932 for a campaign against Abyssinia.[24] Mussolini was seeking to realign European power relations in order to give Italy a dominant voice in the maintenance of European peace through the establishment of a four-power directorate of Europe.[25]

The Holy See had been pleased when Grandi was removed from the Foreign Ministry and when Mussolini took personal direction of affairs once again.[26] After July 1932, in fact, the Pope appeared to be much more in sympathy with Italian foreign policy, intent as it now seemed to be on securing an Italian sphere of influence in central Europe and thereby bringing together the Catholic powers on the Danube. This would adequately and safely fill the power vacuum in central and eastern Europe and, in particular, prevent the spread of Russian influence. The Pope and Cardinal Pacelli sought, therefore, to reassure both the Yugoslavs[27] and the French that they had nothing to fear from Italy providing it was not provoked[28] and, on the morrow of Mussolini's Turin speech in October, the *Osservatore Romano* hailed it as 'a programme of true and just peace'.[29] By mid-January 1933 the Pope was openly delighted with Mussolini and with the state of relations between Italy and the Vatican.[30]

The Lika Raid and its Consequences

Since 1929 the *Ustasa* had been receiving subsidies and assistance from the Hungarian and Italian Governments.[31] In the summer of 1932 Mussolini had been supplied with a programme for *Ustasa* action by Pavelic,[32] which depended on growing domestic unrest in Yugoslavia and, presumably, included a series of *Ustasa* raids into Croatia designed to rally the people to revolt. Thus, when unrest developed in Yugoslavia in the spring and summer of 1932, Mussolini did not so much believe that Yugoslavia was about to disintegrate as that the conditions were developing which might well sustain a concerted attack by the Croat opposition.

In the middle of October a number of the *Ustasa* entered Yugoslavia from a camp at Zara in Italy and advanced twenty miles before they were routed by police and peasants at Lika.[33] As Italian weapons and ammunition were left behind, the raid was immediately associated with Italy.[34] On 2 December, as an anti-Italian gesture, a group of people loyal to Belgrade destroyed the Venetian lions at Trau in Dalmatia and, later in the month, the Little Entente gave support to Yugoslavia and decided on the terms of a Pact of Organization to make their links with one another more secure.[35]

Given the international situation in 1932, the French not only sought a pact with Russia but they were also interested in reaching some kind of agreement with Italy. Herriot, in August, had sought the help of Sir Austen Chamberlain in arranging an informal meeting with Mussolini, but to no avail.[36] Following Mussolini's Turin speech, Herriot made kindly references to Italy in a speech to the Radical-Socialist congress at Toulouse on 5 November, during which he also announced his intent to sign the Franco-Soviet Non-Aggression Pact.[37]

Herriot, however, had taken this initiative against criticism from within his party and government and needed some Italian public acknowledgement of his goodwill. As this was not forthcoming by the beginning of December, he became markedly cool toward the Italians and his attempts to woo Italy came to an abrupt halt.[38] On 2 December, in the midst of the Italo-Yugoslav tension, the Franco-Yugoslav Pact was renewed for a further five years.

The renewal of this pact meant that Mussolini's lack of reply had left Herriot no choice but to give these further guarantees to the Yugoslavs.[39] Mussolini's reaction was to reply to the attack on the lions of Trau with a blistering attack in the Senate on 14 December against the Yugoslav political leadership.[40] All of this worried Aloisi immensely, as he particularly feared that Mussolini might give final approval to Pavelic's plan of attack which would definitely compromise Italy internationally.[41] In fact, where Aloisi and Suvich were inclined to be cautious, Mussolini seemed determined to make use of the fears of Italian intentions and to exert full pressure on Yugoslavia.

This heightened tension between Italy and Yugoslavia had not been without effect on the position of the Catholic Church in Yugoslavia. It would appear that many Serbs identified the Church with any restiveness on the part of the Croats and Slovenes and, as suspicion of an Italian-financed Croat rising developed in November, much of the resentment of the Belgrade Serbs was directed against the Catholic Church. Thus, between a report of 12 November that the Church in Croatia was uninvolved in the political situation[42] and 19 December, when Charles-Roux reported that Pius XI was suggesting that France might give the Church more help in Yugoslavia,[43] it would appear that the Catholic Church had been brought into the political conflict. Certainly, Yugoslav persecution of the Church had been one of the themes taken up by the Italian press at the end of December as part of their anti-Yugoslav campaign.[44] The arrest and internment of the Slovene leader Father Korosec early in 1933 for his proposal of Catholic home rule in western Yugoslavia[45] was certainly not well received by the Vatican. If France would not stand by the Church, Italy could be counted on to do so. At times like this, reasoned the Vatican, if the Belgrade

Government wished to consign the Holy See to the same camp as the Italians, then Belgrade could pay the price.

Whether directly inspired by the Holy See or not, the pastoral letter of the Yugoslav bishops, read throughout Yugoslavia on 8 January 1933, denouncing the *Sokol* certainly had papal support.[46] This pastoral attacked the *Sokol* on the grounds that it was an areligious institution and, in these days, it was argued that such organizations soon tended to become anti-religious. Catholic youth was therefore forbidden to participate in *Sokol* and its attendance at church services was prohibited. While it was claimed that the pastoral had been in the offing for some time, it was undoubtedly timed to remind Belgrade that the rights of the Catholics must continue to be respected. The reaction, however, of the Yugoslav Government and press was strong and the Archbishop replied in kind. Where the issue had arisen on religious grounds, the behaviour of the Serbians helped to create a united Catholic political opposition in Yugoslavia, tied in as this controversy also was with the arrest of the Croat and Slovene opposition leaders.[47] This seemed to be especially true as the pastoral provoked some members of the Yugoslav Government to draft and introduce bills for the expropriation of church lands[48] and for the suppression of the Jesuits.[49] The Pope was understood by the French to have been particularly annoyed at this behaviour of the Yugoslav Government which, they felt, had touched his national pride – 'Il a réagi comme un Italien; comme un vrai Milanais[50] – and was, consequently, fanning the flames of discontent in Yugoslavia.[51]

The Four-Power Pact and European Pacification

A shipment of arms to the Croatian *Ustasa*, probably originating in Italy, was discovered in Austria in early January 1933 and was made public by the Austrian Social Democrats in what came to be known as the Hirtenberg Weapons affair. Whether or not these weapons had been designed to be used by the Croats in an attack on Yugoslavia, their discovery came just at the time when King Alexander was openly contemplating the possibility of war with Italy[52] and it only served to heighten his suspicions of Mussolini's intentions.[53] In fact, the situation in early Janaury was so tense that even Mussolini felt obliged to issue a statement that he favoured good relations with Yugoslavia.[54]

Hitler's appointment as Chancellor of Germany on 30 January 1933 required Mussolini to clarify his own policy as the revelation of the Hirtenberg arms shipments had caused the states of the Little Entente to tighten their alliance further. Accordingly, on 4 March Mussolini drafted his plan for a great power *entente* designed to promote peaceful revision[55] which was launched formally during a visit to Rome by Ramsay MacDonald on 18 March.[56]

The Four-Power Pact, at least in draft form, represented the institutionalization of the substance of Italian foreign policy since July 1932. Italy, through her ties with Austria and Hungary, and through the pressure she was able to exert on Yugoslavia, had increased her European power and influence, whereas the rise of Hitler and the international instransigence of the Nazis had weakened French influence. A new European power relationship was developing and the Four-Power Pact was an attempt both to institutionalize this relationship and to shape it in a manner favourable to Italy. Mussolini's intention was that the concert of the four great powers should then preside over a just revision of European frontiers on a basis of equality.[57]

Given the state of international tension in February 1933, the Pope, as part of the opening of the 1933 Holy Year, also sought a basis for unity among the Western powers and launched what can only be termed a call to arms against Bolshevism. In an interview with Charles-Roux on 7 March, the Pope squarely put the blame on France for the troubled state of international relations and advised that peace would easily follow a change in the French attitude. Hitler, after all, had joined the Pope in his denunciations of Bolshevism and was, therefore, not to be feared, and Mussolini would be prepared for better relations with France if the latter would only stop encouraging the Little Entente.[58] The implication was that no reliance should be placed on the Soviet tie.

It was in the consistorial allocution* delivered on 13 March, however, that the Pope spelled out his views on the international situation. Bolshevism, according to Pius XI, was the real threat of the times. It was advancing at this time because the energies of the Europeans were concentrated on international conflicts and

---

* A consistory is, today, a 'ceremony or solemn occasion for special announcements', attended by cardinals (Robert Graham, pp. 145–6).

on economic ideologies, rather than on getting down to serious decisions designed to deal with the economic crisis and with problems of international peace. If the non-Communist states could cooperate with one another under the spiritual guidance of Rome, then the Bolshevik peril might well be averted.[59]

Agreement on disarmament would be one way of recognizing a new Western accord but, as the Pope warned Ramsay Mac-Donald on 19 March, 'do not disarm order to the profit of disorder'.[60] It was Mussolini's Four-Power Pact which met with the Pope's strongest approval. While he kept his own counsel during the negotiations,[61] this pact, which united the four leading non-Communist powers of Europe with the intention of treaty revision, was directly in line with Pius XI's views of immediate international needs. It was a decisive reaction to a growing crisis and, once the Pact had been initialled on 7 June, the Vatican lost no time in congratulating the participants.[62]

The Pope had deliberately sought to welcome Hitler's accession to power in Germany. Hitler and the Nazis, after all, were the product of the allied treatment of Germany since the 1919 Peace Conference; now that Germany once again had an assertive government, it might at last be possible to secure the stability offered by a balance of European power. Hitler also had the virtue of his anti-Communism and this made him acceptable to the Pope. As Cardinal Faulhaber, Archbishop of Munich, reported after his meeting with the Pope in March 1933: 'Let us meditate on the words of the Holy Father, who, in a consistory, without mentioning his name, indicated before the whole world in Adolf Hitler the statesman who first, after the Pope himself, has raised his voice against Bolshevism'.[63]

This papal assessment of Hitler created consternation within German Catholicism, since, as recently as the March 1933 election campaign, the German Catholic bishops had unanimously denounced National Socialism and had given their support to the important Catholic Centre Party, the *Zentrum*, against the Nazi Government. Following Cardinal Faulhaber's meeting with the Pope on 12 March and his attendance at the consistory on 13 March, however, first the *Zentrum* and the Bavarian Catholic Party voted for Hitler and then, on 28 March, the German bishops themselves announced their support for the Nazi Chancellor.[64]

The result of these shifts of position was the opening of negotiations for a concordat with Hitler in April. The Concordat which was signed on 20 July, provided for the sacrifice of the *Zentrum* in return for protection of church privileges in Germany. This hastily arranged Concordat, which offered gratuitous papal recognition to Hitler, was offered up to encourage pacification and *détente* among the Western powers in order to resist the pressure of Moscow.[65] On the eve of Soviet Foreign Minister Litvinov's arrival in Paris in July to discuss closer ties between France and the Soviet Union,[66] the Pope told Charles-Roux that he hoped that someone, preferably the Japanese, would now attack Russia so that Stalin would thereby be forced to arm his own people who would proceed to overthrow him.[67]

Dilemma over Anschluss: Rapprochement with Yugoslavia

As Mussolini sought to clarify his relationship with France and Germany in the spring of 1933, he was being faced with the unwelcome prospect of having to resist German expansion into Austria and pressure for the *Anschluss*. With Hitler's accession in Germany, the campaign of the Austrian Nazis against Engelbert Dollfuss, Chancellor of Austria since 1932, had been stepped up and Dollfuss, having suspended the operation of the Austrian Parliament in early March, visited Mussolini in April to ask for *Heimwehr* support of his new authoritarian regime. Mussolini was thereby faced with the dilemma of accepting the *Anschluss*, friendship with Hitler and the loss of considerable Italian freedom of manoeurvre or of supporting Dollfuss, conceivably losing German friendship and being forced to toe the French line on treaty revision. The problem for Mussolini basically was how to prevent the *Anschluss* while retaining his own freedom of manoevre between Germany and France.

The most obvious way of defending Austrian independence would have been for Mussolini to have urged Dollfuss to work in cooperation with the Social Democrats, restore parliamentary democracy and pose the direct challenge of Austrian democracy to German authoritarianism. Such an approach was advocated by a number of Austrians, even those close to Dollfuss,[68] yet was unacceptable to Mussolini because such a policy would have put him into direct confrontation with Hitler and this the Duce sought to avoid at all costs. He therefore agreed to support

Dollfuss, on condition that he maintain and develop his authoritarian regime more and more along Fascist lines and that, in so doing, he cut the ground from under the Austrian Nazis and prove himself more anti-Marxist than them by taking decisive action against the Social Democrats. It was expected that, in doing this, Dollfuss would rely largely on the *Heimwehr*.[69]

Yet Mussolini also accepted that it might ultimately be necessary to concede the *Anschluss* and thus, at the same time as he was advising Dollfuss in April 1933, he was also thinking of an alternative defence line running from Rome through Belgrade to Budapest.[70] Consequently, Italo-Yugoslav relations underwent an abrupt change after the advent of the Nazi Government in Germany. Since Mussolini needed Little Entente acquiescence in the Four-Power Pact if it were to be effective, Yugoslavia was, in April, assured by Italy that the latter had no territorial claims to make,[71] assurances which were continued into the summer.[72] Moreover, Mussolini reassured the Little Entente, ever wary of an Austro-Hungarian union or a restoration of the Habsburgs,[73] that his negotiations with Austria and Hungary had no such intent.[74] In fact, Mussolini now wanted the Austro-Hungarian bloc to be open to adhesion by the states of the Little Entente.[75] The German thrust toward the south-east which endangered the continued independence of Austria had, thereby, served to remove Yugoslavia as an issue between France and Italy and to pave the way to an eventual *rapprochement* between those two powers.

During this period, it was also essential to the Pope that the French should improve their relations with Italy and thus, after the war scares of late February, he had not only warned the French that their support of Yugoslavia was responsible for Italian hostility,[76] but Cardinal Pacelli showed the reports of the Paris Nuncio to Count De Vecchi, the Italian Ambassador to the Holy See, to persuade the Italians that the French did not have any really hostile intents. Charles-Roux was kept fully informed of these mediatory moves by the Vatican.[77] Into the summer of 1933, Pacelli acted as intermediary between De Vecchi and Charles-Roux, assuring the one of the peaceful intentions of the other.[78] According to Charles-Roux' memoirs, however, Cardinal Pacelli, throughout this time, was particularly pessimistic about a Franco-Italian *rapprochement*, feeling the ideological affinity between Mussolini and Hitler to be too strong.[79]

As the Pope was thus acting to help European peace, so also was the French Government insisting that the Yugoslavs give satisfaction to the Holy See.[80] Apparently, the French intervention had certain results as on 24 March, the Yugoslav Prime Minister and the Acting Foreign Minister made conciliatory gestures toward the Catholics during parliamentary debate on the budget, inviting the reopening of negotiations for a concordat.[81] The Nuncio responded with alacrity to this offer and negotiations were resumed within the month, the Yugoslav Government making considerable concessions in the opening stages of these negotiations. The negotiations were conducted with a great deal of secrecy, however, not only to avoid Serb Orthodox interference but also, presumably, to keep their existence hidden from Mussolini.

At the end of April, a delegation of Yugoslav parliamentarians visited Rome to attend the Inter-Parliamentary Economic Conference. While there they had been instructed to seek an audience of the Pope to 'present the respectful greetings of the King and the Yugoslav Parliament'. In spite of Pacelli's optimism about the prospect for such an interview, Pius XI flatly refused to receive them, even though the Yugoslav Government had made considerable concessions in the renewed concordat negotiations a few days earlier.[82] This refusal could either be interpreted as an attempt by the Pope to cover the existence of the negotiations or could indicate that the Pope was not yet convinced of the sincerity of the Yugoslavs and expected more extensive concessions. King Alexander was furious and interpreted this as clear evidence of the concordance of Italian policy with that of the Vatican.[83]

The Albanian Schools Question

King Zog's refusal to renew the 1926 Treaty of Tirana when it expired at the end of 1931 had marked the beginning of a prolonged phase of Italo-Albanian conflict. One of the immediate results of Zog's refusal to renew the treaty had been the cutting down of available Italian funds for Albania under the 1931 Italo-Albanian Loan Agreement. In retaliation, Zog, in September 1932, had begun a campaign to exclude Italian cultural influence from Albania by passing a law prohibiting Albanians from sending their children to foreign schools of any kind. Following on the Lika uprising and the increasing Croat agitation in Yugo-slavia, Zog gave another demonstration of his independence by announcing on 21 November his plan for a complete reorganiza-tion of Albanian education on national lines.[84]

As Mussolini decided in the spring of 1933, to reverse his re-lationship with Yugoslavia and seek a degree of *rapprochement*, General Pariani, the Italian military advisor to King Zog, was re-called in March and was not replaced. Pariani's removal served two purposes: as a sign of friendship to Yugoslavia and as a warning to Zog who no longer had a reliable foreigner to preserve domestic order.

In April Zog legislated his educational programme, making education the monopoly of the state and closing all private schools, including four very good technical schools which had been set up by the Italians and which they had refused to allow the Albanians to control. This legislation also resulted in the closing of all Catholic confessional schools. Italian teachers, therefore, were forced to follow the military advisors back to Italy.[85]

Both Italy and the Holy See wanted and expected Zog to back down. The Italian Minister in Tirana let Zog know in June that 'unless King Zog agrees to recall the insult to Italian culture which the abrupt closing of the Italian schools in Albania implied', there would be no assistance, especially financial, pro-vided to the Albanian Government;[86] Mussolini 'wanted Zog to go to Canossa'.[87] They were, however, in no rush and were pre-pared to wait for Zog to change his tune.[88] When in August the Albanians offered to reopen the technical schools and make Italian compulsory in all secondary schools, the Italians held out for the reopening of the confessional schools.[89]

The Catholic bishops, as was to be expected, reacted strongly to the closing of their schools. On 11 July 1933 a pastoral letter from the Albanian bishops was read throughout the country: 'condemning the Albanian Government as anti-clerical and treating as excommunicate those Catholics who had had a hand in passing the new legislation'. The effect was most noticeable among the Catholic tribesmen of the North who had never had much time for the Moslem-dominated Tirana Government[90] but the installation of additional troops in Scutari immediately fol-lowing the pastoral ensured calm.[91]

10 The Anti-Nazi Alliance 1933–5

Dollfuss and the Defence of Austria

By June 1933, in spite of the Four-Power Pact, Nazi terrorism was on the increase in Austria. An unheralded meeting between Gömbös and Hitler in Berlin in the middle of the month[1] upset Mussolini[2] and gave fresh impetus to his Danubian policy. At the end of June Mussolini moved to bring both the Hungarians and the Austrians into line and, on 1 July, Mussolini sent Dollfuss a long letter, in which he advised him to 'carry through a programme of effective and basic internal reforms in the decisive Fascist sense', 'to strike a blow at the Social Democrats' in order to gain the anti-Marxist advantage over the Austrian Nazis and to enter a close working relationship with the Hungarian Government. Particularly significant was the speed with which Mussolini now wanted Dollfuss to act.[3]

Dollfuss, however, had his own ideas about what he wanted to achieve. The offensive of the German and Austrian Nazis, the hostility of the Social Democrats and the absence of a personal power base had indicated to Dollfuss that the parliamentary regime would be a liability in his attempt to protect Austrian independence. While he looked immediately to the *Heimwehr* and to Mussolini for assistance against Hitler, he ultimately hoped to fashion a new social order which could give Austria the inner cohesion necessary to resist external pressures for the *Anschluss*. Dollfuss' search for a new social order involved the creation of a non-party authoritarian regime which would seek accommodation between all classes in society and which would be based on the principle of the 1931 papal encyclical, *Quadragesimo Anno*. This clerical corporate programme was announced by Dollfuss on 2 April 1933 to a meeting of Catholic associations in Vienna, and he was strongly supported by the Archbishop of Vienna, Cardinal

Innitzer.[4]

To Dollfuss, Catholic corporatism seemed to offer the solution to the problems confronting Austria. The Austrian people could be rallied behind their common Catholic heritage; corporatism offered a social programme which could appeal to the working classes; the corporate structure could serve to eliminate political strife in favour of efficient administration; and, by raising high the Catholic banner, Austria could be assured of extensive international sympathy and assistance, notably from Italy and from France. Once negotiations for a Concordat were approaching completion, therefore, Dollfuss announced, on 20 May, the formation of the Fatherland Front, a movement which was designed to stand above politics and to which all persons and political parties were invited to subordinate themselves for the reconstruction of Austria.

Through the creation of the Fatherland Front, Dollfuss hoped to open new possibilities for political reconciliation in Austria, by having a new institution to which persons of all political shades could subscribe for the purpose of Catholic social reconstruction. Not only did he hope that the *Heimwehr* and the Christian Socials would adhere, but he also hoped that, if not the Social Democrats themselves, at least various working-class organizations would voluntarily subscribe to this body, and thereby heal the rift which had bedevilled Austrian politics for so many years. It proved impossible, however, for the idea and the ideal to father a new political movement and, at first, the Fatherland Front did not acquire the support for which Dollfuss had hoped.[5]

Neither the Christian Social Party nor the *Heimwehr* were prepared initially to support Dollfuss' conception of the Fatherland Front, largely out of suspicion of one another. Even though Dollfuss had spoken publicly of his intention to follow a policy based on *Quadragesimo Anno*, the Christian Socials, in a deliberate slight, did not choose Dollfuss as their party chairman at their congress in May 1933,[6] and when he tried to establish a national youth movement under the Fatherland Front he met strong and persistent opposition from the Austrian hierarchy.[7] The Church was not prepared to sacrifice their traditional privileges for this social experiment – albeit a Catholic one. Moreover, the Christian Social Party resisted efforts by Dollfuss to get them to dissolve themselves into the Fatherland Front.[8]

Nor, for that matter, did the *Heimwehr* see in the Fatherland

Front anything other than a vehicle for their own political domi-
nance of Austria through the creation of a Fascist state on the
Italian model. They found, however, that Dollfuss' interest in
Catholic corporatism blocked many of their more extreme plans.[9]

Where Mussolini had never been willing to accept Catholicism
as an organizing principle for his influence in the Danube basin,
he was completely unsympathetic to Dollfuss' goals. The Italian
dictator insisted that Dollfuss should create a regime on the
Fascist model[10] instead of a Catholic corporate state and stressed
this in his letter of 1 July to Dollfuss. Dollfuss, however, was
interested in Catholic authoritarianism not Fascism, and, in this
respect, sought to conciliate the workers not to alienate them.
Yet, in the climate of 1933, neither Mussolini nor the *Heimwehr*
would tolerate such a conciliation and thus Dollfuss could make
no overt moves in this direction lest he should lose their support
against Hitler and the Nazis.

Dollfuss, nevertheless, tried to stem the increasing Italian and
Heimwehr pressure. He replied to Mussolini's letter on 22 July and
defended his programme of corporatism, pointing out that the
popular acceptance of this programme would serve to undermine
Austro-Marxism as effectively as would a public confrontation.[11]

In August Mussolini invited Dollfuss to a meeting at Riccione,
where he offered him a military alliance and put greater pressure
on him to change course in his domestic policy. In return for his
continued assistance, Mussolini now wanted 'the beginning of a
new course in Austrian domestic and foreign policy'. Early in
September Dollfuss would be expected to make a public statement of his intention of working closely with Hungary and Italy
and of the development of the Fatherland Front along Fascist
lines. This was to be followed by the *Heimwehr* leaders being taken
into his Cabinet and the institution of a Fascist dictatorship
which, as one of its first acts, should suppress the Socialists.[12]
While Dollfuss was agreeable to making such a public statement
and to the development of the Fatherland Front, he side-stepped
any promise to include the *Heimwehr* and thus felt he had retained
a free hand in an increasingly constricted situation.[13] Mussolini,
however, had made the price of his continued support perfectly
clear.

At the same time as this, Dollfuss failed to receive the support
he might have expected from the Catholic Church. Although
Cardinal Innitzer, a man noted for his interest in the welfare of

the working classes,[14] acted as Dollfuss' mentor in his programmes, the Cardinal was forced to tell Otto Bauer, the Socialist
leader, in December 1933 that 'he could do nothing' in effecting a
rapprochement between Dollfuss and the Socialists. It seems that
Innitzer was strongly opposed in this respect by the Bishop of
Linz and, more importantly, by Monsignor Sibylla, the Papal
Nuncio, both of whom felt that the moment had arrived 'to
destroy socialism forever'.[15] While Sibylla was known to be a
rabid anti-Socialist,[16] it is fair to assume that Innitzer's hands
were being tied not so much by Sibylla as by Rome itself.

By 1933 Pius XI had moved some distance from his proposals
for social reconstruction and conciliation of 1931. The interven-
ing years of depression and political extremism had brought him,
rather, to favour any policies which could reduce the possible
extension of Marxist influence. The agonies of the Church in
Spain under the Republic were before him as an example of the
results of misguided social reform.[17] In this context, Dollfuss'
suspension of Parliament and his plan to transform Austria into a
Catholic corporate state were initially received warmly by the
Vatican, who rushed through the negotiations for the Concordat
at Dollfuss' request.[18] Dollfuss' close association with Mussolini
through the *Heimwehr* was also supported and encouraged by the
Vatican.[19]

The issue of the *Anschluss*, however, was not initially of such
great consequence to the Pope. While sympathetic to Austrian
desires for independence the Pope, like Mussolini, did not want to
be forced to choose between the two German nations and, also
like Mussolini, hoped to divert German ambitions elsewhere.
Vatican acceptance of the German offer of a Concordat had been
based on the assumption that the experience with the Italian
Concordat could be repeated in Germany.[20]

And yet, by giving such gratuitous recognition to Hitler, Pius
XI gave considerable injury to Dollfuss. Not only did the German
Concordat of 20 July overshadow the Austrian Concordat of 2
June and thereby rob Dollfuss of a chance of standing as the
guardian of Catholicism against Nazi barbarism, but it also
created a dilemma for many of the clerical supporters of Dollfuss
who had, up to this time, served as 'a strong element of resistance
to the Reich'.[21] Pius XI, in following Mussolini's foreign policy
closely, never really seemed to understand the true intentions of
Dollfuss and Cardinal Innitzer. Initially, the Pope believed that

Dollfuss was launching an anti-Marxist crusade and thus could not understand Dollfuss' hostility to Germany and his scruples about too close an association with Italy or the need to conciliate the Socialists. However, once Hitler showed, within months of signing the Concordat, that he had little intention of respecting it,[22] the Pope was more sympathetic to Dollfuss' aversion to the *Anschluss*. Yet now Pius XI failed to understand why Dollfuss would not fall in line with Mussolini and why he was reluctant to suppress Socialism. Toward the end of 1933, the loyalties of the Austrian hierarchy were seriously divided.

As Dollfuss was reluctant to follow Italian direction, so too were the Hungarians. While prepared for closer relations with Austria and economic negotiations with Austria and Italy, Gömbös would not allow Mussolini to turn any Austro-Hungaro-Italian agreement against Germany nor to expand it to bring in the Little Entente.[23] Mussolini was thus pushed more and more into reliance on Dollfuss and on his willingness to create a Fascist Austria.

Yet, Dollfuss continued to resist Italian pressure. While he made the speech he had promised Mussolini on 11 September, when he announced his plans to reform Austria as 'a Social Christian German state with a corporative basis'[24] and indicated the Fatherland Front as the vehicle for this reform, he did not bring the *Heimwehr* into his Government as Mussolini wanted. Instead, in a Cabinet shuffle on 20 September, Dollfuss took many portfolios for himself and only appointed Fey, the leader of the Viennese *Heimwehr*, as Vice-Chancellor.[25] Dollfuss did not want to be forced to move against the Socialists and, on 15 September, assured the French Minister 'that he would not change his attitude to the Socialists while they kept their neutrality'.[26] In a desperate attempt to escape Italian control, Dollfuss even approached the Germans with proposals for direct negotiations at the end of September.[27]

Among his domestic supporters, Dollfuss continued to have difficulty in convincing either the *Heimwehr* or the Christian Socials to submit to the Fatherland Front.[28] Ultimately, on 6 December, the Austrian bishops came to his assistance when they 'temporarily' withdrew the permission which had been granted to the clergy to participate in public life. This meant that the numerous members of the clergy who worked for the Christian Social Party at all levels of government were forced to resign their positions.[29] Fearful lest this should be interpreted as indicating their displeasure with Dollfuss, the episcopate, in a Christmas pastoral, denounced the German Government and stated their unambiguous support for the present Government of Austria and its politics.[30] This move by the Church, apparently with Dollfuss' full concurrence,[31] was designed to facilitate the incorporation of the Christian Socials within the Fatherland Front. The Church had withdrawn its support from one political party in favour of support for the newly-devised non-political Government of Dollfuss.

Behind the action of the Austrian bishops now lay the growing concern of the Vatican about Nazi Germany. At the end of August Pius XI had been distressed by the immediate series of violations of the German Concordat and also had been annoyed by Hitler's continuing attack on Austria and by his persecution of German Jews.[32] In Germany, the Church was in a weakened position because it had originally been identified with the Centre Party in opposition to the Nazi Government. Now, the indications in Austria were that too close a political identification with the Dollfuss Government was causing opponents of that Government to abandon the Church.[33] By the end of 1933, the Pope was completely disillusioned with the Nazis[34] and felt that the *Anschluss* could only be prevented if Austria were to align herself with Italy. He was quite prepared, therefore, to sacrifice the Christian Socials in favour of the *Heimwehr* if Austria could thereby be saved.

Yugoslavia between Germany and Italy

Whereas the Four-Power Pact had been emasculated in the summer of 1933 as a result of the objections of Poland and the Little Entente, the withdrawal of Germany from the Disarmament Conference and the League of Nations in October of that year had virtually destroyed Mussolini's attempts to create a Franco-German equilibrium in Europe. Being engaged in the conflict with Hitler over Austria and having no longer any institutions through which he could juxtapose French and German interests, Mussolini was highly resentful of Hitler's actions and, after October 1933, joined France in the anti-German camp.[35]

One of the necessary preconditions for any *rapprochement* with the Little Entente, however, was an improvement of Italo-

Yugoslav relations. While Mussolini expected France, in line with improved Franco-Italian relations, to bring Yugoslavia to better terms with Italy during the winter of 1933–4, such was not the intention of King Alexander and, in fact, it was now the Yugoslav King and Government which blocked Mussolini's desired *rapprochement* with France.

In looking away from France for support, Alexander had looked to the other states of the Balkans, to Greece, Turkey and Rumania and to Bulgaria. The result of his diplomacy was the Balkan Pact between Yugoslavia, Greece, Turkey and Rumania, signed on 9 February 1934. Although not a member, Bulgaria associated itself with the Pact, especially after the coup of 19 May 1934 installed a pro-Yugoslav Government at Sofia. Alexander thus brought together the Balkan states to exclude Italian influence from the Balkans.[36]

Another new source of support for Yugoslavia was to be found in Nazi Germany and, in November 1933, after the isolation occasioned by Germany's withdrawal from the Disarmament Conference and the League of Nations, Hitler gave orders that Germany was to seek friendship with the Belgrade Government, and was therefore not to support the Croat cause.[37] Friendly German approaches to Belgrade date from this time.[38]

Early in January 1934 Dollfuss cancelled his negotiations with the Germans and, on 11 January appointed Fey to the control of defence and public security,[39] thereby placing substantial power and initiative in the hands of the *Heimwehr*. With Fey's appointment, the *Heimwehr* were in a position to provoke the Socialists into armed reaction, thereby giving the Austrian Government justification for suppressing this Marxist insurrection.[40] Such was the origin of the Austrian Civil War of February 1934. By crushing the Socialists, both Dollfuss and the *Heimwehr* had finally fallen in with Mussolini's programme for Austria.

Whereas Dollfuss complied with Mussolini's terms, the Hungarians, on the contrary, were simultaneously binding themselves more closely to Germany. The Hungarians opened negotiations with Germany for a preferential trade agreement immediately after Fey's appointment on 11 January[41] and concluded the agreement on 21 February.[42] As Mussolini invited both Dollfuss and Gömbös to Rome in the middle of March, the Hungarians could point out that they had little intention of tying themselves solely to Italy.[43]

The Rome Protocols of 17 March 1934 represented the consolidation by Mussolini of an anti-German front in the Danube basin. The key issue in the area was now the preservation of Austrian independence to which Mussolini was fully committed by his pledges to Dollfuss. On 21 February, Mussolini even made overtures to Yugoslavia to join this entente[44] only to be told that Yugoslavia would make no agreement with Italy until the latter had promised to expel the *Ustasa* nor until the other members of the Little Entente had been consulted.[45]

It was against a background of increasing Italian and French pressure for an Italo-Yugoslav *rapprochement* that the Yugoslavs made their first direct approach to Germany for the opening of commercial negotiations on 9 March.[46] At the same time, they let the Germans know that they wanted to use Germany as a counterweight to Italian aspirations on the Danube.[47] The German–Yugoslav negotiations resulted in the conclusion of a commercial agreement on 1 May, which was designed to give Yugloslavia such trade privileges with Germany that she could not afford to break the treaty and lose the markets. These economic terms were, in German eyes, the prelude to a political *rapprochement*.[48]

Relations between the Holy See and Yugoslavia improved toward the end of 1933, partly because of the Pope's fear of the *Anschluss*,[49] but primarily because of King Alexander's open attempts at a *rapprochement*. In December, he celebrated his 45th birthday in Zagreb and attended High Mass in the Cathedral where Archbishop Bauer preached the sermon.[50] Throughout 1934, complete tranquillity prevailed in relations between Yugoslavia and the Holy See. In fact, negotiations for a concordat were continuing in the utmost secrecy with the King himself assisting in setting aside the objections of the Serb Orthodox Patriarch. The Concordat was ready for signing prior to Alexander's assassination in October 1934 and was thereby delayed until 25 July 1935.[51]

Barthou

The French riots of 6 February 1934 brought a change of government and the replacement of Paul-Boncour by Louis Barthou at the Quai d'Orsay. With the advent of Barthou came a new orientation in French policy as he, rather than merely seeking a new formula to ensnare Hitler, set about to restore the French eastern alliances and, this time, to bring the Soviet Union into the anti-German combination. In terms of Franco-Italian relations, this meant that France was now less interested in Italian goodwill and, particularly, in sacrificing the Little Entente to an Italian-dominated eastern Europe.

Barthou came to office just as Mussolini's programmes in Danubian Europe had reached fruition with the Rome Protocols. In his major speech to the Fascist Congress on 18 March 1934, Mussolini sought to orient Italian long-term aspirations away from Europe and toward the East and South – to Asia and Africa:

> ... I prefer ... to point out to you the historical objectives towards which our generation and those which follow must be oriented in this century.... The historical objectives of Italy have two names: Asia and Africa. South and East are the cardinal points which must rouse the interest and the will of the Italians. To the North there is little or nothing to be done, nor is there to the West; nor in Europe nor across the Oceans.... We are not speaking about territorial conquest, let this be understood by all both near and far, but about a natural expansion which must lead to collaboration between Italy and the peoples of Africa, between Italy and the nations of the Near and Middle East.... We do not intend to claim monopolies or privileges but we ask and we seek that those who have arrived, are satisfied and conservative, should not work in any way to block the spiritual, political, and economic expansion of Fascist Italy.[52]

This speech was followed in April by the first appropriations to finance preparations for an Abyssinian campaign.[53]

If colonial expansion were now to have a higher priority, it was necessary that the *entente* with France be consummated. Mussolini, therefore, anxiously awaited Barthou's resumption of Franco-Italian talks.

Austria: The Corporate Constitution

Because Berlin was unsure of Italian intentions, Vice-Chancellor von Papen was despatched to Rome at the end of March 1934 with the suggestion that a meeting should take place between Hitler and Mussolini.[54] This meeting, which took place at Venice in mid-June, was notable only for the lack of results 'because none of the problems in existence received even the beginning of a solution'.[55] Austria was too great a barrier between them and Mussolini had not been pleased by the recent German trade agreements with Yugoslavia.[56]

The security of Italian support for Austrian independence, once accounts seemed to have been settled with the Socialists, allowed Dollfuss to proceed with his arrangements for a new constitution, and this was promulgated on 1 May 1934. The constitution represented the Austrian attempt to erect a corporate state on the lines of *Quadragesimo Anno* and, therefore, was tied closely to the provisions of the Austrian Concordat, with 9 of the 23 articles of the Concordat being written into the text of the Constitution.[57]

As an added insurance for his new state, Dollfuss removed the anti-Habsburg laws and allowed members of the Habsburg family to return to Austria as private citizens if they so wished. In this venture, which occasioned great concern in Hungary and Czechoslovakia, Dollfuss had the strong support of the Austrian Church.[58] Moreover, as a result of the cooling of Italian interest in the Croats,[59] Croat separatists now looked to the Dollfuss regime for possible support. On 11 March, Dollfuss and Innitzer received a delegation of Croats who had 'pledged Croat loyalty to Austria' and had, in turn, been urged to remain 'good Catholics, good Croats and good Austrians'. Dollfuss had assured them 'Our common fatherland, Austria, shall also be your paternal roof, all the more so because now we can begin to recreate Austria in the spirit of Christendom'.[60] As the possibility of a Habsburg restoration could serve to rally the Croats, so it could also still attract a considerable amount of Hungarian sympathy which would now be promoted by the Hungarian higher clergy for Otto's cause.[61]

This policy was devised by Dollfuss and the Austrian hierarchy to bring the Catholic constitution eventually to its logical conclusion in a restoration.[62] While the Vatican gave the new constitution its fullest support,[63] it gave no evidence of sympathy for this revival of the Habsburg cause.[64] Similarly, the Italians appeared unconcerned by this new development.[65]

The time was long past, in fact, when such a venture could have had any hope of success, especially since a generation was now coming of age in Austria which did not remember the days of the Empire.[66] The clerical constitution, married to a deluge of pro-Habsburg propaganda, did not achieve much popularity with the Austrian people, who were treated to the full effects of clerical repression during 1934.[67] In fact, what was particularly notice-able at the end of the year was that the close association of the Church with the Constitution had led many Austrians to convert to Protestantism in protest against the Government and, in many cases, to show their affiliation to 'Protestant' Germany.[68]

Negotiations with Albania

At the end of August 1933, King Zog made the study of Italian compulsory in all secondary, technical and vocational schools of Albania and required that 80 per cent of all scholarship students going abroad must go to Italy. This gesture was still insufficient to satisfy the Italians, who insisted that the confessional schools must also be reopened.[69] This insistence on the importance of the confessional schools created a stumbling block to the negotiations between Rome and Tirana. Mussolini insisted that Catholicism be accepted as part of Italian culture. At the same time, Zog found this particularly difficult to accept because the majority of the population were either Moslem or Orthodox and expected him at least to resist this Italian religious imperialism. By 1934 the confessional schools had become the bargaining counter between Italy and Albania.

Once again Zog had sought alternatives and, in November 1933, had found the Yugoslavs, intent as they were on Balkan organization, willing to open commercial negotiations.[70] Zog then attempted to use these Yugoslav ties to put pressure on Italy to resume her loan payments,[71] only to run into continued Italian insistence on the opening of the Catholic schools of Scutari and the conclusion of an Albanian Concordat.[72] The conclusion of the Balkan Pact in February, excluding Albania as a gesture to Muss-olini, annoyed Zog who saw the collapse of his Yugoslav ties and complained that he had no chance of being considered indepen-dent of Italy.[73]

Early in June a rumour reached Aloisi that Zog had concluded a secret treaty with Yugoslavia designed to reduce the number of his Italian advisors.[74] On 23 June a squadron of the Italian Navy anchored in the Bay of Durazzo for a few days, presumably as a warning – at least it was interpreted as such by the Albanian and foreign press.[75] This was followed by the decision by the Italian Foreign Ministry to settle the dispute with Albania.[76] At the end of July Mussolini gave the go ahead and charged Aloisi with the negotiations.[77] Accordingly, Aloisi received Sereggi, Zog's *aide-de-camp* who had been sent as a special emissary on 14 August.[78] Discussions continued until 20 August when Aloisi told Sereggi that the opening of the Catholic schools and the conclusion of a concordat with Italian support were still expected of Albania.[79] The rest of the negotiations did not go at all well, owing to Zog's continuing refusal to lift the ban on denominational schools, allowing only seminaries to take in the occasional lay pupil.[81] In spite of Aloisi's influence with Cardinal Dolci, a personal friend of his, the Vatican rejected Zog's proposals[82] and the Italo-Albanian negotiations went into abeyance at the beginning of 1935.[83]

The Return of Laval

The murder of Dollfuss on 25 July by Austrian Nazis provoked Mussolini's fear that there might have been a German–Yugoslav plot directed against Italy in the event of *Anschluss*. Thus, as he moved troops to the Austrian frontier, the bulk of them were designed not to oppose Hitler but, rather, to prevent any Yugoslav move into Carinthia in support of the Nazis.[84] On 11 September Galli had an audience with Mussolini when he pointed out that, should Mussolini drop Italian support of the *Ustasa* and make some friendly overtures, a *rapprochement* with Yugoslavia was still possible. Mussolini refused to countenance this but did tell Galli to return to Belgrade and convince the Yugoslavs of his willingness to reach an agreement.[85] Barthou, now intending to take a direct hand in developing an Italo-Yugoslav *rapprochement*, invited Alexander to France for discussions prior to the French Minister's visit to Rome[86] and, on 6 October, Mussolini, in a speech in Milan, made conciliatory gestures toward Yugoslavia.[87]

The assassination of King Alexander and Louis Barthou at Marseilles on 9 October threatened to make Italy a diplomatic outcast and to destroy many Italian plans. This would have been the case if the members of the *Ustasa* who committed the murder could have been traced to the Croat camps in Italy. While the complicity of the Italian Government in the Marseilles crime has never been established, Mussolini clearly had motives for disposing of Alexander, who had been deliberately hampering a Franco-Italian *rapprochement* for over a year. At the news of the assassination the Italian leaders held their breath.[88] Many of the Italian fears were mitigated, however, with the appointment of Pierre Laval as Barthou's successor. 'The nomination [of Laval]', noted Aloisi, 'is good for us'.[89] Laval, who had initiated a Franco-Italian *rapprochement* in 1931, was a man who understood Italy and her colonial aspirations, and a man who had a reputation within the Fascist leadership of being a 'straight-shooter' with whom one could deal easily.[90] Laval had the additional advantage that he was interested in Franco-Italian *rapprochement* for its own sake, rather than as part of the larger arrangement envisaged by Barthou.

Early in December a border incident occurred between Abyssinia and Italian Somaliland at Wal-Wal. As the Abyssinians brought the matter to the League of Nations, Mussolini saw this as the issue on which the Abyssinian campaign could be opened. Orders were given that the agreement with France, which was a necessary preliminary, must be completed as quickly as possible.[91] By the end of the month, Italy had accepted the French position over Austria[92] and, on 31 December, Mussolini decided that, in order to hasten the negotiations, only a general agreement was necessary before Laval came to Rome, on the understanding that details could be worked out between Mussolini and Laval in private meetings.[93] Thus, from Laval's arrival on 4 January 1935 until the signing of the Franco-Italian Agreement on 7 January the time was spent in complex negotiations.[94]

The resulting Franco-Italian Agreement brought Rome and Paris together in support of Austrian independence and against the possibility of unilateral German rearmament, realized a settlement of matters relating to the Libyan frontier and to the Italian population of Tunisia and, most importantly, acknowledged a free hand for Italian expansion into Abyssinia. The agreement represented the final achievement of Mussolini's central diplomatic objective of the past few years; France had at last recognized an Italian sphere of influence centring on the eastern Mediterranean. The secret agreement to hold military staff talks between France and Italy following on the agreement was a clear indication of its fundamental importance to both Laval and Mussolini.[95]

The brutal murder of Dollfuss had helped to drive Mussolini firmly into the Anglo-French camp and into the Franco-Italian Agreement. The creation of this anti-German alliance was welcomed by the Holy See, to whom the murder of Dollfuss had only confirmed their view of the Nazi regime as 'the negation of Christianity'.[96] Not only was the Vatican very satisfied with this agreement which brought France into line with Italian policy, but it was also pleased that it enhanced the *rapprochement* between France and the Holy See. Laval was the first Foreign Minister of France to visit the Vatican since 1870.[97] Laval's visit to Rome was, therefore, the occasion for a great papal display of enthusiasm for France, which continued well into 1935,[98] since the two leading Catholic nations of Europe had finally come together in defence of Catholic Austria.

11 The Impact on Italian Foreign Policy

What is initially striking about relations between the Italian Fascist Government and the Papacy under Pius XI is the extent to which they were in agreement on the basic international problems of the inter-war period. Both the Pope and Mussolini had blamed the French obsession to secure and maintain her own continental hegemony for the failure to restore genuine peace to Europe after 1919. At the same time, neither believed in the efficacy of the League of Nations or the system of collective security, wedded as these institutions were to the French-dominated *status quo*. Both felt, rather, that the aspirations and needs of all the powers should be recognized so that a real accommodation could be achieved; genuine pacification could only arise from continuing review and on-going revision of the peace treaties.

However, Mussolini and the Pope had not reached these conclusions in the same way. As many Italians believed that Italy had not received adequate compensation in the peace settlements for its wartime sacrifices, so Mussolini, in seeking to assert the Italian national interest in the 1920s, was bound to stand opposed to the existing European *status quo*. He sought treaty revisions to attempt to secure Italy's deserved territories, but, more important, he also sought to create new principles and structures for the conduct of European diplomacy which could give Italy, recognized as one of the great powers, a more permanent influence in international affairs. The Pope, on the other hand, was seeking the establishment of real and continuing peace, and was in strong disagreement with the liberal legalism which informed much of the peace settlement. Disputes were left unresolved and the bitterness of the dissatisfied powers continued to fester. The Pope discerned few genuine attempts at mutual accommodation and reconciliation in the post-war world.

This basic similarity of view in the 1920s forms the background to any assessment of the implications of the Lateran Agreements for Italian foreign policy. Consensus between Italy and the Holy See had been well established before concrete moves were made to settle the Roman Question; the Vatican had even been lending Italy a considerable amount of practical support before the domestic differences were finally resolved. The result was that, with fundamental agreement already in existence, the Lateran Agreements produced subtle shifts of emphasis in Italian foreign policy rather than striking new directions, and their impact must be judged in relation to the far more important international stimuli of the Depression and the re-emergence of an activist Germany in the early 1930s.

From 1927 Mussolini's foreign policy had been oriented to defining a sphere for the independent exercise of Italian influence. This area was to include the Balkan peninsula, the eastern half of the Mediterranean basin and the north-eastern corner of Africa. While other powers, especially Great Britain and France, had interests in the area, Mussolini wanted the predominance of Italian interests to be recognized by these powers, just as the predominance of French interests was already recognized in the western Mediterranean.

In the wake of the collapse of the Austro-Hungarian Empire in 1918, a power vacuum had been created on the Danube and in the Balkan peninsula. Because of the Italian acquisition of the South Tyrol from Austria in 1919 and because of the Italianization programmes imposed on the German-speaking residents of that area, relations between Austria and Italy had been cool in the 1920s. With Germany, Austria and Hungary all weak and isolated after the war, Mussolini had sensed little threat to Italian interests in the Danube basin and, consequently, had not conceived it desirable for Italy to play any significant role in that area. Instead, he had concentrated his attention on the Balkans.

Yugoslavia, under French patronage, was the central and potentially the dominant power in the Balkans. Mussolini sought to establish Italian control over that peninsula by isolating Yugoslavia from her neighbours and, if possible, by forcing the internal disintegration of this kingdom of the Serbs, Croats and Slovenes. Such a policy required, first, Italian friendship with the Balkan countries surrounding Yugoslavia – Rumania, Bulgaria and Greece – and special treaty arrangements with Hungary and

Albania. Although Mussolini advocated the revision of the peace treaties in Hungary's favour, in practice he was only prepared to support such a revision if it were to be directed against Yugoslavia. Secondly, Mussolini's anti-Yugoslav policy involved the subsidization and encouragement of dissident Croatians in an attempt to foster internal movements for separation from Belgrade.

In the eastern Mediterranean, Mussolini sought the pacification of Libya, friendship with Greece, Turkey and the Soviet Union, and influence in Egypt and Palestine. In east Africa, Italy controlled Eritrea, sought to pacify Somalia, and intrigued for influence in Abyssinia and, across the Red Sea, in the Yemen.

When Sir Austen Chamberlain was Foreign Secretary, Britain was prepared to condone and even to support this Italian policy, so long as the peace of Europe and Britain's own interests were not threatened. France, on the other hand, did not feel that it could condone either Italian support of Hungarian revisionism or Italian threats to Yugoslavia, both of which endangered that European *status quo* which France was determined to maintain by exercising her preponderant power. France, therefore, signed a treaty of friendship with Yugoslavia in November 1927, in a direct intervention to block Mussolini's Balkan manoeuvres. This Franco-Yugoslav Pact thereafter became the pivotal factor in Franco-Italian relations. Until Yugoslavia was removed as an issue between France and Italy, Mussolini was not prepared to reach any final settlement of outstanding issues with Paris.

The Holy See had been interested in its missionary outreach in the 1920s and had provided Mussolini with considerable support for his policy before 1929. The Vatican was actively involved in the Balkans in trying to bring branches of Orthodox Christianity into communion with Rome and, in the Levant, having been forced to restore to France its position as protector of the Latin Catholics in 1926, the Holy See sought to encourage the Italians by using them to counter this restored and rather unwelcome French patronage of the Church. Consequently, on the Red Sea, in Egypt and Palestine and in Bulgaria, Church representatives frequently worked closely with the Italians and informally helped to promote Italian influence. In Albania, the co-operation was more deliberate and more direct, as Italy had subsidized and supported the work of the Catholic Church in that country since 1927 as one of the agencies of Italian cultural influence. By these favours, the Church assisted Italy in extending the circle of its diplomatic friendship in the Balkans and the Middle East.

Such cooperation pre-dated the domestic settlement between Church and State and, in fact, was to decline immediately after the signing of the Lateran Agreements. Presumably alarmed by the squabbling between France and Italy over who could best represent the Catholic interest in the Middle East, the Pope deliberately cut loose from Italian patronage in this area in 1929, in favour of direct dealings with the indigenous populations. In December 1929 he warned his missionaries about the danger of excessive nationalism in their work.

While the Holy See had willingly assisted in the extension of peaceful Italian influence in the 1920s, it had been disconcerted by Italian hostility to Yugoslavia and, particularly, by Italian attempts to foment the internal crisis of that country from 1929 onwards. The Yugoslav situation was a particularly difficult one for the Holy See. The Pope wanted a concordat with Belgrade to guarantee the Catholic position in Yugoslavia, but negotiations had been sporadic because members of the Belgrade Government were always suspicious that the Church was supporting the Croat separatists. The Catholic Croats sought separation from the Orthodox Serbs of Belgrade but, at the same time, the Croats, together with the Catholic Slovenes, took little comfort from the persecution of their fellow Slavs in Italy as a result of the Fascist Government's Italianization policy. The situation was further complicated by the fact that, in the Italian eastern provinces of Venezia Giulia, the Slav opposition to Italianization was being led in many cases by the Catholic clergy. Needing a concordat, the Holy See sought to maintain correct relations with Belgrade and would not allow the Croat clergy to support separatism.

The conclusion of the Lateran Agreements took place at the same time as the Yugoslav crisis came to a head with the institution of a dictatorship by King Alexander to control the sectional rivalries of that country. This placed the Holy See in a position where it would eventually be forced to choose between the two countries unless Italian policy changed in some way.

The Vatican would have preferred Mussolini to take an interest in the Catholic states and regions of central Europe – Austria, Hungary, Poland and, possibly, Bavaria – which had lost their central focus with the 1918 collapse of the Austro-Hungarian Monarchy. The restoration of some Catholic *Mittel-*

europa might now be possible under Italian patronage. The most significant outcome of the Lateran Agreements for Italian foreign policy was that the *Conciliazione* smoothed the way for Italian involvement with Austria and made such a Danubian policy possible.

The Lateran Agreements immediately made Mussolini *persona grata* to the Catholic political parties of Austria and Hungary. Such a new outlook on the part of the Austrian Christian Socials, the dominant party in the government of that country, facilitated a *rapprochement* with Italy once Johannes Schober had become Chancellor of Austria in September 1929 and led, after the conclusion of the Austro-Italian Agreement of February 1930, to a resolution of the conflict between the two countries over the South Tyrol. In Hungary, the Catholic Legitimists (supporters of the claims of the Archduke Otto of Habsburg) also looked to Mussolini as a possible patron for a restoration of the Monarchy or a reunion of Austria and Hungary.

Mussolini, however, had not initially been very interested in developing a general policy for the Danube. His religious policy was not designed to apply to international relations and he was aware of the Vatican interest in a Catholic *Mitteleuropa*. Mussolini did not seek to exploit the possibilities of such a programme after 1929, just as he avoided becoming ensnared with Britain over Malta as a result of the Pope's campaign against Lord Strickland in 1929 and 1930.

Mussolini did expect some support from the Church in the Balkans, however. The imposition of King Alexander's dictatorship in Yugoslavia had initially been so effective in driving the Croat separatist political leaders into exile that the Italians were coming to depend on the ability of the Catholic clergy in Croatia to keep the sense of Croatian separatism alive. In Yugoslavia, where the Church had become the only tolerated voice of Croatia, Mussolini expected the Church to show loyalty to its new Italian patron and the Catholic clergy in Yugoslavia to show the same zeal in resisting Belgrade's centralization as the Catholic clergy of Venezia Giulia had shown in resisting his own.

The Holy See and the Catholic hierarchy of Yugoslavia tried to remain aloof from these controversies as best they could but, in 1930 and 1931, the possibility existed for negotiating a concordat with Belgrade if the Church made some public gesture of loyalty to Yugoslavia. Such a gesture was accordingly provided by the pastoral of Archbishop Bauer of Zagreb in February 1931, calling for prayers for the persecuted Slavs in Italy.

This pastoral had a decisive influence in bringing the Italian domestic dispute over *Azione Cattolica* to a head in 1931. Already under pressure from the Fascist Party to put some controls on the operation of the increasingly popular Catholic lay association, Mussolini was now witnessing a deliberate Catholic move to hamper his anti-Yugoslav campaign by direct interference in both his domestic and his foreign policy. He thus decided to limit *Azione Cattolica* and to force the Church to support his foreign policy in the Balkans. The experience of the lack of Catholic support for the abdicating Spanish monarch in 1931 served as a lesson to Mussolini that the Church would always look to its own needs before those of any political regime.

Yet, as Mussolini sought to secure what he could of his Balkan policy in 1931, one of the effects of the onset of the Depression had been a renewal of radicalism in Germany. In 1931, with the plan for a German-Austrian customs union, Germany made an abortive first gesture toward the forbidden *Anschluss*. Up to this time, Mussolini had not sensed any threat to Austrian independence and, consequently, had not formulated any consistent Italian policy for the Danube, in spite of Vatican attempts to nudge him in that direction. Now, with a restive Germany and the growing strength of the radical National Socialists in that country, Mussolini now found it necessary to formulate a Danubian policy lest Italy suddenly find itself with the power of Germany resting on her Alpine frontier.

Accordingly, in the summer of 1932, Mussolini resumed direct control of the Foreign Ministry and redefined Italian foreign policy. He was still interested in securing an Italian sphere of influence and he therefore sought to capitalize on internal Yugoslav discontent by unleashing the *Ustasa* terrorists in the autumn of 1932 for a futile raid into Croatia. Mussolini also made belligerent gestures to the Yugoslavs. As late as January 1933 he still expected a French withdrawal from the Balkans. Plans were also initiated for an Italian takeover of Abyssinia should such an option prove feasible in the near future.

This Italian sphere was, however, to be extended and placed in a larger context in 1932. It was to be extended to include an Austria and Hungary independent of German influence and working together under Italian patronage and it was to serve as the base for Italian participation in a four-power directorate of Europe. This directorate, incorporating Britain, France, Germany and Italy, as the four great powers, would serve to re-adjust European relations to permit the peaceful incorporation of a resurgent Germany into the European system. By taking a pos-ition 'equidistant' from both France and Germany, Italy and Britain would balance conflicting interests.

For a variety of reasons, the Pope gave enthusiastic support to this new Italian policy. The advent of the Depression, with its social disruption, had caused a change in Vatican policy as well. In place of the expansive missionary work of the 1920s, the Pope, in 1930, had launched his crusade against Soviet persecution of the Church and, in the years that followed, sought to rally and defend Catholics against the threats posed to Christianity by Moscow and the Comintern. The Pope now supported any initia-tive such as the one Mussolini was proposing, toward a settling of differences between the non-Communist powers, so that the Christian West could better withstand the onslaught of Bolshevik atheism. In addition, the Pope was pleased that Mussolini was at last supporting and uniting Austria and Hungary. To encourage Italian action on the Danube and to maintain peace in Italy, it was worth siding with Italy against Yugoslavia as it appeared that the German threat was pushing Mussolini toward a union of Catholic central Europe. With the one looking at Germany and the other at the Soviet Union, Mussolini and the Pope were once again in accord on foreign policy.

The accession of Hitler to the Chancellorship of Germany and his immediate threats to the independence of Austria occasioned yet a further shift of policy on Italy's part. Once Mussolini had secured the signatures of Britain, France and Germany to his Four-Power Pact in the summer of 1933, he dropped his emphasis on 'equidistance' in favour of participation in an anti-German alliance. This meant that Mussolini suddenly dropped his hos-tility to Yugoslavia and shifted the Italian focus completely from the Balkans to the Danube. As Mussolini encouraged Dollfuss and the *Heimwehr* to resist Hitler in the summer of 1933, he simul-taneously sought friendly relations with Belgrade. This, in turn, opened the way for serious negotiations with France once bila-teral discussions were resumed after the signing of the Four-Power Pact in July 1933.

Yugoslavia, however, would not remove itself as an issue as

quickly as Mussolini desired. King Alexander first sought to unite the Balkan countries against outside interference and, then, in 1934, he reached out to Nazi Germany for protection against any Franco-Italian settlement at Yugoslav expense.

The murder of King Alexander and Louis Barthou at Marseilles in October 1934 and the accession of the pliable Pierre Laval as French Foreign Minister brought about an agreement in January 1935 whereby Italy would join France in resisting German expansion and rearmament in return for French concession of an Italian sphere of influence: Italy would henceforth exercise its influence from Austria to Abyssinia with French blessing.

Having first welcomed Hitler as German Chancellor and signed a concordat with him in order to encourage the unity of the Western powers, the Pope soon became disillusioned by immediate Nazi violations of the Concordat. Like Mussolini, he too shifted his support from the scheme for a four-power directorate to an anti-Nazi alliance in defence of Austria. Hitler's behaviour had demonstrated to the Pope that the Nazis were as great an immediate danger to Christian Europe as were the Communists and it proved, in fact, to be Hitler rather than Stalin who forced a consolidation of the Catholic position in Europe. Not only did Catholic France and Catholic Italy unite in 1935 in defence of Catholic Austria, but decreased Italian hostility to Yugoslavia facilitated the secret negotiation of a concordat with that country, which was signed in 1935.

For the Holy See, the Franco-Italian *rapprochement* of 1935 represented the ideal diplomatic organization of Europe, uniting European Catholicism, as it did, initially against the anti-clerical Nazis and ultimately against the anti-Christian Bolsheviks. The Franco-Italian Agreement was popularly rooted in Catholic sympathy. Once Mussolini had invaded Abyssinia in October 1935, in line with his understanding with Laval, Catholic bitterness was great when the British Government forced France to choose between the continued support of Britain and the continued support of Italy. Within a year, the Franco-Italian alliance had collapsed with the result that France and Britain looked to Moscow and the Popular Front movement as the best defence against Hitler, while Mussolini was backed into the same corner as the Nazi dictator.

Appendices

Appendix A: Dino Grandi's Report to the Council of Ministers, 5 November 1929*

In the months of September and October some events of notable international interest took place. They affect international affairs in general. Some of them affect Italy directly.

1. New direction of British policy toward America
2. The death of Stresemann
3. The internal Austrian crisis
4. Anti-Italian demonstrations in Yugoslavia
5. The fall of the Briand Cabinet
6. The London Naval Conference
7. The attempted assassination of the Crown Prince in Brussels on October 24

The advent of the Labour Party to power was a novelty in European politics, and also a brusque change in what had been the static and fixed direction of British policy during the five years of the Baldwin Cabinet. British action at the Hague Conference, resumption of diplomatic relations with the USSR, plans for new constitutions for Egypt, Iraq and India, MacDonald's trip to Washington. The *entente cordiale* with France is finished. The prudent reserve of Conservative policy toward Germany and the cold aversion toward America are also finished. The Labour Party declares itself a friend of Germany and does not conceal the intention to veer the axis of British European policy toward Berlin. In imperial policy, the Labour Party overcomes the

---

* *Source:* Collection of Italian Documents, St Antony's College, Oxford (job 329/112722–42). Translation by the author.

Conservative hesitations and realizes, at least in the theatrical choreography designed to impress the distant states of the Empire, the new Anglo-American collaboration. The price of this collaboration: the concession of naval parity and the renunciation of naval supremacy. The new system of supreme world sea power will, in Anglo-American plans, be sanctioned at the London Naval Conference, *whose specific intention is not the well-understood one of making another attempt at the reduction of armaments, but rather of internationally sanctioning a type of hierarchy of the world naval powers.* This is – we shall discuss it soon – one of the basic reasons why Italy cannot accept anything less than absolute parity with France. The policy of MacDonald, which strangely resembles that of the last Sultans of the Ottoman Empire, signals a diminution of British prestige but helps, undoubtedly, to slow down temporarily the centrifugal movements in the Empire. The policy of Anglo-American collaboration, in fact, reassures Canada and Australia. The tranquillity of the sea routes in the Pacific and the Atlantic makes it possible to concentrate imperial activity in the two continents where new and old anti-British ferments react: Africa and Asia.

What is the repercussion of this new British orientation on Italian policy? No direct repercussions. Favourable indirect repercussions. The end of the Anglo-French *entente cordiale* weakens France and enriches with new and unforeseen elements the European chess-board, which the Locarno policies had rendered fixed, static and stagnant. The mobility of the international situation is always of advantage to the necessarily dynamic and necessarily changing policy of Italy. It is a great illusion to believe that the English Conservative Government was a sincere friend of Fascist Italy. In the last five years, London has always endured the policy of the Fascist Government and when it has not blocked it, it was only from fear of worse. The policy of Fascist Italy in the Balkans has always found the London Government hostile, heavily dragging the weight of the Paris Government.

It is enough to remember the English attitude to the Italo-Albanian alliance, which Chamberlain did not want at any cost, and the philo-Serb attitude of the British representative in Belgrade, Mr Kennard, during and after the acute phase of Italo-Yugoslav relations.

The truth is that the London Government has never had any

other preoccupation than to give right to might. And as the strongest was Italy and she was taking the right for herself, then Italy had, for Chamberlain, the right. That's all. And yet this illusion still lives among many of those circles which do not conceive of Italy's international life except as a function of a vassalage to this or that of the three great powers, towards which they have stretched the past and the present 'threads' of Italian spirit. The German thread is past and the French thread reduced; today it is the British thread. I shall never forget the murmurs which were echoed by certain venerable members of the Senate (first of all the president of the Italian Academy) when the Fascist Government two years ago 'dared' to answer a dry '*no*' to the invitation to adhere to the Anglo-French naval agreement and to the Anglo-French move against the philo-Macedonian policy of the Sofia Government. They spoke of 'ruin'. Our declaration, simple enough and natural for the autonomy of our foreign policy even from Great Britain, was judged a reckless move without precedent. The Italian 'no' provoked the failure of the two proposals. *But this, if it was the true victory of our policy* of that moment, made these afore-mentioned circles tremble even more in fear of the 'vendetta' (their word) which would come from Albion. No vendetta arrived. On the contrary. Under such an aspect – of internal instruction – a little Socialism in England will suit the Italians well. And as the Labour Party is the open and declared enemy of Fascism, then Italy will accustom itself to believe less in the illusion of English friendship.

The death of Stresemann has placed in peril for a moment that present policy of Germany which a French newspaper has termed 'bigamous'. A bitter conflict is being unchained in Germany between the parties of both the nationalist associations and of the right who do not want the approval of the Young Plan and the deliberations of the Hague Conference against the parties of the governing coalition who intend to have these accords ratified. The conflict which truly appears destined to assume there the character of a civil war has been somewhat appeased by the unchaining in France of a campaign against Briand and against the acceptance of the deliberations of the Hague. The fall of Briand has made the German extremists recover their wits. The Young Plan will be accepted and ratified, then. Stresemann continues, even dead, to follow the right policy, which – beyond doubt – indicates an improving position to Germany. Stresemann has had the funeral honours of the Consuls. The German people compare him to Bismarck. The London Conference; Dawes Plan, Locarno Treaty; entry of Germany into the League of Nations; Young Plan; final evacuation of the Rhineland – these are the clear steps on the road made by Germany, as advised by Stresemann. His death is an advantage for us. Stresemann hated Italy and hated Fascism. Through calculation and through instinct. He was a German who judged Fascist Italy to be in the same guise as the Italy of the Triple Alliance. A convinced Mason, he was logically a convinced anti-Fascist. Italy did not count as an element in his international policy. Thus, Italy counted exclusively in his wretched parliamentary game, where the question and the polemics of the Alto Adige, put forward exclusively by him at the opportune moment, served to pacify the intransigent attitude of the Right who were sympathetic to Fascism. Now we definitely know that the irredentist organizations of the Tyrol were subsidized by the German Government. This is not to deceive ourselves that his death will greatly change things in Germany, but he is one less enemy of Fascism in the world. The death of Stresemann and the fall of Chamberlain have taken from the scene two of the three patrons of the pacific development of the last five years, from Locarno to the Hague.

This almost simultaneous disappearance of Chamberlain and Stresemann has weakened the remaining Briand, whose action appears, at the present moment, determined more than ever by temporization and by uncertainty.

A recent event is the advent in Austria of the Schober Cabinet with the support of the Heimwehr. The internal Austrian situation strangely offers some analogies to the Italian situation of 1922. Except that the March on Rome, sweeping away all attempts at compromise and intermediate solutions, carried Mussolini and Fascism directly and all at once to the Government of the Nation. Chancellor Schober seems, at least for today not to have decided to drop his tentative and temporary tactics. [*Crossed out*: We urge him almost daily to make a show of courage and to give a decisive rhythm to his action.] Before the Jewish Bank hand in hand with the social democrats of Prague, Berlin and Paris makes the task more difficult for him. The victory of the Heimwehr in Austria signifies for Italy some important and useful things. One deals in the first place, with an anti-democratic regime which joins itself to the other regimes existing in Europe, regimes which for intuitive and intrinsic reasons cannot move themselves into the orbit of the Fascist regime, and constitute therefore a series of convergent forces in the struggle against the common enemy, European social-democratic Masonry. In the second place, the advent of the Heimwehr to power signifies a weakening, at least for a certain period, of the tendency to an Anschluss and to irredentism in the Tyrol. The Heimwehr, at least for now, is not Pan-German, and sustains differentiated characteristics within the confines of the German race, of Austrian civilization from that more rigidly teutonic. In the third place, the power in the hands of the Heimwehr signifies, besides the discomfiture of Berlin, the discomfiture of Benes and of the Little Entente, and therefore of France, who was last trying for several years to realize the great programme of a vast confederation of Danube states, under the auspices of Paris and the direction of the Little Entente. The entry of Austria into the orbit of French policy would have obliged Hungary to surrender unconditionally. On the contrary, a government of the Right in Austria signifies for Hungary the breaking of the circle which was suffocating her [*crossed out*: *stabilizing a corridor with Italy, determining a possible road for the transport of war materials*]. A friendly Austria is for Hungary an open breach to the world. From Vienna one acts directly on Prague and above all on Zagreb. Even the Croat revolution will draw advantage from it.

The incidents and the demonstrations which were reported all over Yugoslavia after the sentence of Pola have returned to the carpet the problem of our relations with Yugoslavia which some have had the impression of being improved in recent times. In reality, the tension between us and Yugoslavia is the same as three years ago, when the Italian Government suddenly broke the spell of Italo-Serb friendship with the international denunciation of Yugoslav armaments. The situation has not changed greatly since then. If only Serbia has understood, after the hammering of Italian policy, continued without respite for two years, that a provocative and arrogant attitude instead of intimidating Italy only makes her resist the action more and more. It understands that the advice of London and Paris means little to Italy and that the policy of British or French support at Belgrade does not intimidate Italy. At the same time, Wall Street and the City declare that their own hesitation to concede a loan to Serbia until Serbia modifies and improves her relationship with Italy. For a certain time, Serbia pretended to make a change, and, while continuing to arm herself feverishly, showed Italy a penitent face and offered a respectful demeanour. But while the government and the press of King Alexander were representing this new part of the Serbian tragicomedy, the peripheral organizations continued their destructive and criminal action against Italy. It is enough to quote the statistics of the crimes committed by the Oriuna from June 1928 to October 1929 in Venezia Guilia as the following: 36 homicides, 7 attempted homicides, 9 woundings.

As the Fascist Government has not changed its attitude at all, Serbia, confronted with the inanity of its policy, again puts on its mask. This is the savage anti-Italian outbreak of the demonstrations after the Pola sentence. Grotesque and savage, but very instructive and symptomatic for us. Serbia is already well advanced in its military preparations, feverishly intensified in 1926, after the Treaty of Tirana. If Wall Street and the City have made difficulty up to now in conceding a large loan for internal reconstruction, it is certain nevertheless that Serbia has found all the credits it wished, both in France and England, for its supply of arms. In 1930 the preparation of the Yugoslav army will be almost completed. It is from that moment that our situation in Albania will begin to be delicate again. Serbia resumes its courage and modifies its strategic preparation on our frontiers. The Yugoslavian military readiness of these last months, defensive in the Dalmatian–Bosnian sector, defensive and offensive in the Julian sector, exclusively offensive in the Albanian and Macedonian sectors must be reason for serious reflection by us. Serbia shows that it no longer intends to wait for the Italian army north of Zagreb, as in the earlier plan of the Yugoslav General Staff, and instead, it is counting on resisting to the bitter end and to counter-attack, probably, on the same Julian frontiers. At the same time, the Belgrade Government tries to use the ground of common hate for Italy as an idea which serves as the cement of the races, conflicting and divided among themselves, of the Yugoslav State. Already the Croats are protesting at the attempt made at Belgrade to make the anti-Italian demonstrations of Zagreb, Ragusa and Spalato appear as Croat initiatives, and therefore to throw a shadow on the relations of confidence which Belgrade well knows exists between the Croat patriots and us. These demonstrations, in a large part organized by the Serb associations, rather than relaxing, *must intensify our action of attempting to plant our influence beyond the Adriatic and beyond the Illyrian mountains*. Because this is the 'sense' of our present fascist policy.

The Adriatic is no longer sufficient to defend our independence as a Mediterranean race from the Slav races. Beyond the Adriatic and on the shores of the Adriatic, which is truly a trench which divides the Orient from the Occident, there is a chain of states which must be, from the Canal of Otranto to Nevoso, bridgeheads commanded by Italy. We have made Albania, we must make Croatia. It is the old policy of Caesar, it is the contemporary policy of Napoleon, it is the present policy of Mussolini. Destiny wishes that the borders between the Occident and the Orient remain on the Sava, which was the border indicated by Diocletian between the Eastern Empire and the Western Empire. The Sava is also the border which divides, from the Congress of Nicea to today, Roman Catholicism from the Eastern Churches.

Our relations with France have not changed much in the last two months. The Italo-French collaboration at the Hague Conference on the specific terrain of reparations must not be considered with the optimism with which some have judged it. We know too well the French tendency to nourish illusions. The Franco-Italian negotiations to resolve the questions of Tunis and Libya have not advanced far. The French reception of our offer of preliminary discussions on naval disarmament has been cold, and one cannot hope for much good even on this terrain where agreement would be easiest. The attempted assassination of the Crown Prince in Brussels on 24 October has once again raised the delicate question of the *fuorusciti*. It is not, and will never be, possible to have a calm agreement between Italy and France as long as France tolerates on its territory the organization of crimes which strike a direct blow at the life of the State. We wait, therefore, without illusions, for the work of the new Tardieu Cabinet.

I said before that the French attitude to our offer of preliminary conversations to try and reach an Italo-French agreement on naval disarmament before the London Conference had been very reserved and prudent. These conversations have taken place, however. The Fascist Government advanced as precondition for a Franco-Italian naval agreement the criterion of parity with

France, not only in battleships but for all types of ships. We are not able to accept anything less than this condition. However, we are disposed to accept that level which France will indicate as necessary for her maritime defence. We are, besides, eventually disposed to support France in the question of submarines.

It must be clear by now, contrary to what some French writers have claimed, that the Italian attitude to the next London Conference on the matter of submarines will depend exclusively on how many France will make in our regard. The Marine Minister had concluded, with regard to this proposal, that in order to retain Italian advantage, Italy must keep full liberty over the construction of submarines. It is scarcely necessary for me to stress that our participation at the London Naval Conference, with or without the agreement with France, does not change in any way the criteria of the attitude followed up to today by Italy on the general problem of disarmament. These criteria are and remain those stated by the Head of the Government in his speech to the Senate of June 1928, and confirmed in the note of 6 October 1928 to the British Government, in reply to the invitation to adhere to the Anglo-French naval compromise.

The eventual results of the London Conference remain, for us, conditional and subordinate to the results of the general conference on disarmament, and, as everyone knows, the laborious studies and preparatory work for this is carried out at the League of Nations.

Another important question is represented by the various committees required by the Young Plan, the greatest of which are the Committee for the constitution of the Bank of International Payments (which now sits at Baden Baden) and the Committee for the regulation of the Eastern Reparations (which sits in Paris). The work of the first committee is of a primarily technical and financial character and this is coming to an end. The Committee for the regulation of the Eastern Reparations had been examining and discussing the complex questions relative to the payments due from Austria, Hungary, Bulgaria as well as to the Successor States for the ceded goods and the cost of liberation. In spite of the general desire to complete this work the results achieved so far have been rather sparse. In reference to *Austria*, there is a Franco-British proposal for the complete cancellation of Austrian reparations. The Italian delegation has been opposed to this proposition up to now and has asked that the problem be returned for examination at the next plenary conference. We are interested in keeping the question open and are saving our decision for the moment when it will have value as a card in the political game with Chancellor Schober. Regarding *Bulgaria*, the Italian, French and British delegations have presented a common plan of regulation, which is however opposed, in a joint and like-minded fashion, by the states of the Little Entente. The questions relating to the *Hungarian reparations* are still far from a possible solution. The Little Entente has posed as condition for its acceptance of a regulation which will arrange definitively the problem of Hungarian reparations, the requirement that Hungary accept the compensation between its debts for reparations and its credits due for the payment for the expropriated Hungarian optants. The Hungarian Government has definitely refused to deal on this basis and the whole question will, consequently, be examined by the plenary Conference. The Fascist Government has supported Hungary without reserve and has worked to reduce the opposition of the Little Entente. But the situation is as delicate and difficult as ever. One the one hand Hungary, agitated and diffident, could choose a direction which Italy has already strongly warned would be catastrophic and unlikely, at the same time, to undermine the general agreements of the Young Plan. On the other hand, Czechoslovakia, from whom we await the payment of the sums which are due to us to satisfy the pledges made at the Hague towards England, profited from our delicate situation in relation to Hungary to withdraw the concrete offer of a definitive settlement, advanced some weeks ago and accepted in principle by us, declaring, suddenly, its solidarity with Yugoslavia and Rumania. The Hague Conference will thus resume its work, probably in the second half of the current month, in an atmosphere full of perplexity and dissent.

To conclude, we have, as mentioned earlier, a greater concentration of European social democracy in the fight against Fascism. That is beyond doubt. There is only one front on which the Labourites of MacDonald and Henderson, the populist democrats and socialists of Müller and the French Left are perfectly in agreement: *the struggle against Fascism*. On the other side, the situation is bad in Spain where General De Rivera [*crossed out*: making the dictatorship a joke] has a difficult situation; in Poland where Marshal Pilsudski has not succeeded in transforming his paradoxical political–military revolution into either a doctrine or judicial institutions, no matter how rudimentary. The situation is particularly delicate in Hungary, where the regime of Count Bethlen is having its difficulties, both from the economic crisis and from the repercussions on the sensitive Hungarian public conscience of the results of the Paris Conference on Eastern Reparations. At this time, the Labour MP Smith, secretary to Henderson, has made a mysterious trip through the Danube and Balkan capitals, with extended stops in Budapest and Belgrade. The declared scope of the trip is to carry the support of the Labour Party to those political parties which are preparing to struggle against domestic dictatorship and which have as a programme a great Danubian conference on a democratic base. These are significant symptoms which one must not overlook and which indicate that *Anno VIII* offers a vast and complex battlefield on which our action must be more than ever attentive and vigilant.

Appendix B: B. Mussolini: 'Aphorisms' (21 May 1931)*

1. A monarchy justifies its existence when the first to feel himself a monarchist is the king; the opposite case is when these same monarchists cannot pretend to be less republican than the king.
2. When a king abdicates, he resigns and, therefore, must be replaced, either by another king, if one exists, or by a president. In the latter case, it is necessary, whether one wants it or not, to proclaim a republic. A new regime is never born from the dismissal of a sovereign. Its appearance is more complicated, more noble, more grand; it is born from implicit or explicit nomination by the people or from a victory.
3. The Spanish republic has not had, in general, a good press: no one in Europe feels the urgent necessity for it. In European eyes, the naval agreement or the Austro-German move are infinitely more important events.
4. In Paris, the ex-king has had a formidable welcome. Explanation: in Madrid, they are bored with the monarchy,

---

* *Source*: Autografi del Duce, Archivio Centrale dello Stato, Rome, busta 6, fasc. IX, sotto-fasc. 'E'. Published in Italian in Renzo De Felice, *Mussolini il duce*, vol. I. *Gli anni del consenso, 1929–1936*, pp. 824–5. Translation by the author.

in Paris with the republic.

5. The Spanish republic is not a revolution; it is a plagiarism.
A plagiarism 150 years too late. To make a parliamentary
republic today is like using gas lamps when electric lighting
is available.

6. Revolution? But the revolution is above all a movement of
ideas which develop and universalize themselves. Where is
all this in Spain? The republic announces a series of
retrospective trials: the leaders are – in fact – great lawyers.

7. A regime does not defend itself at the last hour: it defends
itself from the first hours and successively in all the hours
and in all the minutes, right up to the last hour, but in this
case with the most ruthless decisions; what are thousands of
dead (it would be but enough to deliver a volley) if one is
concerned that the triumph of a certain principle signifies
the ruin of a people and the probability of an infinitely
greater number of victims tomorrow?

8. Kerensky did not bring Nicholas back. He prepared for
Lenin.

9. Today, it is no longer a question of a republic or of a
monarchy, but of communism or fascism.

10. Even in Italy, people are surprised that the Spanish clergy
and the Spanish Catholics have let the monarchy go. That
happened exactly one week after the Easter ceremonies
during which the king washed the feet of the beggars and
walked in the procession. His Catholic Majesty of Spain had
no defenders among the Catholics. This is the fact. But what
are the motives? The motive is of an historical order: the
Church does not make à true and proper issue of political
instruction except on extremely theoretical lines: it judges
institutions by the attitude they hold to the Church. There is
no doubt that the Spanish monarchy favoured the Church.
And yet, the support is wanting. It is necessary to convince
them that the Bishops are not political leaders or army
generals, but pastors: the men that they direct form the
flock: a flock of sheep. Now a lone wolf scatters a million
sheep.

11. The stupidity of democracy, which lives on an enormous lie
producing a wonderful humbug for the so-called sovereign
people, is made public once again in the comparisons that
some people are making between Italy and Spain. In order

to do that, it is necessary to be sublimely stupid.

12. The paradox in all this is that the democrats have not respected the wish of the majority: Zamora has vilified, therefore, one of the dogmas of democracy; the answer of the urns has been nullified: and the cities have overhwelmed the countryside. To establish the reigme of the immortal principles, it is necessary to begin by denying them. It is necessary to be unintelligent to take all this seriously!

Appendix C: Minute by Mussolini on his Meeting with Pope Pius XI*†

The first exchanges were rather embarrassing. The Holy Father held out his hand to me and invited me to sit. 'We offer you welcome to this house which, being the House of the Father, is the house of all.' He first asked me for news of Edda in Shanghai. The gesture is very kind and I thank him profoundly. 'I am very pleased with this meeting, both for the fact in itself and for the day.' That gives me the opportunity to express to him my gratification, my satisfaction and my *recognition* of the way in which matters have improved to this present state of affairs. 'It pleases me that the Director of the *Araldo della Verità* of Florence, who had used absolutely unworthy language in the face of the Holy See and myself, should have been tried and punished.

'But my attention is drawn to Protestant propaganda, which appears to be making progress in all dioceses according to an inquiry which I have had the Bishops make. The Protestants behave audaciously and speak of "missionary" tasks in Italy. The laws on the admitted cults – instead of the tolerated – have helped in this.'

I observe that, according to the data of the last census, the Protestants are hardly one hundred and thirty-five thousand, of which thirty-seven thousand are foreigners against forty-two million Catholics.

* The meeting took place in the Vatican at 11.00 a.m. on 11 February 1932.

† *Source*: Collection of Italian Documents, St Antony's College, Oxford – Job 1/3; published in Italian in Angelo Corsetti, 'Dalla preconciliazione ai patti del Laterano: Note e documenti', *Annuario 1968 della Biblioteca Civica di Massa*, pp. 149–225. Translation by the author.

'It is true', continues the Holy Father, 'that Italy is fundamentally Catholic and this is also a condition of privilege from the national point of view, but precisely because of this it is necessary to be vigilant.'

When I asked him which were the points most particularly afflicted by this situation, the Holy Father cited to me Florence, Spezia, Piazza Armeria (Riesi) and gave me a suitable memorial on the question.

'Those measures also please me whereby youths of the paramilitary and of the Balilla may participate in the observance of their festive duties, but a certain *vade mecum* which has been distributed among the paramilitary and the Avanguardisti is the origin and the beginning of corruption. It is the Christian fathers who first advised me of this matter. I understand that in this world one can neither do everything nor avoid everything bad. I am also satisfied that the licentiousness of certain papers which circulate among the young, with harmful effects, has been restricted. I am pleased with the interest of the Government in the construction or reconstruction in the earthquake zones of the parochial houses, whch are almost totally lacking in some zones of Italy. There are four thousand and more which need to be constructed. With the aid of Providence, we hope to succeed. But there will also be work there for our successors. An open Church is a safeguard not only for souls but also for the nation. Good Catholic Christians can be only the best citizens.

'I must also express my satisfaction with the rapidity with which the Government has recently answered the nomination of Bishops. Some young dioceses are thereby filled without long holidays, which benefit no one. I hope that this practice will be continued.

'I am happy that compatibility has been re-established between the Fascist Party and Catholic Action. If ever, the difficulties have disappeared for the Catholics. But I do not see, in the whole of Fascist doctrine – with its affirmation of the principles of order, authority and discipline – anything contrary to Catholic conceptions.'

I note also his repeated affirmation – a little less frequent in these recent times – of Fascist totalitarianism. 'This totalitarianism is in the circle of the State but, besides material interests, there are also spiritual ones and it is here that Catholic totalitarianism enters.'

The Holy Father at this point takes a book, looks for a page, and thus recommences. 'Here is a book by Manzoni, not well known, *La Morale Cattolica*. Manzoni, generally, is a cautious and moderate writer but, in this period, he seems to clench his fist. "When", says Manzoni, "Christ said to the Apostles, '*Eunte et docete* [sic] *omnes gentes*', I entrusted to the Church a divine mandate, an order which the Church must execute".'

I share the opinion of the Holy Father – State and Church act on two 'different levels' and are able, thus – limiting their reciprocal spheres of activity – to collaborate together.

The Holy Father considers this collaboration to be even more necessary in these times of crisis and great misery.

'I receive', continues the Holy Father, 'letters of all types and all asking for help. The nations which at one time were offering, are now asking. The world is disturbed. What happens in the Far East gives birth, perhaps, to a greater struggle for control of the Pacific.'

The Holy Father asks then for news of Geneva. I answer him that, especially after Grandi's speech, the actions for disarmament have been augmented.

'It was I,' says the Holy Father, 'who advised the *Osservatore Romano* to call Grandi's speech "courageous".'

I: 'Certainly a word from Your Holiness would give a most strong impulse to the problem.'

The Holy Father: 'I shall say something on the matter in St Peter's tomorrow without, naturally, going into detail.'

At this point, I add that beside the reduction of arms, there is also the cancellation of debts – reparations, the lowering of tariff barriers, the devaluation of gold because the crisis is working itself out.

The Holy Father agrees and observes that, in history, there are states of crisis whose chronic condition has lasted for centuries like that which upset the world in the fifth, sixth and seventh centuries and which resolved itself at the time of Charlemagne. Certainly, a crisis cannot become 'chronic' without endangering the very life of the people.

'Besides these general problems which sadden us', continues the Holy Father, 'there is a sorrowful triangle which augments our grief: Mexico, a country totally absorbed by Masonry; Spain, where Bolshevism and Masonry work together, and Russia, which proceeds in its work of de-Christianizing that people. I have received this very day the 36th volume of the Russian anti-religious library. There is also the underlying anti-Christian aversion of Judaism. When I was in Warsaw, I saw that, in all the Bolshevik regiments, the commissar or commissaria was Jewish. In Italy, however, the Jews are different. At one time, I was friendly with old Massaroni, who was the master of Balsamo Monzese, and who endowed the Church of the country with a Way of the Cross; also with Elia Prottes and I was also a student of the rabbi of Milan, Di Zano, when I wished to penetrate certain "nuances" of the Hebrew language.

'Now I wish to give you, in remembrance of this day, three medals, two of which recall the Crucifixion and the third, the radio. Sometimes I think how the message of Peter and Paul could have been facilitated had they had this means at their disposal. It is incredible what they accomplished availing themselves only of the means of their time.

'In these days, I have prayed for and caused to have prayed for the souls of your brother and of your nephew.'

Notes

NOTES TO CHAPTER ONE: 'A VERY DETERMINED ANTAGONIST'

1. Carlo Falconi, *The Popes in the Twentieth Century: From Pius X to John XXIII* (London, 1967) p. 181.
2. Adrian Lyttleton, *The Seizure of Power: Fascism in Italy, 1919–1929* (London, 1973) p. 429; Renzo De Felice, *Mussolini il fascista*, vol. II: *L'organizzazione dello stato fascista, 1925–1929* (Turin, 1968) [hereafter cited as *De Felice III*] p. 382.
3. *De Felice III*, pp. 382–3.
4. Ibid., and Renzo De Felice, *Mussolini il duce*, vol. I, *Gli anni del consenso, 1929–1936* (Turin, 1974) [hereafter cited as *De Felice IV*].
5. *Mandements, lettres pastorales et circulaires des évêques de Québec*, vol. XIII, p. 440.
6. See René Rémond, 'Il fascismo italiano visto dalla cultura cattolica francese', *Storia contemporanea*, no. 4 (1971) pp. 685–96.
7. Robert A. Graham, S. J., *Vatican Diplomacy: A Study of Church and State on the International Plane* (Princeton, 1959) p. 216.
8. Falconi, pp. 197–9, 214.
9. Like the Apostolic Nuncios, Apostolic Delegates also have ecclesiastical responsibilities, but, unlike the nuncios, they do not have corresponding political duties.
10. The framework of papal diplomacy is discussed thoroughly in Robert Graham, *Vatican Diplomacy* (see especially Chapters 4 and 5).
11. *De Felice III*, p. 383.
12. D. A. Binchy, *Church and State in Fascist Italy* (London, 1941) p. 105.
13. Ibid., p. 106.
14. Pietro Scoppola, *La Chiesa e il fascismo: documenti e interpretazioni* (Bari, 1973) pp. 52–3; Francesco Margiotta Broglio, *Italia e Santa Sede dalla Grande Guerra alla conciliazione* (Bari, 1966) pp. 71–86.
15. Margiotta Broglio, pp. 43–71.
16. Ibid., pp. 82–6; *De Felice III*, pp. 386–8.
17. Luigi Federzoni, *Italia de ieri per la storia di domani* (Verona, 1967) pp. 115–24; Scoppola, pp. 31–6.
18. Margiotta Broglio, pp. 82–6.
19. Ibid., pp. 107–11.
20. Christopher Seton-Watson, *Italy from Liberalism to Fascism, 1870–1925* (London, 1967) pp. 656–7.

21. Margiotta Broglio, pp. 127–30.
22. Ibid., pp. 140–51.
23. *De Felice IV*, pp. 331–4.
24. Margiotta Broglio, p. 82.
25. *De Felice III*, pp. 391–2.
26. Ibid., pp. 401–2.
27. Ibid., pp. 415–16.
28. Ibid., p. 394.
29. The most concise, analytical biography of Pius XI is that in Falconi, 'Pius XI: Achille Ratti', in *The Popes in the Twentieth Century*, pp. 151–233, from which most of the following biographical details are taken.
30. Binchy, pp. 79–81; on Pius XI's papal style, see also papers of the British Foreign Office, Public Record Office, London [hereafter cited as *FO*], e.g. Wingfield to Simon, 3 January 1935 (R273/81/22).
31. Falconi, pp. 200–1.
32. Ibid., p. 201.
33. Margiotta Broglio, pp. 43–58.
34. Falconi, p. 183.
35. Binchy, pp. 245–6.
36. *De Felice III*, pp. 400–2.
37. Ibid., pp. 428–36.
38. Falconi, pp. 7–14.
39. Ibid., p. 203.
40. Anthony Rhodes, *The Vatican in the Age of the Dictators, 1922–1945* (London, 1973) pp. 131–6; Robert Graham, ch. 13.

NOTES TO CHAPTER TWO: AREAS OF COOPERATION BEFORE 1929

1. Giampiero Carocci, *La politica estera dell'Italia fascista (1925–1928)* (Bari, 1969) ch. x; the best general discussion of Italian foreign policy is C. J. Lowe and F. Marzari, *Italian Foreign Policy, 1870–1940* (London, 1975).
2. Gordon Wright, *France in Modern Times: From the Enlightenment to the Present* (Chicago, 1974) p. 335.
3. Ibid., p. 335
4. Rhodes, pp. 83–4.
5. Ibid., p. 84.
6. *FO*, Randall to Chamberlain, 24 October 1928 (W10318/2153/17).
7. *Documenti diplomatici italiani* [hereafter cited as *DDI*], 7th series, vol. v, no. 63, Piacentini to Mussolini, 8 March 1927.
8. Mario Bendiscioli, *La politica della Santa Sede (direttive – organi – realizzazioni), 1918–1938* (Florence, 1939) p. 85.
9. Terence P. McLaughlin (ed.), *The Church and the Reconstruction of the Modern World: The Social Encyclicals of Pius XI* (New York, 1957) p. 32.
10. Rhodes, pp. 89–93.
11. Falconi, p. 126.
12. Rhodes, pp. 89–93.
13. François Charles-Roux, *Huit ans au Vatican, 1932–1940* (Paris, 1947) p. 52.
14. Letter from Sir Alec Randall to the author, 23 November 1973.

15. Ronald Jasper, *Arthur Cayley Headlam: Life and Letters of a Bishop* (London, 1960) especially pp. 165–7.
16. *FO*, report of Foreign Research and Press Office, 'The Uniate Roman Catholic Churches', 4 November 1942 (R7376/7376/57).
17. *FO*, Russell to Chamberlain, 29 January 1927 (E427/417/65).
18. *FO*, Randall to Cushendun, 17 September 1928 (E4679/843/65); annual report for 1928 from the Holy See, 9 May 1929 (C3397/3397/22).
19. Rhodes, p. 132.
20. *FO*, annual report for 1929 from the Holy See, 27 March 1930 (C2470/2470/22); Rhodes, pp. 131–8; Nicolas Zernov, *The Russian Religious Renaissance of the Twentieth Century* (New York, 1963) pp. 254–5.
21. Maria Ormos, 'L'opinione del Conte Stefano Bethlen sui rapporti Italo-Ungherese (1927–31)', *Storia contemporanea*, no. 2 (1971) pp. 297–9.
22. Carocci, ch. VIII.
23. *DDI*, 7th series, vol. v, no. 407, Mussolini to Piacentini, 11 September 1927.
24. Ibid., no. 273, Ivo Frank to Durini di Monza, 13 June 1927.
25. Ibid., no. 168, Ricciardi to Mussolini, 27 April 1927.
26. Carocci, ch. XIII; *DDI*, 7th series, vol. v, no. 123, minute by Mussolini on his conversation with Bethlen, 4 April 1927.
27. *DDI*, 7th series, vol. v, no. 123, minute by Mussolini on his conversation with Bethlen, 4 April 1927.
28. Ormos, pp. 300–1.
29. *De Felice IV*, pp. 358–9.
30. Nicholas M. Nagy-Talavera, *The Green Shirts and the Others: A History of Fascism in Hungary and Rumania* (Stanford, 1970) p. 80.
31. Edward Crankshaw, *The Habsburgs* (London, 1971) pp. 168–9.
32. *DDI*, 7th series, vol. vii, no. 195, Durini di Monza to Mussolini, 20 January 1929.
33. Gordon Brook-Shepherd, *The Last Habsburg* (London, 1968) p. 184.
34. Letter from the Archduke Otto (Dr Otto von Habsburg) to the author, 11 April 1974.
35. Bendiscioli, p. 130.
36. *FO*, Phipps to Cushendun, 1 November 1928 (C8220/34/21).
37. Nagy-Talavera, pp. 51–2.
38. Ormos, p. 286.
39. C. A. Macartney, *October Fifteenth: A History of Modern Hungary, 1929–1945*, vol. i (Edinburgh, 1956) p. 85.
40. Letter from the Archduke Otto to the author, 11 April 1974.
41. Macartney, pp. 76–7.
42. C. A. Macartney and A. W. Palmer, *Independent Eastern Europe: A History* (London, 1962) pp. 266–7.
43. *DDI*, 7th series, vol. viii, no. 8, De Astis to Grandi, 18 September 1929.
44. Macartney and Palmer, p. 278.
45. Carocci, p. 194.
46. Ibid., ch. v.
47. *FO*, annual report for 1928 from the Holy See, 9 May 1929 (C3397/3397/22); annual report for 1929 from the Holy See, 27 March 1930 (C2470/2470/22).

48. *FO*, Randall to Cushendun, 17 September 1928 (E4679/843/65).
49. Stavro Skendi (ed.), *Albania* (New York, 1956) p. 14.
50. *DDI*, 7th series, vol. iv, no. 561, Aloisi to Mussolini, 30 December 1926.
51. *DDI*, 7th series, vol. v, no. 41, Aloisi to Mussolini, 3 March 1927.
52. Ibid., no. 65. Memo by Grandi, 9 March 1927.
53. Ibid., no. 439, Sola to Mussolini, 26 Sepember 1927.
54. *FO*, Seeds to Chamberlain, 20 December 1927 (C146/146/90).
55. *FO*, Seeds to Chamberlain, 28 July 1927 (C6655/6655/90); Seeds to Chamberlain, 3 February 1928 (C1351/146/90).
56. *DDI*, 7th series, vol. vii, no. 152, Sola to Mussolini, 8 January 1929; Pietro Quaroni, *Diplomatic Bags: An Ambassador's Memoirs* (London, 1966) p. 64.
57. *DDI*, 7th series, vol. vii, no. 244, Sola to Mussolini, 11 February 1929.
58. Ibid., no. 152, Sola to Mussolini, 8 January 1929.
59. *DDI*, 7th series, vol. iv, no. 438, Piacentini to Mussolini, 21 September 1926.
60. *DDI*, 7th series, vol. v, no. 63, Piacentini to Mussolini, 8 March 1927.
61. Ibid., no. 86, Grandi to Piacentini, 21 March 1927.
62. Ibid., no. 516, Grandi to Rocco, 9 November 1927.
63. Ibid., no. 434, Mussolini to Piacentini, 23 September 1927.
64. Ibid., no. 668, Piacentini to Mussolini, 11 December 1927.
65. Ibid., no. 669, Piacentini to Mussolini, 11 December 1927.
66. *DDI*, 7th series, vol. vi, no. 31, Piacentini to Mussolini, 19 January 1928.
67. Ibid., no. 355, Grandi to Count Roncalli, 24 May 1928.
68. Ibid., no. 646, Piacentini to Mussolini, 12 September 1928.
69. Ibid., no. 647, Piacentini to Mussolini, 12 September 1928.
70. Giorgio Rumi, *L'imperialismo fascista* (Milan, 1974) p. 51.
71. This colonial war in Libya is discussed in Giorgio Rochat, 'La repressione della resistenza Araba in Cirenaica nel 1930–31, nei documenti dell 'archivio Graziani', *Il movimento di liberazione in Italia* (January–March 1973) pp. 3–39, and in E. E. Evans-Pritchard, *The Sanusi of Cyrenaica* (Oxford 1949).
72. Emilio De Bono, *Anno XIII: The Conquest of an Empire* (London, 1937) p. 3.
73. Robert L. Hess, *Italian Colonialism in Somalia* (Chicago, 1966) ch. vii.
74. C. G. Baeta, 'Missionary and Humanitarian Interests, 1914 to 1960'. in L. H. Gann and Peter Diugnan (eds), *Colonialism in Africa 1870–1960*, vol. ii: *The History and Politics of Colonialism 1914–1960* (Cambridge, 1970) p. 427.
75. *DDI*, 7th series, vol. v, no. 433, Pedrazzi to Mussolini, 22 September 1927.
76. P. G. Edwards, 'Anglo-Italian Relations 1924–1929, unpublished D. Phil. thesis, University of Oxford (1971) ch. IV.
77. *DDI*, 7th series, vol. v, no. 88, report for Grandi, 21 March 1927.
78. *FO*, Russell to Chamberlain 8 April 1926 (C4465/660/22).
79. *DDI*, 7th series, vol. v, no. 136, Federzoni to Mussolini, 11 April 1927. While Ethiopian Christianity had only a tenuous connection with the Coptic Church in Alexandria, they did share the common theology of Monophysitism. 'In addition to this theological unity, the head of the Church in Ethiopia and usually the only bishop, the *Abuna*, was tradition-

ally an Egyptian monk appointed by the Patriarch of Alexandria. This custom, which dates back to the fourth century, was changed in 1929, when additional bishops were appointed and came to an end on July 13, 1948', Robert L. Hess, *Ethiopia: The Modernization of Autocracy* (Ithaca, 1970) p. 20.

80. *DDI*, 7th series, vol. v. no. 482, Gasparini to Federzoni, 22 October 1927.
81. Ibid., no. 673, Grandi to Federzoni, 12 December 1927.
82. *FO*, Russell to Chamberlain, 8 April 1926 (C4465/660/22).
83. *FO*, Fontana to Perrin, 22 February 1927, in report of 5 February 1942 (R1205/509/57).
84. Archivio Centrale dello Stato, Rome [hereafter cited as *ACS*], Segreteria Particolare del Duce, Carteggio Riservato [hereafter cited as *SPD*], busta 34, 'Bastianini', Bastianini to Mussolini, 17 March 1926.
85. Rhodes, pp. 66–7.
86. *FO*, Hopkinson to Howard, 'The Church in the Near East', 15 February 1942 (R1452/509/57).
87. *DDI*, 7th series, vol. v, no. 215, Pedrazzi to Mussolini, 19 May 1927.
88. Ibid., no. 433, Pedrazzi to Mussolini, 22 September 1927.
89. Ibid., no. 436, Mussolini to Pedrazzi, 24 September 1927.
90. Carocci, ch. XIX.
91. *DDI*, 7th series, vol. vi, no. 165, Cora to Mussolini, 18 March 1928; no. 186, Mussolini to Cora, 26 March 1928.
92. *DDI*, 7th series, vol. vii, no. 12, Porta to Mussolini, 29 September 1928; no. 120, Cora to Mussolini, 20 December 1928.
93. *DDI*, 7th series, vol. vi, no. 88, memo by Mussolini, 8 February 1928.
94. *DDI*, 7th series, vol. vii, no. 63, Orsini Baroni to Mussolini, 11 November 1928.
95. *FO*, minute by Howard-Smith, 17 December 1928 (C9578/9578/90).
96. *DDI*, 7th series, vol. vi, no. 119, Orsini Baroni to Mussolini, 20 February, 1928; *FO*, annual report for 1928 from the Holy See, 9 May 1929 (C3397/3397/22).
97. *DDI*, 7th series, vol. vii, no. 2, Orsini Baroni to Mussolini, 14 February 1929.
98. Ibid., no. 282, Orsini Baroni to Mussolini, 25 February 1929.
99. *FO*, Russell to Chamberlain, 31 May 1928 (C4264/31/22).
100. *ACS*, *SPD*, busta 22, 'Federzoni', Federzoni to Mussolini, 6 February 1928.
101. *DDI*, 7th series, vol. vi, no. 119, Orsini Baroni to Mussolini, 20 February 1928; no. 128, Grandi to Orsini Baroni, 24 February 1928.
102. *FO*, Russell to Chamberlain, 12 April 1928 (E1992/577/65).
103. *DDI*, 7th series, vol. vi, no. 226, Pedrazzi to Mussolini, 5 April 1928.
104. Ibid., no. 468, Mussolini to Bordonaro, 10 July 1928; *FO*, Bordonaro to Oliphant, 2 August 1928 (E3885/95/65).
105. *FO*, Oliphant to Bordonaro, 4 December 1928, (E5616/95/65).
106. *DDI*, 7th series, vol. vii, no. 125, Mussolini to Bordonaro, 22 December 1928.
107. *FO*, Russell to Chamberlain, 12 April 1928 (E1992/577/65).
108. *FO*, Barlassina to Mussolini, 11 February 1929, in report of 5 February 1942 (R1205/509/57).

109.   *FO*, annual report from the Holy See for 1929, 27 March 1930 (C2470/2470/22); Hopkinson to Howard, 'the Church in the Near East', 15 February 1942 (R1452/509/57).
110.   *FO*, Randall to Cushendun, 23 August 1928, (C6484/976/22); 28 August, 1928 (C6626/976/22).

NOTES TO CHAPTER THREE: AREAS OF CONFLICT BEFORE 1929

1.   *De Felice IV*, p.358.
2.   *DDI*, 7th series, vol. IV, no. 550, Vannutelli Rey to Bordonaro, 18 December 1926.
3.   *DDI*, 7th series, vol. V, no. 653, memo by Mussolini, 4 December 1927.
4.   *DDI*, 7th series, vol. VI, no. 68, minute by Mussolini on his conversation with Beaumarchais, 30 January, 1928.
5.   Ibid, no. 167, minute by Mussolini on his conversation with Beaumarchais, 19 March, 1928.
6.   Raffaele Guariglia, *Ricordi, 1922–1946* (Naples, 1950) pp. 67–74.
7.   *DDI*, 7th series, vol. VI, no. 208, memo by Office V, Europe and the Levant, 30 March, 1928.
8.   Robert L. Hess, 'Italy and Africa: Colonial Ambitions in the First World War', *Journal of African History*, vol. IV, no. 1 (1963) pp. 105–26.
9.   *DDI*, 7th series, vol. VI, no. 264, Manzoni to Mussolini, 19 April, 1928.
10.   *DDI*, 7th series, vol. VII, no. 121, Beaumarchais to Mussolini, 21 December, 1928.
11.   Ibid., no. 126, Mussolini to De Cicco, 22 December, 1928.
12.   Guariglia, pp. 74–82; Carocci, chs. VIII and IX.
13.   Carocci, ch. 11.
14.   Dennison I. Rusinow, *Italy's Austrian Heritage, 1919–1946* (Oxford, 1969), pp. 185–210; Binchy (p. 556) reports that there were about 500,000 Slavs in Venezia Giulia, of which 350,000 were Slovenes and 150,000 were Croats.
15.   Margiotta Broglio, pp. 136–40.
16.   C. A. Macartney, *Hungary and her Successors: The Treaty of Trianon and its Consequences, 1919–1937* (London, 1937), pp. 364–9.
17.   Carocci, ch. XVII; Ladislaus Hory and Martin Broszat, *Der Kroatische Ustascha-Staat, 1941–1945* (Stuttgart, 1964), pp. 15–17.
18.   Carocci, ch. XVII; Stephen Graham, *Alexander of Yugoslavia: The Story of the King who was Murdered at Marseilles* (Hamden, Conn., 1972), pp. 139–42.
19.   *DDI*, 7th series, vol. V, no. 273, Ivo Frank to Durini di Monza, 13 June, 1927.
20.   Ibid., no. 324, Grandi to Durini di Monza, 14 July 1927; Carocci, ch. XVII.
21.   *DDI*, 7th series, vol. VI, no. 441, Rochira to Mussolini, 28 June, 1928.
22.   Ibid., no. 522, Galli to Mussolini, 27 July, 1928.
23.   Ibid., no. 604, Mussolini to Galli, 31 August, 1928.
24.   Ibid., no. 658, Mussolini to Aldrovandi, Franklin, Orsini Baroni *et al.*, 17 September, 1928.
25.   Ibid., no. 550, De Astis to Mussolini, 12 August, 1928.

26. Ibid., no. 581, De Astis to Grandi, 24 August, 1928.
27. *DDI*, 7th series, vol. VII, no. 169, Durini di Monza to Mussolini, 14 January, 1929.
28. *FO*, Chilton to Cushendun, 17 October 1928 (C7871/34/21).
29. *DDI*, 7th series, vol. VII, no. 43, De Astis to Mussolini. 17 October, 1928; no. 47, Mussolini to De Astis, 23 October, 1928.
30. Ibid., no. 47, Mussolini to De Astis, 23 October, 1928.
31. Ibid., no. 25, Mussolini to Manzoni, 9 October, 1928.
32. Ibid., no. 121, Beaumarchais to Mussolini, 21 December, 1928.
33. *FO*, Graham to Chamberlain, 7 February 1929 (C1141/368/22).
34. *DDI*, 7th series, vol. VII, no. 53, Petrucci to Mussolini, 2 November, 1928.
35. *FO*, Chamberlain to Graham 8 April 1929, (C2504/2462/22).
36. Malbone W. Graham, 'Constitutional Development, 1914–1941' in Robert J. Kerner (ed.), *Yugoslavia* (Berkeley and Los Angeles, Calif., 1949).
37. Macartney, *Hungary and her Successors*, pp. 370–1; Stephen Graham, pp. 158–63.
38. *DDI*, 7th series, vol. VII, no. 158, Rochira to Mussolini, 8 January, 1929.
39. Hory and Broszat, pp. 19–20.
40. *DDI*, 7th series, vol. VII, no. 209, Rochira to Mussolini, 24 January, 1929.
41. Ibid., no. 286, Galli to Mussolini, 26 February, 1929.
42. Stephen Clissold (ed.), *A Short History of Yugoslavia From Early Times to 1966* (Cambridge, 1966), p. 165; Royal Institute of International Affairs, *South Eastern Europe: A Political and Economic Survey* (London, 1939), p. 76.
43. Rhodes, pp. 157–8.
44. Ibid., pp. 158–9.
45. Ibid., pp. 157–8; Jasper, pp. 166–7.
46. Stephen Graham, p. 137.
47. *DDI*, 7th series, vol. VII, no. 46, Memo by Rochira, 22 October, 1928.
48. Ibid., no. 53, Petrucci to Mussolini, 2 November, 1928.
49. Rusinow, ch. VII.
50. *FO*, Phipps to Chamberlain, 3 January 1929 (C150/149/3).
51. *DDI*, 7th series, vol. VIII, no. 8, De Astis to Grandi, 18 September, 1929.
52. Klemens Von Klemperer, *Ignaz Seipel: Christian Statesman in a Time of Crisis* (Princeton, 1972), p. 335.
53. Carocci, p. 194.
54. Carocci, p. 194; *DDI*, 7th series, vol. VI, no. 560, De Astis to Grandi, 17 August, 1928, ibid.; no. 581, De Astis to Grandi, 24 August 1928.
55. *DDI*, 7th series, vol. VII, no. 321, Durini di Monza to Mussolini, 16 March, 1929.
56. Von Klemperer, *Seipel*, p. 289; *DDI*, 7th series, vol. VII, no. 80, Auriti to Mussolini, 20 November, 1928.
57. *DDI*, 7th series, vol. VII, no. 17, Auriti to Mussolini, 3 October, 1928.
58. Ibid., no. 128, Auriti to Mussolini, 24 December, 1928.
59. Ibid., no. 129, Ricciardi to Mussolini, 4 January, 1929.
60. Ibid., no. 139, Ricciardi to Mussolini, 4 January 1929.
61. Ibid., no. 236, Grandi to Auriti, 5 February, 1929.
62. Ibid., no. 257, Mussolini to Manzoni, 16 February 1929.
63. Binchy, p. 309.

64. Orme Sargent, private papers, Public Record Office, London, vol. I (Au/ 28/2), Phipps to Sargent, 15 November, 1928.
65. *FO*, Phipps to Cushendun, 1 November, 1928 (C8220/34/21).
66. *DDI*, 7th series, vol. VII, no. 226, De Astis to Mussolini, 30 January, 1929.
67. *FO*, Phipps to Sargent, 17 November, 1931 (C8767/150/3).

NOTES TO CHAPTER FOUR: CHANGING PERSPECTIVES IN 1929

1. Rhodes, p. 84.
2. *FO*, Randall to Chamberlain, 24 October 1928 (W10318/2153/17).
3. *DDI*, 7th series, vol. V, no. 88, report for Grandi, 21 March 1927.
4. Ibid.
5. Ibid., no. 175, Mussolini to Medici, 2 May 1927.
6. *FO*, Dobbs to Amery, 11 December 1928 (E162/162/65).
7. *FO*, Russell to Chamberlain, 31 May 1928 (C4264/31/22).
8. *FO*, Randall to Cushendun, 11 October 1928 (W9858/2153/17); *FO*, Tyrrell to Cushendun, 31 October 1928 (W10421/2153/17).
9. *FO*, Chilton to Chamberlain, 3 January 1929 (W198/198/17).
10. *FO*, Tyrrell to Chamberlain, 25 February 1929 (C1455/116/22); *FO*, Chilton to Chamberlain, 14 February 1929 (C1349/116/22).
11. *FO*, Tyrrell to Chamberlain, 25 February 1929 (C1455/116/22); *FO*, annual report for 1929 from the Holy See, 27 March 1930 (C2470/2470/ 22).
12. *DDI*, 7th series, vol. VII, no. 253, Paulucci de Calboni Barone to Mussolini, 15 February 1929.
13. *FO*, Chilton to Chamberlain, 21 February 1929 (C1517/116/22).
14. *DDI*, 7th series, vol. VII, no. 403, Manzoni to Mussolini, 2 May 1929.
15. *FO*, Tyrrell to Chamberlain, 27 March 1929 (W2898/9/17); *FO*, Tyrrell to Chamberlain, 2 April 1929 (W3036/9/17).
16. *FO*, Graham to Chamberlain, 22 February 1929 (C1542/116/22).
17. Ibid.
18. *FO*, minute by Chamberlain, 12 February 1929 (C1118/116/22).
19. *DDI*, 7th series, vol. VII, no. 274, Grandi to Manzoni, De Cicco and San Martin, 21 February 1929.
20. *FO*, Hoare to Chamberlain, 22 February 1929 (E1141/162/65).
21. *DDI*, 7th series, vol. VII, no. 314, San Martin to Mussolini, 13 March 1929.
22. Ibid., no. 317, Grandi to De Cicco and San Martin, 15 March 1929.
23. *FO*, Tyrrell to Chamberlain, 2 April 1929 (W3036/9/17).
24. *FO*, Chilton to A. Henderson, 25 July 1929 (W7320/198/17).
25. *FO*, Holman to the Eastern Department, 18 September 1929 (E4805/ 1908/93).
26. *DDI*, 7th series, vol. VIII, no. 190, De Vecchi to Grandi, 25 November 1929.
27. *FO*, Chilton to A. Henderson, 25 July 1929 (W7320/198/17).
28. *DDI*, 7th series, vol. VII, no. 282, Orsini Baroni to Mussolini, 25 February 1929.
29. *FO*, Randall to A. Henderson, 7 November 1928 (J3118/6/1); Barton to A. Henderson, 15 November 1929 (J3370/6/1).

30. *DDI*, 7th series, vol. VIII, no. 190, De Vecchi to Grandi, 25 November 1929.
31. *FO*, Randall to A. Henderson, 13 December 1929 (C9634/727/22).
32. *FO*, annual report from the Holy See for 1930, 13 February 1931 (C1077/1077/22).
33. *DDI*, 7th series, vol. IX, no. 57, De Bono to Grandi, 23 May 1930.
34. *FO*, minute by Howard-Smith, 17 December 1928 (C9578/9578/90).
35. *FO*, Hodgson to Chamberlain, 10 January 1929 (C565/565/90).
36. *DDI*, 7th series, vol. VII, no. 176, Sola to Grandi, 16 January 1929.
37. Ibid., no. 322, Sola to Mussolini, 16 March 1929.
38. *FO*, Jordan to A. Henderson, 21 September 1929 (C7459/565/90).
39. *FO*, Jordan to A. Henderson, 21 September 1929 (C7458/565/90).
40. *FO*, Jordan to A. Henderson, 7 October 1929 (C7789/565/90).
41. Binchy, pp. 558–60.
42. *DDI*, 7th series, vol. IX, no. 354, Sandicchi to Grandi, 10 November 1930.
43. *DDI*, 7th series, vol. VII, no. 381, Galli to Mussolini, 22 April 1929.
44. Ibid., no. 329, Grandi to Galli, 20 March 1929.
45. *FO*, Chamberlain to Graham, 8 April 1929 (C2504/2462/22); *DDI*, 7th series, vol. VII, no. 348, minute by Mussolini on his meeting with Chamberlain, 2 April 1929.
46. *FO*, memo respecting Franco-Italian relations, 18 January 1930 (C576/29/22).
47. *DDI*, 7th series, vol. VII, no. 477, Galli to Mussolini, 7 June 1929.
48. Ibid., no. 379, Galli to Mussolini, 22 April 1929.
49. Ibid., no. 435, memo by Predic (?), May 1929.
50. Ibid., no. 438, Sola to Mussolini, 20 May 1929.
51. Ibid., no. 477, Galli to Mussolini, 7 June 1929.
52. Ibid., no. 515, Mussolini to Beaumarchais, 29 June 1929.
53. Ibid., no. 560, Guariglia to Grandi, 25 July 1929.
54. Ibid., no. 531, Manzoni to Mussolini, 10 July 1929.
55. This is thoroughly discussed in David Carlton, *MacDonald versus Henderson: The Foreign Policy of the Second Labour Government* (London, 1970).
56. *DDI*, 7th series, vol. VII, no. 531, Manzoni to Mussolini, 10 July, 1929; vol. VIII, no. 3, Boscarelli to Grandi, 22 September 1929.
57. *DDI*, 7th series, vol. VII, no. 458, Morreale to Ghigi, 30 May 1929.
58. Hory and Broszat, p. 20.
59. *DDI*, 7th series, vol. VII, no. 286, Galli to Mussolini, 26 February 1929.
60. Ibid., no. 267, Durini di Monza to Mussolini, 19 February 1929.
61. Ibid., no. 350, Durini di Monza to Mussolini, 2 April 1929.
62. Ibid., no. 350, Durini di Monza to Mussolini, 2 April 1929.
63. Ibid., no. 169, Durini di Monza to Mussolini, 14 January 1929.
64. Ibid., no. 195, Durini di Monza to Mussolini, 20 January 1929.
65. Ibid., no. 226, De Astis to Mussolini, 30 January 1929.
66. Ibid., no. 252, De Astis to Mussolini, 14 February, 1929.
67. Ibid., no. 275, Mussolini to Durini di Monza, 21 February 1929.
68. Ibid., no. 276, Mussolini to Durini di Monza, 22 February 1929.
69. Ibid., p. 84n.
70. Ibid., no. 408, memo for Grandi from Oxilia, probably 2 May 1929.
71. Ibid., no. 459, Mussolini to Durini di Monza, 31 May 1929.

72. Ibid., no. 468, Guariglia to the War Minister, 3 June 1929.
73. Ibid., no. 491, Grandi to Manzoni and Durini di Monza, 17 June 1929.
74. Ibid., no. 543, Durini di Monza to Mussolini, 16 July 1929.
75. *FO*, Phipps to Chamberlain, 12 February 1929 (C1254/116/22).
76. *DDI*, 7th series, vol. vii, no. 271, Auriti to Mussolini, 20 February 1929.
77. Von Klemperer, *Seipel*, pp. 333–5; see also Friedrich Engel-Janosi, *Il Vaticano fra Fascismo e Nazismo* (Florence, 1973), p. 88.
78. Binchy, p. 560.
79. Scoppola, pp. 241–3.
80. *FO*, Phipps to Chamberlain, 13 March 1929 (C2017/116/22).
81. Von Klemperer, *Seipel*, p. 395.
82. *DDI*, 7th series, vol. vii, no. 387, Auriti to Mussolini, 26 April 1929.
83. Ibid., no. 433, Mussolini to Auriti, 18 May 1929; no. 439, Auriti to Mussolini, 21 May 1929.
84. Ibid., no. 321, Durini di Monza to Mussolini, 16 March 1929.
85. Ibid., no. 499, memo by Toselli for Grandi, 19 June 1929; no. 501, memo by Guariglia, 21 June 1929.
86. Ibid., no. 321, Durini di Monza to Mussolini, 16 March 1929.
87. Ibid., no. 536, Auriti to Mussolini, 12 July 1929.
88. *FO*, Chamberlain to Graham, 8 April 1929 (C2504/2462/22).
89. *DDI*, 7th series, vol. vii, no. 499, memo by Toselli for Grandi, 19 June 1929; no. 501, memo by Guariglia, 21 June 1929.
90. Ibid., no. 529, Auriti to Mussolini, 8 July 1929; no, 580, Geisser Celesia to Mussolini, 5 August 1929.
91. Ibid., no. 559, Ricciardi to Mussolini, 23 July 1929.
92. Ibid., p. 587n.
93. Ibid., no. 613, memorandum, 4 September 1929.
94. *DDI*, 7th series, vol. viii, no. 8, De Astis to Grandi, 18 September 1929.

NOTES TO CHAPTER FIVE: CRISIS OVER MALTA

1. Arthur Marder, 'The Royal Navy and the Ethiopian Crisis of 1935–36', *American Historical Review* (June 1970) pp. 1130–1.
2. J. G. Lockhart, *Cosmo Gordon Lang* (London, 1949) pp. 365–6.
3. This dominant role of the Church in Maltese society is made abundantly clear in Jeremy Boissevain's socio-anthropological study of rural Malta, *Saints and Fireworks: Religion and Politics in Rural Malta* (London, 1965).
4. W. K. Hancock, *Survey of British Commonwealth Affairs*, vol. i, *Problems of Nationality, 1918–1937* (London, 1937) p. 422.
5. Brian Blouet, *The Story of Malta* (London, 1967) p. 194.
6. Hancock, p. 410.
7. Boissevain, p. 8.
8. Edith Dobie, *Malta's Road to Independence* (Norman, Okla., 1967) pp. 32–4.
9. Ibid., p. 80.
10. Ibid., p. 89.
11. Hancock, p. 424.
12. Dennis Austin, *Malta and the End of Empire* (London, 1971) pp. 7–8.
13. As explained in Boissevain.

14. *FO*, Acting Governor of Malta to the Colonial Secretary, 19 October 1927 (C9114/7030/22).
15. Dobie, pp. 88–9.
16. Ibid., pp. 87–9.
17. Ibid., pp. 80, 84–5.
18. Austin, pp. 9–10.
19. Henry Hornyold-Strickland, 'Strickland, Gerald', *Dictionary of National Biography, 1931–1940*, p. 839.
20. Hon. Mabel Strickland, in conversation with the author on 9 November 1973, claimed that the Church hierarchy had been very much the equal of her father in the intensity with which they sought their political goals.
21. *FO*, Ormsby-Gore to Chamberlain, 9 November 1927 (C9059/7030/22).
22. *FO*, Graham to Sargent, 26 July 1929 (C5784/24/22).
23. Austen Chamberlain Papers, University of Birmingham (Ac54/230) Chamberlain to Graham, 22 December 1927. Sir Harry Luke, in *Cities and Men: An Autobiography*, vol. III (London, 1956) p. 62, and Viscount Swindon in *I Remember* (London, n.d.) pp. 88–9.
24. Blouet, p. 186; Austin, p. 9.
25. Boissevain, pp. 10–11.
26. Dobie, p. 9.
27. *FO*, Acting Governor of Malta to the Colonial Secretary, 7 September 1927 (C7809/7030/22).
28. Carocci, ch. 11, pp. 18–31.
29. *FO*, Wingfield to Chamberlain, 17 August 1927 (C7030/7030/22); 26 August 1927 (C7174/7030/22).
30. *FO*, Acting Governor of Malta to the Colonial Secretary, 6 September 1927 (C7667/7030/22).
31. *FO*, Acting Governor of Malta to the Colonial Secretary, 7 September 1927 (C7809/7030/22).
32. *DDI*, 7th series, vol. V, no. 400, Grandi to Fileti, 8 September 1927.
33. Ibid., no. 418, Grandi to Bordonaro, 14 September 1927.
34. *A. Chamberlain Papers* (AC 50/377), Chamberlain to Graham, 2 November 1927.
35. *A. Chamberlain Papers* (AC 54/230), Chamberlain to Graham, 22 December 1927.
36. Edwards, ch. IX and X.
37. *Documents on British Foreign Policy, 1919–1939*, series IA, vol. V, no. 427, Chamberlain to A. Henderson, 27 July 1928; *DDI*, 7th series, vol. VI, no. 640, Manzoni to Mussolini, 10 September 1928.
38. *DDI*, 7th series, vol. VII, no. 35, Bordonaro to Mussolini, 12 October 1928; *FO*, memo by Sargent, 16 October 1928 (C7738/121/22).
39. Ibid., no. 66, Guariglia to Mussolini, 12 November 1928.
40. *A. Chamberlain Papers* (AC 55/210), Graham to Chamberlain, 24 May 1928.
41. *FO*, Russell to Chamberlain, 28 October 1927 (C8812/7030/22).
42. *FO*, Randall to Cushendun, 23 August 1928 (C6484/976/22); 28 August 1928 (C6626/976/22).
43. *FO*, Randall to Cushendun, 28 August 1928 (C6626/976/22).
44. *FO*, Randall to Cushendun, 15 November 1928 (C8585/121/22).

45. Hancock, pp. 413–4.
46. Ibid., p. 414.
47. *FO*, minute by Howard-Smith, 5 September 1928 (C6749/121/22).
48. Hancock, p. 412.
49. Boissevain, p. 11.
50. Hancock, p. 415.
51. *FO*, Graham to Chamberlain, 22 February 1929 (C1542/116/22).
52. The pro-Catholic *Tribuna* was one of the few papers to direct its attacks against England at this time. *FO*, Graham to Chamberlain, 22 February 1929 (C1542/116/22).
53. *FO*, Chilton to Chamberlain, 1 March 1929 (C1742/24/22).
54. Lockhart, p. 321.
55. *FO*, Chilton to Chamberlain, 25 February 1929 (C1535/24/22).
56. *FO*, Chilton to Chamberlain, 1 March 1929 (C1742/24/22).
57. *FO*, Chilton to A. Henderson, 11 July 1929 (C5322/24/22).
58. Witness his behaviour in the dispute with Italy over Catholic Action in 1931.
59. *FO*, Chilton to Chamberlain, 1 March 1929 (C1742/24/33).
60. *FO*, telegram from Chilton, 8 March 1929 (C1720/24/22).
61. *FO*, Chilton to Chamberlain, 30 March 1929 (C2378/24/22).
62. *FO*, Colonial Office to Foreign Office, 19 February 1929 (C1273/24/22).
63. *FO*, Foreign Office memo, 'The Malta Dispute', 16 February 1932 (C1475/1027/22); telegram from Chilton, 8 March 1929 (C1720/24/22).
64. *FO*, telegram from Chilton, 9 March 1929 (C1748/24/22).
65. *FO*, annual report for 1929 from the Holy See, 27 March 1930 (C2470/2470/22).
66. For full text, see *Exposition of the Malta Question with Documents (February 1929–June 1930)*, Vatican White Paper on Malta (Vatican City, 1930) pp. 80–6.
67. *FO*, Foreign Office minute by O'Malley, 26 June 1929 (C4921/24/22).
68. The text of this section of Robinson's report may be found in the Vatican White Paper on Malta, pp. 86–93.
69. *FO*, Chilton to A. Henderson, 31 January 1930 (C913/30/22); Foreign Office memo, 16 February 1932 (C1475/1027/22); Sir Alec Randall, *Vatican Assignment* (London, 1956) pp. 39–40.
70. *FO*, Ogilvie-Forbes to Simon, 11 December 1931 (C9404/3/22).
71. *FO*, annual report for 1929 from the Holy See, 27 March 1930 (C2470/2470/22).
72. *FO*, Chilton to A. Henderson, 5 July 1929 (C5524/24/22).
73. *FO*, Chilton to Lindsay, 11 July 1929 (C5270/24/22).
74. *FO*, Chilton to A. Henderson, 18 July 1929 (C5523/24/22).
75. *FO*, A. Henderson to Chilton, 5 August 1929 (C5524/24/22).
76. *FO*, Chilton to Lindsay, 19 July 1929 (C5570/24/22).
77. *FO*, A. Henderson to Chilton, 5 August 1929 (C5524/24/22); Randall to A. Henderson, 13 August 1929 (C6437/24/22); A. Henderson to Randall, 8 September 1929 (C7384/24/22); Randall to A. Henderson, 15 October 1929 (C7989/24/22), etc.
78. *FO*, Chilton to A. Henderson, 20 December 1929 (C9883/24/22).
79. *FO*, Chilton to A. Henderson, 31 January 1930 (C913/30/22).

80. *FO*, telegram from Randall, 7 March 1930 (C1852/30/22).
81. *FO*, Chilton to A. Henderson, 14 March 1930 (C2059/30/22).
82. *DDI*, 7th series, vol. VII, no. 304, Rey di Villarey to Mussolini, 9 March 1929.
83. Ibid., no. 305, Guariglia to Grandi, March 1929.
84. Ibid., no. 348, minute by Mussolini on his meeting with Chamberlain, 2 April 1929.
85. Collection of Italian documents, St Antony's College, Oxford [hereafter cited as *StA*], unsigned letter to Grandi, probably written by Mussolini, April 1929 (job 26/012606).
86. *DDI*, 7th series, vol. VII, no. 305, Guariglia to Grandi, March 1929.
87. *StA*, report by Grandi to the Council of Ministers, 5 November 1929 (job 329/112722–42).
88. *FO*, telegram from Graham, 24 July 1929 (C5638/24/22); *DDI*, 7th series, vol. VII, no. 592, Bordonaro to Mussolini, 13 August 1929.
89. *FO*, Colonial Office note, 22 March 1932 (C2965/491/22).
90. *DDI*, 7th series, vol. VII, no. 572, Mussolini to Bordonaro, 2 August 1929.
91. Carocci, pp. 200–1.
92. *DDI*, 7th series, vol. VII, no. 592, Bordonaro to Mussolini, 13 August 1929.
93. *FO*, Graham to Sargent, 26 July 1929 (C5784/24/22).
94. *FO*, telegram from Graham, 24 July 1929 (C5638/24/22).
95. *FO*, Graham to Sargent, 26 July 1929 (C5784/24/22).
96. *FO*, Graham to A. Henderson, 11 November 1929 (C8743/24/22).
97. *FO*, Colonial Office note, 22 March 1932 (C2965/491/22).
98. *FO*, Graham to A. Henderson, 11 November 1929 (C8743/24/22).
99. *FO*, Colonial Office note, 22 March 1932 (C2965/491/22).
100. *FO*, Colonial Office to Foreign Office, 1 May 1930 (C3364/30/22).
101. *FO*, telegram from Chilton, 2 May 1930 (C3400/30/22).
102. *FO*, Passfield to the Governor of Malta, 3 May 1930 (C3428/30/22).
103. *FO*, telegram from Chilton, 7 May 1930 (C3562/30/22).
104. *FO*, telegram from Chilton, 22 May 1930 (C4031/30/22).
105. *FO*, 24 May 1930 (C4070/30/22).
106. *FO*, telegram from Ogilvie-Forbes, 16 June 1930 (C4803/30/22).
107. *FO*, report from the Cabinet minutes, 18 June 1930 (C4882/30/22).
108. Arthur Henderson Papers, Public Record Office (London), Graham to A. Henderson, 6 May 1930 (FO 800/281).
109. *FO*, Graham to A. Henderson, 13 June 1930 (C4791/30/22); *DDI*, 7th series, vol. IX, no. 100, Bordonaro to Grandi, 16 June 1930.
110. Arthur Henderson Papers, Graham to A. Henderson, 6 May 1930 (FO 800/281).
111. *FO*, A. Henderson to Graham, 23 May 1930 (C4052/30/22).
112. *FO*, Ogilvie-Forbes to Simon, 11 December 1931 (C9404/3/22).
113. *FO*, Ogilvie-Forbes to A. Henderson, 27 June 1930 (C5204/30/22).
114. *FO*, report from the Cabinet minutes, 4 February 1931 (C823/3/22).
115. *FO*, 5 March 1931 (C2211/3/22).
116. *FO*, telegram from Graham, 12 May 1931 (C3249/3/22).
117. *FO*, A. Henderson to Graham, 2 July 1931 (C4765/3/22).
118. *FO*, Governor of Malta to Passfield, 27 April 1931 (C2895/3/22).

119. *FO*, Fitzalan to Vansittart, 20 April 1931 (C2670/3/22).
120. *FO*, Governor of Malta to Passfield, 27 April 1931 (C2895/3/22).
121. *FO*, Ogilvie-Forbes to Sargent, 30 October 1931 (C8188/3/22).
122. *ACS*, *SPD*, busta 17, 'D'Annunzio', Mussolini to D'Annunzio, 20 May 1931.
123. *ACS*, *SPD*, busta 17, Rizzo to Chiavolini, 23 May 1931.
124. *ACS*, *SPD*, busta 17, Rizzo to Chiavolini, 11 June 1931.
125. *ACS*, *SPD*, busta 17, report from Rizzo, 30 April 1929.
126. *ACS*, *SPD*, busta 17, D'Annunzio to Mussolini, 16 July 1931.
127. *ACS*, *SPD*, busta 17, Mussolini to D'Annunzio, 18 July 1931.
128. In her initial report to the Foreign Office about these discussions, the Hon. Mabel Strickland gave the impression that the initiative had been taken by Mussolini, although Sir Robert Vansittart, the Permanent Under-Secretary, believed that Strickland had taken the initiative. *FO*, minute by Sargent, 26 September 1931 (C7343/3/22). In conversation with the author in 1973, Miss Strickland said that it was, in fact, Prince Orsini, Chamberlain to the Pope and an old school friend of Strickland's who had set up the meetings and called on his friend Guglielmo Marconi to act as intermediary with Mussolini. The meetings took place in the Park Lane Hotel in London.
129. *FO*, minute by Sargent, 26 September 1931 (C7343/3/22).
130. *FO*, Murray to Sargent, 27 November 1931 (C8856/3/22).
131. *FO*, Colonial Office note, 22 March 1932 (C2965/491/22); Graham to Sargent, 21 January 1933 (C718/7/22); telegram from Graham, 7 August 1933 (C6991/7/22).
132. *FO*, Colonial Office note, 14 January 1932 (C491/491/22).
133. Hancock, p. 420.
134. *FO*, Foreign Office minute by Sargent, 22 February 1932 (C1474/1027/22).
135. *FO*, Colonial Office note, 14 January 1932 (C491/491/22); Colonial Office note, 22 March 1932 (C2965/491/22).
136. *FO*, Parliamentary question, 2 March 1932 (C1737/1027/22).
137. *FO*, Graham to Simon, 24 March 1932 (C2506/1027/22).
138. *FO*, Graham to Vansittart, 25 March 1932 (C2560/1027/22).
139. *FO*, Graham to Simon, 2 August 1932 (C6849/141/22).
140. *FO*, Simon to Graham, 8 April 1932 (C2866/1027/22).
141. *ACS*, Presidenza del Consiglio dei Ministri 1937–39, fascicolo 15/sotto-fascicolo 2/1817; Celesia to Giunta, 2 May 1932; Giunta to Mussolini, 6 May 1932; circular of the Società Nazionale 'Dante Alighieri', 19 May 1932.
142. *FO*, Graham to Simon, 2 August 1932 (C6849/141/22).
143. *FO*, Simon to Graham, 8 April 1932 (C2866/1027/22).
144. *FO*, Graham to Simon, 5 June 1932 (C4890/2868/22).
145. *FO*, telegram from Graham, 6 May 1932 (C3712/1027/22).
146. *FO*, Graham to Simon, 5 June 1932 (C4890/141/22).
147. *FO*, Graham to Simon, 2 August 1932 (C6849/141/22).
148. *FO*, Ogilvie-Forbes to Simon, 20 February 1932 (C1551/1027/22); telegram from the Governor of Malta, 30 May 1932 (C4427/1027/22); Ogilvie-Forbes to Sargent, 25 June 1932 (C5341/1027/22); telegram

from the Governor of Malta, 1 June 1932 (C4441/1027/22).
149. *FO*, report from the Cabinet minutes, 8 June 1932 (C4799/1027/22).
150. *FO*, Colonial Office note, 31 October 1932 (C9036/491/22).
151. *FO*, Graham to Simon, 14 October 1932 (C8719/491/22), Graham to Vansittart, 5 November 1932 (C9349/1027/22).
152. *FO*, Graham to Vansittart, 10 March 1933 (C2379/7/22).
153. *FO*, Ogilvie-Forbes to Sargent, 9 July 1932 (C5856/1027/22).
154. *FO*, memo by Perowne, 17 January 1933 (C2232/7/22).
155. *FO*, 4 November 1932 (C10549/1027/22); Ogilvie-Forbes to Simon, 8 November 1932 (C9418/491/22).
156. *FO*, Colonial Office note, 4 January 1933 (C167/7/22).
157. *FO*, Colonial Office note, 28 February 1933 (C2015/7/22).
158. *FO*, telegram from Clive, 15 July 1933 (C6371/7/22).
159. *FO*, Clive to Simon, 7 August 1933 (C7367/7/22); Fitzalan to Cunliffe-Lister, 12 September 1933 (C8523/7/22); Montgomery to Carr, 27 September 1934 (R5371/8/22).
160. *FO*, Montgomery to Carr, 27 September 1934 (R5371/8/22).
161. *FO*, Wingfield to Simon, 6 November 1934 (R6337/8/22).
162. *FO*, Colonial Office note, 4 October 1932 (C8355/1027/22).
163. *FO*, Governor of Malta to the Colonial Secretary, 25 October 1932 (C9489/1027/22).
164. *FO*, report from the Cabinet minutes, 7 July 1933 (C6160/7/22).
165. *FO*, telegram from Graham, 26 July 1933 (C6645/7/22).
166. *FO*, telegram from Graham, 5 August 1933 (C6961/7/22).
167. *FO*, Vansittart to Graham, 21 August 1933 (C7428/7/22); report from the Cabinet minutes, 5 September 1933 (C7821/7/22); telegram from Murray, 19 September 1933 (C8319/7/22).
168. *FO*, Drummond to Simon, 9 December 1933 (C10849/7/22); Drummond to Vansittart, 29 December 1933 (R56/8/22).
169. *FO*, telegram from Drummond, 12 December 1933 (C10876/7/22).
170. *FO*, memo by Simon, 4 January 1934 (R166/8/22).
171. *FO*, telegram from Murray, 23 August 1934 (R4689/8/22); Drummond to Simon, 10 November 1934 (R6329/8/22).

NOTES TO CHAPTER SIX: THE ONSET OF THE DEPRESSION, 1929–30

1. *De Felice IV*, pp. 365–9.
2. Klemens Von Klemperer, 'Chancellor Seipel and the Crisis of Democracy in Austria', *Journal of Central European Affairs*, vol. 22 (January 1963), p. 477.
3. *FO*, Phipps to A. Henderson, 17 December, 1929 (C9905/149/3).
4. *DDI*, 7th series, vol. VIII, no. 25, Auriti to Grandi, 27 September, 1929.
5. Ibid., no. 25, Auriti to Grandi, 27 September, 1929.
6. Ibid., no. 37, Auriti to Grandi, 2 October, 1929.
7. *FO*, Phipps to A. Henderson, 17 De ember, 1929, (C9905/149/3).
8. *DDI*, 7th series, vol. VIII, no. 37, Auriti to Grandi, 2 October, 1929.
9. Ibid., no. 64, Auriti to Grandi, 11 October, 1929.
10. Ibid., no. 82, Grandi to Auriti, 17 October, 1929.

11. Ibid., no. 40, De Astis to Grandi, 2–3 October, 1929.
12. Ibid., no. 61, De Astis to Grandi, 10 October, 1929.
13. Ibid., no. 47, Grandi to De Astis, 5 October, 1929.
14. Ibid., no. 65, Ricciardi to Grandi, 11 October, 1929.
15. Ibid., no. 73, Grandi to De Astis, 14 October, 1929.
16. Ibid., no. 108, Auriti to Grandi, 25 October, 1929.
17. Ibid., no. 196, Ricciardi to Grandi, 28 November, 1929.
18. Ibid., no. 194, Grandi to Brocchi, 28 November, 1929.
19. Ibid., no. 225, Auriti to Grandi, 8 December, 1929.
20. Ibid., no. 219, Auriti to Grandi, 5 December, 1929; no. 246, Auriti to Grandi, 13 December, 1929.
21. Ibid., no. 113, Auriti to Grandi, 26 October, 1929.
22. Ibid., no. 305, Grandi to Auriti, 11 January, 1930.
23. Ibid., no. 334, Auriti to Grandi, 28 January 1930.
24. Ibid., no. 347, minute by Mussolini on his conversations with Schober, 4 February 1930.
25. *FO*, Phipps to A. Henderson, 10 February 1930 (C1147/1014/3).
26. *FO*, Graham to A. Henderson, 22 February 1930 (C1493/1014/3).
27. *FO*, Phipps to A. Henderson, 12 April 1930 (C3101/1014/3).
28. *DDI*, 7th series, vol. vii, no. 556, Mussolini to De Vecchi, 22 July 1929.
29. Binchy, p. 561.
30. Ibid., p. 562.
31. See Carlton.
32. *DDI*, 7th series, vol. viii, no. 33, Rosso to Grandi, 30 September 1929.
33. Ibid., no. 81, Grandi to Bordonaro, Aloisi and De Martino, 17 October 1929.
34. Ibid., no. 152, Grandi to Manzoni, 12 November 1929; no. 171, Manzoni to Grandi, 19 November 1929.
35. Ibid., no. 215, Manzoni to Grandi, 4 December 1929.
36. Ibid., no. 261, Grandi to Manzoni, 18 December 1929.
37. Ibid., no. 304, Mussolini to Grandi, 10 January 1930.
38. Ibid., no. 481, Grandi to Mussolini, 10 April 1930.
39. *StA*, report by Grandi to the Council of Ministers, 5 November 1929 (job 329/112722–42).
40. *DDI*, 7th series, vol. viii, no. 258, Visconti Prasca to the General Staff of the Army, 17 December 1929
41. *DDI*, 7th series, vol. ix, no. 29, minute by Grandi, 12 May 1930.
42. *DDI*, 7th series, vol. viii, no. 302, minute by Grandi on his conversation with Jeftic, 8 January 1930.
43. Ibid., no. 360, Guariglia to Galli, 12 February 1930.
44. *FO*, N. Henderson to Vansittart, 13 March 1930, (C2643/141/92).
45. *DDI*, 7th series, vol. ix, no. 29, minute by Grandi, 12 May 1930.
46. Clissold, p. 179; *FO*, N. Henderson to A. Henderson, 7 February 1930 (C1144/1142/92).
47. *FO*, N. Henderson to A. Henderson, 7 February, 1930 (C1144/1142/92).
48. *DDI*, 7th series, vol. viii, nos 251 and 252, Galli to Grandi, 14 December 1929.
49. *FO*, N. Henderson to A. Henderson, 7 February 1930 (C1144/1142/92).
50. Ibid.

51. Ibid.
52. *DDI,* 7th series, vol. VIII, no. 380, Fani to De Vecchi, 21 February 1930, especially n. 1.
53. Ibid.
54. Ibid., no. 396, De Vecchi to Grandi, 28 February 1930.
55. Guariglia, *Ricordi,* pp. 74–82.
56. *StA,* Mazzotti to Mussolini, 14 April 1930 (job 130/036614–5); Guariglia, *Ricordi,* pp. 86–7.
57. On Mussolini's continuing control of Yugoslav policy, see *FO,* Graham to A. Henderson, 3 February 1931 (C918/129/92).
58. *ACS, SPD,* busta 13, 'Grandi', Grandi to Mussolini, 4 August 1932; Mussolini to Grandi, 14 August 1932.
59. Guariglia, *Ricordi,* pp. 111–27.
60. K. St. Pavlowitch, *La Yougoslavie et l'Italie entre les deux guerres: les conversations Marinkovitch–Grandi (1930–31),* (Paris, 1967) pp. 6–7.
61. *DDI,* 7th series, vol. VIII, no. 227, Piacentini to Grandi, 9 December 1929.
62. *DDI,* 7th series, vol. IX, no. 148, minute by Grandi, 14 July 1930; no. 234, Grandi to Mussolini, 31 August 1930.
63. Ibid., no. 241, minute by Grandi, 9 September 1930.
64. Ibid., no. 243, Mussolini to Borgoncini Duca, 11 September 1930; no. 274, Grandi to Galli, 27 September 1930.
65. Stephen Graham, p. 170.
66. *DDI,* 7th series, vol. IX, no. 425, Galli to Grandi, 29 November 1930; no 479, Galli to Grandi, 28 December 1930.
67. *StA,* report by Grandi to the Council of Ministers, 5 November 1929 (job 329/112722–42).
68. Stanley Suval, *The Anschluss Question in the Weimar Era: A Study of Nationalism in Germany and Austria, 1918–1932,* (Baltimore, Md., 1974) pp. 148–9.
69. See Carocci; Alan Cassels, *Mussolini's Early Diplomacy* (Princeton, N.J., 1970); Renzo De Felice, *I rapporti tra fascismo e nazionalsocialismo fino all'andata al potere di Hitler (1922–1933); appunti e documenti* (Naples, 1971).
70. *DDI,* 7th series, vol. VIII, no. 469, Auriti to Grandi, 4 April 1930.
71. F. G. Stambrook, 'The German-Austrian Customs Union Project of 1931: A Study of German Methods and Motives', *Journal of Central European Affairs,* vol. 21 (April 1961) p. 25.
72. *DDI,* 7th series, vol. VIII, no. 390, Orsini Baroni to Grandi, 26 February 1930.
73. *FO,* Phipps to Sargent, 5 March 1930 (C1884/1014/3).
74. Ludwig Jedlicka, 'The Austrian Heimwehr', *Journal of Contemporary History,* vol. I, no. 1, pp. 138–9.
75. Guariglia, *Ricordi,* pp. 86–7.
76. *StA,* report by Mazzotti, May–June 1932 (job 132/036648–52).
77. *StA,* Mazzotti to Mussolini, 14 April 1930 (job 132/036614–5).
78. Guariglia, *Ricordi,* pp. 86–7.
79. *DDI,* 7th series, vol. IX, no. 191, Arlotta to Mussolini, 2 August 1943.
80. Ibid., no. 326, Auriti to Grandi, 25 October 1930; no. 377, Auriti to Grandi, 15 November 1930.
81. Ibid., no. 318, Geisser Celesia to Grandi, 21 October 1930.
82. *FO,* Phipps to A. Henderson, 2 June 1930 (C4465/3929/21); Stambrook,

p. 27; *DDI*, 7th series, vol. IX, no. 191, Arlotta to Mussolini, 2 August 1930.

83. *DDI*, 7th series, vol. IX, no. 317, Geisser Celesia to Grandi, 20 October 1930.
84. Ibid., p. 450, n. 1 (Auriti to Grandi, 25 September 1931).
85. Ibid., no. 191, Arlotta to Mussolini, 2 August 1930.
86. Ibid., no. 329, Auriti to Grandi, 27 October 1930; p. 450, n. 1 (Auriti to Grandi, 25 September 1931).
87. *De Felice IV*, ch. 5.
88. Edoardo and Duilio Susmel (eds), *Opera Omnia di Benito Mussolini* [hereafter cited as *Opera Omnia*], vol. XXIV, pp. 278–85; *De Felice IV*, pp. 104–11; Ormos, p. 289; Guariglia, *Ricordi*, pp. 109–10.
89. *FO*, annual report for 1930 from the Holy See, 13 February 1931 (C1077/1077/22).
90. *ACS*, Grandi papers, fasc. 4, sotto-fasc. 3, minutes of the Grandi–Liapceff–Buroff meeting, 21 January 1931.
91. *DDI*, 7th series, vol. IX, 425, Galli to Grandi, 29 November 1930; *FO*, Graham to A. Henderson, 4 November 1930 (E6092/463/44).
92. *DDI*, 7th series, vol. IX, no. 344, Aloisi to Grandi, 2 November 1930.
93. Guariglia, *Ricordi*, pp. 109–10.
94. *DDI*, 7th series, vol. IX, no. 370, Grandi to Mussolini, 12 November 1930.
95. Ibid., no. 425, Galli to Grandi, 29 November 1930; no. 479, Galli to Grandi, 28 December 1930.
96. *ACS*, Grandi papers, fasc. 4, sotto-fasc. 3, minutes of the Grandi–Marinkovic conversation, 22 January 1931; see also Pavlowitch, pp. 10–11.
97. *FO*, annual report for 1930 from the Holy See, 13 February 1931 (C1077/1077/22); Rhodes, ch. IX; Robert Graham, ch. XIII.
98. *FO*, annual report for 1930 from the Holy See, 13 February 1930 (C1077/1077/22).
99. *DDI*, 7th series, vol. IX, no. 411, minute by Grandi, 26 November 1930.
100. *ACS*, Grandi papers, fasc. 4, sotto-fasc. 3, minutes of the Grandi-Curtius meetings of 19 January 1931, and 25 January 1931; *SPD*, busta 13, 'Grandi', Grandi to Mussolini, 4 August 1932.

NOTES TO CHAPTER SEVEN: CONFLICT OVER CATHOLIC ACTION, 1931–2

1. *ACS*, Grandi papers, fasc. 4, sotto-fasc. 3, minutes of the Grandi-Curtius meetings of 19 January and 25 January 1931; fasc. 5, minutes of the Grandi–Curtius meeting, 15 May 1931.
2. *ACS*, Grandi papers, fasc. 5, minute on Grandi–Von Schubert meeting, 21 March 1931.
3. Stambrook.
4. Guariglia, *Ricordi*, p. 80.
5. Ibid., p. 81.
6. *ACS*, Grandi papers, fasc. 5, minutes of the Grandi–Curtius meeting, 15 May 1931.
7. *FO*, N. Henderson to A. Henderson, 29 April 1930 (C3446/1142/92).

8. *FO*, Leigh-Smith to A. Henderson, 28 August 1930 (C6741/1142/92).
9. Stephen Graham, p. 167.
10. *FO*, N. Henderson to A. Henderson, 17 October 1930 (C7880/1142/92).
11. *FO*, Ogilvie-Forbes to A. Henderson, 30 October 1930 (C8138/1142/92).
12. *FO*, Leigh-Smith to A. Henderson, 5 December 1930 (C8994/1142/92); *FO*, annual report for 1930 from the Holy See, 13 February 1931 (C1077/1077/22).
13. *La Tribuna*, 10 March 1931.
14. *DDI*, 7th series, vol. IX, no. 240, note, 6 September 1930.
15. Ibid., no. 243, Mussolini to Borgoncini Duca, 11 September 1930; no. 245, Borgoncini Duca to Mussolini, 12 September 1930.
16. *StA*, Head of Militia to Minister of Justice, 21 March and 25 March 1931 (jobs 102/027395–6 and 102/027397–9); *DDI*, 7th series, vol. IX, no. 382, De Vecchi to Grandi, 18 November 1930, and no. 476, Borgoncini Duca to Grandi, 26 December 1930.
17. *De Felice IV*, p. 254.
18. *FO*, annual report for 1931 from the Holy See, 19 February 1932 (C1550/1550/22).
19. *De Felice IV*, pp. 248–52.
20. Rusinow, p. 204.
21. *DDI*, 7th series, vol. IX, no. 382, De Vecchi to Grandi, 18 November 1930.
22. *Berliner Tageblatt*, 25 February 1931.
23. *ACS, SPD*, busta 28, 'Gran Consiglio del Fascismo'.
24. No minutes of the meetings of the Fascist Grand Council are to be found in the files of Mussolini's Secretariat (*SPD*) in Rome. There is, however, evidence that Mussolini had certain parts of the minutes destroyed in 1932 (*ACS, SPD*, busta 29, 'Gran Consiglio del Fascismo', Starace to Chiavolini, 5 August 1932), while Renzo De Felice, in conversation with the author on 31 May 1974, indicated that, according to his information, no minutes were kept of Fascist Grand Council meetings after 1924, both to prevent leaks and to encourage free discussion.
25. The 1931 conflict over Catholic Action is discussed in Scoppola, pp. 255–80; *De Felice IV*, pp. 246–76; and, using material from the Vatican archives, in Angelo Martini, S. J., *Studi sulla questione romana e la Conciliazione* (Rome, 1963) pp. 131–46.
26. *De Felice IV*, pp. 263–8.
27. *StA*, Procurator-General of Trieste to Minister of Justice, 10 May and 27 August 1931 (jobs 102/027400–5 and 102/027414–6).
28. Lavo Cermelj, *Life-and-death Struggle of a National Minority (The Jugoslavs in Italy)* (Ljubljana, 1945), pp. 114, 120.
29. Rusinow, p. 203.
30. Binchy, pp. 564–7.
31. *ACS*, Grandi papers, fasc. 3, sotto-fasc. 2, Grandi to Paris, London, Berlin, etc., 1 June 1931.
32. *FO*, Graham to A. Henderson, 3 August 1931 (C6082/87/22); Fulvio D'Amoja, *Declino e prima crisi dell'Europa di Versailles: studio sulla diplomazia Italiana ed Europea (1931–1933)* (Milan, 1967) pp. 36–40.
33. Ormos, p. 309.
34. Macartney, p. 92.

35. *FO*, Ogilvie-Forbes to Vansittart, 17 June 1931 (C4228/187/21).
36. In correspondence with the author on 11 April and 10 May 1974, the Archduke Otto indicated that neither his mother nor the Legitimists had had anything to do with the scheme, that he had never met Pius XI in the summer of 1931 and had deliberately stayed out of Italy lest he seem to give substance to the rumours and that he firmly believed that the rumour originated in Rome and not with the Vatican. The British Chargé d'Affaires, Mr Ogilvie-Forbes, learned of the story through the French Ambassador to the Holy See. (*FO*, Ogilvie-Forbes to Vansittart 17 June 1931, (C4228/187/21).)
37. Ormos, p. 306.
38. *FO*, Ogilvie-Forbes to Vansittart, 17 June 1931 (C4288/187/21).
39. *FO*, Graham to Vansittart, 19 June 1931 (C4449/187/21).
40. *FO*, Addison to A. Henderson, 29 July 1931 (C5967/187/21).
41. *FO*, Schrivener to A. Henderson, 3 August 1931 (C6166/187/21).
42. Geoffrey Warner, *Pierre Laval and the Eclipse of France* (London, 1968) p. 24.
43. William Evans Scott, *Alliance against Hitler: The Origins of the Franco-Soviet Pact* (Durham, N. C., 1962) pp. 10–16.
44. *FO*, Ogilvie-Forbes to A. Henderson, 2 March 1931 (W2699/47/98).
45. D'Amoja, pp. 34–5.
46. *FO*, Graham to A. Henderson, 18 March 1931 (C1934/1672/22).
47. Guariglia, *Ricordi*, pp. 80–2; see also D'Amoja, p. 43, n.11.
48. *Foreign Relations of the United States: 1931*, vol. 1, Garrett to the Secretary of State, 26 May 1931, pp. 419–20.
49. *ACS*, Grandi papers, fasc. 3, sotto-fasc. 2, Grandi to Mussolini, 25 July 1931.

That there was considerable substance to Laval's plan was made clear when Berthelot told the British a few days later that he had proposed to Laval a new approach for resolving Franco-Italian differences, namely that France should offer Italy 'a free hand in Ethiopia' instead of concessions in North Africa, which was after all a French sphere of influence. Italy would be given a mandate in Asia Minor on the break-up of Turkey following the death of Mustapha Kemal and the Yugoslav conflict would be resolved by a tripartite Franco-Italo-Yugoslav pact, directing Yugoslavia away from the Adriatic toward Constantinople. The expectation was that Italy would accept such a scheme if she realized she could no longer play France against Germany after a Franco-German *rapprochement*.

Berthelot, a noted supporter of Anglo-French collaboration and of the Little Entente and an equally noted opponent of Italy (see Hubert Lagardelle, *Mission à Rome–Mussolini* (Paris, 1955) pp. 12–13; Richard Challener, 'The French Foreign Office: The Era of Phillippe Berthelot', in Craig and Gilbert, *The Diplomats 1919–1939*), was, through this leak, seeking to keep Britain fully informed about French policy and, very possibly, also hoping to use a British reaction to stop Laval. If so, he judged the British correctly, as Vansittart, the Permanent Under-Secretary of the Foreign Office, on reading the report, minuted that Berthelot's ideas represented 'the most preposterous stuff of the worst pre-war days:

indeed it is the worst mentality of the *last century*' and suggested that
Foreign Secretary Henderson should lose no time in making his views
known. There is no evidence that the British followed up at this time,
however. [*FO*, Tyrrell to A. Henderson, 1 August 1931 (C6683/1230/
22).]

50. Guariglia, *Ricordi*, pp. 140–1.
51. On these negotiations, see *Documents Diplomatiques Français* [hereafter
    cited as *DDF*], 1st series, vol. II, no. 182, 'Note de la Sous-direction
    d'Afrique-Levant', 10 January 1933; Alberto Theodoli, *A cavallo di due
    secoli* (Rome, 1950) pp. 173–5; D'Amoja, pp. 47–50; Guariglia, *Ricordi*,
    pp. 140–4.
52. *De Felice IV*, pp. 397–400.
53. Guariglia, *Ricordi*, pp. 140–76; Esmonde Robertson, 'Mussolini and
    Ethiopia: The Pre-History of the Rome Agreements of January 1935', in
    Ragnhild Hatton and M. S. Anderson (eds), *Studies in Diplomatic History:
    Essays in Memory of David Bayne Horn* (London, 1970) p. 347.
54. *FO*, Jordan to A. Henderson, 26 August 1930 (C6753/176/90).
55. *FO*, Hodgson to A. Henderson, 20 May 1930 (C4105/176/90).
56. *FO*, Hodgson to Simon, 15 June 1932 (C5150/122/90).
57. *FO*, N. Henderson to Hoare, 17 July 1935 (R4615/241/92); an extensive,
    although unreliable, account of these secret negotiations is given in
    Appendix IV of John Flournoy Montgomery, *Hungary: The Unwilling
    Satellite* (New York, 1947). Montgomery, an American diplomat, was
    reputedly friendly with the Italian who served as the envoy between Alex-
    ander and Mussolini and had access to his files. The other knowledgeable
    source is J. B. Hoptner, *Yugoslavia in Crisis, 1934–1941* (New York, 1962).
    Hoptner has compiled his own private archives from Yugoslav sources.
    The negotiations are also mentioned in Stephen Graham, in C. Fotitch,
    The War We Lost: Yugoslavia's Tragedy and the Failure of the West (New York,
    1948) and in Nevile Henderson, *Water under the Bridges* (London, 1945).
58. Hoptner, pp. 19–20.
59. *StA*, report by Mazzotti, 16 March 1932 (job 132/036632–8).
60. *FO*, N. Henderson to Simon, 9 May 1932 (C4173/433/92).
61. Stephen Graham, p. 177; Montgomery, pp. 260–1; *FO*, N. Henderson to
    Hoare, 17 July 1935 (R4615/241/92).
62. *De Felice IV*, pp. 250–1.
63. *StA*, minute by Mussolini on his meeting with Pius XI, 11 February 1932
    (job 1/3) (see Appendix C).
64. McLaughlin, pp. 280–95.
65. *FO*, annual report for 1934 from the Holy See, 12 January 1935 (R402/
    402/22); see also Wingfield to Simon, 3 January 1935 (R273/81/22).

NOTES TO CHAPTER EIGHT: THE SPANISH CATALYST

1. See Cassels, pp. 201–15.
2. Ibid., pp. 361–2; Guariglia, *Ricordi*, pp. 31–4.
3. Cassels, pp. 214–15.
4. *FO*, R. Graham to Chamberlain, 7 February 1929 (C1141/368/22).

5. *StA*, report by Grandi to the Council of Ministers, 5 November 1929 (job 329/112722–42).
6. José M. Sanchez, *Reform and Reaction: The Politico-Religious Background of the Spanish Civil War* (Chapel Hill, 1964) pp. 13–30.
7. Raymond Carr, *Spain: 1808–1939* (Oxford, 1966) ch. XI.
8. Ibid., chs. XI and XIV.
9. Ramos-Oliviera, *Politics, Economics and Men of Modern Spain, 1808–1946* (1946) p. 438, quoted in Sanchez, p. 68n.
10. *FO*, G. Grahame to A. Henderson, 16 December 1930 (W13892/35/41).
11. Carr, ch. XIV; *ACS, SPD*, busta 67, 'Spagna', Marsenys to Mussolini, 31 March 1930.
12. *FO*, G. Grahame to A. Henderson, 30 December 1930 (C13892/35/41).
13. *FO*, Clive to Simon, 19 January 1934 (W842/27/41).
14. Sanchez, p. 82.
15. Richard A. H. Robinson, *The Origins of Franco's Spain: The Right, the Republic and Revolution, 1931–1936* (Newton Abbot, 1970) p. 27.
16. Sanchez, p. 62.
17. Ibid., p. 107.
18. Ibid., p. 83.
19. *FO*, Clive to Simon, 19 January 1934 (W842/27/41); Charles-Roux, p. 177.
20. *Berliner Tageblatt*, 25 February 1931.
21. *ACS, SPD*, busta 67, 'Spagna', Marsenys to Mussolini, 31 March 1930.
22. *ACS*, Grandi papers, fasc. 4, sotto-fasc. 3, minutes of a meeting between Grandi and Quinones de Leon, 24 January 1931.
23. Sanchez, p. 81.
24. *FO*, telegram from Ogilvie-Forbes, 17 April 1931 (W4312/46/41); *FO*, Ogilvie-Forbes to Henderson, 23 April 1931 (W478/46/41).
25. *FO*, telegram from Ogilvie-Forbes, 1 May 1931 (W4999/46/41).
26. Sanchez, pp. 84–5.
27. Hugh Thomas, *The Spanish Civil War* (London, 1961) pp. 29–30.
28. Sanchez, pp. 91–4.
29. *FO*, Knox to Reading, 1 October 1931 (W11649/46/41).
30. *FO*, telegram from R. Graham, 17 April 1931 (W4345/46/41).
31. *FO*, R. Graham tò A. Henderson, 24 April 1931 (W4790/46/41); R. Graham to A. Henderson, 22 May 1931 (W6087/46/41).
32. *FO*, R. Graham to A. Henderson, 24 April 1931 (W4790/46/41); *La Tribuna*, 14 May 1931.
33. *ACS*, Autografi del Duce, 1931, busta 6, fasc. IX, 'Aforismi', 21 May 1931.
34. Gabriel Jackson, *The Spanish Republic and the Civil War, 1931–1939* (Princeton, N. J., 1965) p. 48.
35. Carlo Confalonieri, *Pio XI visto da vicino* (Turin, 1957) p. 203.
36. *StA*, minute by Mussolini on his meeting with Pius XI, 11 February 1932 (job 1/3).
37. *DDF*, 1st series, vol. III, no. 304, Charles-Roux to Paul-Boncour, 20 May 1933.
38. Richard A. H. Robinson, 'The Parties of the Right and the Republic', in Raymond Carr (ed.), *The Republic and the Civil War in Spain* (London, 1971) p. 55.

39. Juan Antonio Ansaldo, *Mémoires d'un Monarchiste Espagnol, 1931–1952* (Monaco, 1953) pp. 18–21.
40. Guariglia, *Ricordi*, p. 189.
41. Ibid., p. 774.
42. Ibid., pp. 193–9.
43. Robinson, *Origins of Franco's Spain*, p. 174.
44. Ansaldo, p. 27.
45. Antonio de Lizarza Iribarren, *Memorias de la conspiracion, 1931–1936* (Pamplona, 1969) p. 41.
46. *FO*, Ogilvie-Forbes to Reading, 23 October 1931 (W12297/46/41).
47. *FO*, annual report from the Holy See for 1932, 20 February 1933 (C1850/1850/22).
48. *FO*, Kirkpatrick to Smith, 12 January 1933 (W586/586/41).
49. *DDF*, 1st series, vol. I, no. 246, Charles-Roux to Herriot, 16 October 1932; ibid., vol. II, no. 379, Charles-Roux to Paul-Boncour, 7 March 1933; *FO*, Kirkpatrick to Simon, 20 March 1933 (C2887/2887/22).
50. *DDF*, 1st series, vol. II, no. 379, Charles-Roux to Paul-Boncour, 7 March 1933.
51. *FO*, annual report from the Holy See for 1933, 1 January 1934 (R153/153/22).
52. Sanchez, p. 108.
53. *FO*, G. Grahame to Simon, 15 February 1935 (W1487/18/41).
54. Sanchez, p. 174.
55. *FO*, G. Grahame to Simon, 18 December 1933 (W14778/116/41).
56. Sanchez, p. 183.
57. Charles-Roux, p. 179.
58. *FO*, telegram from G. Grahame, 24 January 1934 (W1078/27/41).
59. *FO*, annual report from the Holy See for 1934, 12 January 1935 (R402/402/22).
60. Rhodes, p. 121.
61. Ibid., p. 120.
62. *FO*, Clive to Simon, 23 January 1934 (W842/27/41).
63. *ACS, SPD*, Carteggio Riservato, busta 67, 'Spagna', Carpi to Mussolini, 7 February 1942; for English translation, see William C. Askew, 'Italian Intervention in Spain: The Agreements of March 31, 1934 with the Spanish Monarchist Parties', *Journal of Modern History*, vol. XXIV, no. 2 (1952) pp. 181–3; see also Lizarza Iribarren, pp. 34–40.
64. Sanchez, p. 187.
65. Baron Pompeo Aloisi, *Journal (25 Juillet 1932–14 Juin 1936)* (Paris, 1957), 12 December 1933, p. 167.
66. *DDF*, 1st series, vol. VI, p. 60n.
67. Lizarza Iribarren, pp. 39–40, 48–9.
68. *FO*, Wingfield to Simon, 22 January 1935 (W814/18/41).
69. Sanchez, pp. 185–6.
70. Thomas, p. 226.

NOTES TO CHAPTER NINE: THE QUEST FOR FOUR-POWER UNITY, 1932–3

1. Macartney, pp. 100–1.

2. *FO*, Ogilvie-Forbes to Simon, 13 February 1932 (C1377/321/22).
3. *DDF*, 1st series, vol. I, no. 32, Charles-Roux to Herriot, 17 July 1932.
4. Ibid., no. 70, Charles-Roux to Herriot, 27 July 1932; no. 101, Charles-Roux to Herriot, 12 August 1932.
5. Ibid., no. 101, Charles-Roux to Herriot, 12 August 1932.
6. *StA*, Mazzotti to Mussolini, 28 June 1932 (job 132/036653–61).
7. De Felice, *I rapporti...*, pp. 161–2.
8. *DDF*, 1st series, vol. II, no. 123, Charles-Roux to Paul-Boncour, 19 December 1932.
9. *DDF*, 1st series, vol. I, nos 70, 101, 246, 259, Charles-Roux to Herriot, 27 July, 12 August, 16 October, 20 October 1932.
10. Ibid., no. 246, Charles-Roux to Herriot, 16 October 1932.
11. Ibid., no. 259, Charles-Roux to Herriot, 20 October 1932.
12. Ibid., no. 246, Charles-Roux to Herriot, 16 October 1932; no. 259, Charles-Roux to Herriot, 20 October 1932.
13. *FO*, Ogilvie-Forbes to Sargent, 30 May 1932 (N3501/1792/38).
14. *FO*, telegram from Graham, 1 December 1932 (C1002/1557/22).
15. *FO*, Kirkpatrick to Sargent, 17 January 1933 (C723/723/22); *DDF*, 1st series, vol. III, no. 304, Charles-Roux to Paul-Boncour, 20 May 1933.
16. Guariglia to Grandi, 19 February 1932, printed in Guariglia, *Ricordi*, pp. 144–71.
17. *DDF*, 1st series, vol. I, no. 16, Herriot to Tyrrell, 13 July 1932; *ACS*, Grandi papers, fasc. 6, sotto-fasc. 2, minute by Grandi, 2 July 1932; D'Amoja, p. 69.
18. Macartney and Palmer, p. 299.
19. *FO*, telegram from Graham, 16 July 1932 (C6036/29/62); Aloisi, 26 July 1932, pp. 3–4.
20. Aloisi, 4 October 1932, p. 12.
21. Ibid., pp. 11–13; Carocci, pp. 241–3.
22. *DDF*, 1st series, vol. I, no. 271, Beaumarchais to Herriot, 24 October 1932.
23. *FO*, N. Henderson to Simon, 9 May 1932 (C4173/433/92).
24. Aloisi, 29 July 1932, p. 5.
25. *De Felice IV*, p. 417.
26. *DDF*, 1st series, vol. I, no. 70, Charles-Roux to Herriot, 27 July 1932.
27. Ibid., no. 70, Charles-Roux to Herriot, 27 July 1932.
28. Ibid., no. 101, Charles-Roux to Herriot, 12 August 1932, and no. 285, Charles-Roux to Herriot, 28 October 1932.
29. *Osservatore Romano*, 24–5 October 1932.
30. *FO*, Kirkpatrick to Sargent, 17 January 1933 (C723/723/22).
31. Hory and Broszat, pp. 20–2.
32. Aloisi, 15 December 1932, pp. 39–40.
33. *FO*, N. Henderson to Simon, 17 October 1932 (C8846/433/92).
34. Stephen Graham, pp. 189–90; *FO*, N. Henderson to Sargent, 12 November 1932 (C9640/433/92).
35. *DDF*, 1st series, vol. II, no. 120, Naggiar to Paul-Boncour, 19 December 1932.
36. *FO*, memo by Perowne, 12 October 1932 (C8585/1557/22).
37. Scott, p. 67.

38. Aloisi, 21 November 1932, pp. 20–1; 4 December 1932, p. 28; 6 December 1932, pp. 29–30.
39. Macartney and Palmer, p. 295.
40. *ACS*, Autografi del Duce, busta 7, fasc. X, sotto-fasc. 'A', speech by Mussolini to the Senate, 14 December 1932.
41. Aloisi, 15 December 1932, pp. 39–40.
42. *FO*, N. Henderson to Sargent, 12 November 1932 (C9640/433/92).
43. *DDF*, 1st series, vol. ii, no. 123, Charles-Roux to Paul-Boncour, 19 December 1932.
44. Ibid., no. 142, De Dampierre to Paul-Boncour, 28 December 1932.
45. Stephen Graham, p. 173.
46. *FO*, N. Henderson to Simon, 21 January 1933 (C767/24/92); *DDF*, 1st series, vol. iii, no. 304, Charles-Roux to Paul-Boncour, 20 May 1933.
47. *FO*, N. Henderson to Simon, 4 February 1933 (C1692/24/92).
48. Ibid.
49. *FO*, Kirkpatrick to Simon, 25 February 1933 (C1951/1292/92).
50. Ibid.
51. *FO*, Tyrrell to Simon, 13 March 1933 (C2387/24/92).
52. Aloisi, 7 January 1933, pp. 46–7.
53. *FO*, memorandum respecting Franco-Italo-Yugoslav relations, 23 January 1933 (C376/44/92).
54. *DDF*, 1st series, vol. ii, p. 612n.
55. Aloisi, 8 March 1933, pp. 83–4.
56. *DDF*, 1st series, vol. iii, no. 2, De Jouvenel to Paul-Boncour, 18 March 1933.
57. D'Amoja, p. 262.
58. *DDF*, 1st series, vol. ii, no. 379, Charles-Roux to Paul-Boncour, 7 March 1933.
59. *Osservatore Romano*, 13–14 March and 23 March 1933; *FO*, annual report for 1933 from the Holy See, 1 January 1934 (R153/153/22).
60. *DDF*, 1st series, vol. iii, no. 17, Charles-Roux to Paul-Boncour, 20 March 1933.
61. Ibid., no. 304, Charles-Roux to Paul-Boncour, 20 May 1933.
62. Ibid., no. 380, Charles-Roux to Paul-Boncour, 9 June 1933.
63. Falconi, p. 194.
64. Ibid., pp. 192–7; Rhodes, ch. xii.
65. J. S. Conway, *The Nazi Persecution of the Churches, 1933–45* (Toronto, 1968) p. 61.
66. Scott, pp. 115–21.
67. *DDF*, 1st series, vol. iii, no. 456, Charles-Roux to Paul-Boncour, 5 July 1933.
68. It was advocated by Ernst Karl Winter, the Austrian Catholic publicist and friend of Dollfuss, in a letter to Mussolini on 4 May 1933. The letter is published in Jens Petersen, 'Gesellschaftssystem, Ideologie und Interesse in der Aussenpolitik des Faschistischen Italien', *Quellen und Forschungen aus italienischen Archiven und Bibliotheken*, liv (Tubingen, 1974).
69. Aloisi, 12–14 April 1933, pp. 108–9.
70. Ibid., 17 April 1933, p. 110.
71. Ibid., 22 April 1933, pp. 113–4.

72. Ibid., 24 May 1933, pp. 125–6; *DDF*, 1st series, vol. IV, no. 33, Naggiar to Paul-Boncour, 23 July 1933.
73. *DDF*, 1st series, vol. III, no. 114, Clauzel to Paul-Boncour, 11 April 1933; *FO*, memo by Vansittart, 21 June 1933 (C5661/5661/3).
74. *DDF*, 1st series, vol. IV, no. 53, De Dampierre to Paul-Boncour, 29 July 1933.
75. Julius Braunthal, *The Tragedy of Austria* (London 1948) pp. 192–4.
76. *DDF*, 1st series, vol. II, no. 379, Charles-Roux to Paul-Boncour, 7 March 1933.
77. *DDF*, 1st series, vol. III, no. 21, Charles-Roux to Paul-Boncour, 20 March 1933.
78. Ibid., no. 383, Charles-Roux to Paul-Boncour, 10 June 1933.
79. Charles-Roux, p. 156.
80. *FO*, Tyrrell to Simon, 13 March 1933 (C2387/24/92).
81. *FO*, N. Henderson to Simon, 24 March 1933 (C2877/1292/92).
82. *DDF*, 1st series, vol. III, no. 209, Naggiar to Paul-Boncour, 28 April 1933; *FO*, Clive to Simon, 4 May 1933 (C4213/1292/92).
83. *DDF*, 1st series, vol. III, no. 248, Naggiar to Paul-Boncour, 6–8 May 1933.
84. *FO*, memorandum respecting Italo-Albanian relations, 1925–34, 6 July 1934 (R3775/67/90).
85. Ibid., *DDF*, 1st series, vol. III, no. 279, Degrand to Paul-Boncour, 15 May 1933.
86. *FO*, Hodgson to Simon, 14 June 1933 (C5564/2873/90).
87. Aloisi, 20 June 1933, pp. 134–5.
88. *FO*, Graham to Simon, 24 June 1933 (C5754/2873/90).
89. *FO*, memorandum respecting Italo-Albanian relations, 1925–34, 6 July 1934 (R3775/67/90).
90. *FO*, Hodgson to Simon, 14 June 1933 (C5564/2873/90).
91. *FO*, Hodgson to Simon, 28 June 1933 (C6077/2873/90).

NOTES TO CHAPTER TEN: THE ANTI-NAZI ALLIANCE, 1933–5

1. *DDF*, 1st series, vol. III, no. 485, De Vienne to Paul-Boncour, 13 July 1933.
2. Aloisi, 20 June 1933, p. 135.
3. Braunthal, pp. 184–7.
4. *FO*, Phipps to Simon, 3 April 1933 (C3275/420/3).
5. Gordon Brook-Shepherd, *Dollfuss* (London, 1961) p. 104.
6. Ibid., pp. 108–9.
7. Ibid., p. 107.
8. Charles A. Gulick, *Austria: from Habsburg to Hitler*, vol. II (Berkeley and Los Angeles, Calif.: 1948) pp. 1112–16.
9. Jedlicka, p. 143.
10. Aloisi, 9 May 1933, p. 121.
11. Braunthal, pp. 187–92.
12. Ibid., pp. 192–3; D'Amoja, pp. 395–6.

13. Braunthal, p. 194.
14. *FO*, Phipps to Simon, 22 September 1932, (C8174/8174/3).
15. Gulick, p. 1219.
16. *FO*, Phipps to A. Henderson, 23 January 1931 (C713/713/3).
17. *StA*, minute by Mussolini on his meeting with Pope Pius XI, 11 February 1932, (job 1/3).
18. *DDF*, 1st series, vol. III, no. 304, Charles-Roux to Paul-Boncour, 20 May 1933; *FO*, Clive to Simon, 22 April 1933 (C3851/3244/18).
19. *DDF*, 1st series, vol. III, no. 304, Charles-Roux to Paul-Boncour, 20 May 1933.
20. Conway, p. 14.
21. *DDF*, 1st series, vol. III, p. 866n, Puaux to Paris, 11 July 1933.
22. *Documents on German Foreign Policy* [hereafter cited as *DGFP*), series C, vol. II, no. 149, the Ambassador to the Holy See to the Foreign Ministry, 27 December 1933.
23. Aloisi, 27 July 1933, pp. 141–2; Braunthal, pp. 187–92.
24. Jurgen Gehl, *Austria, Germany and the Anschluss, 1931–1938* (London, 1963) p. 70.
25. Braunthal, pp. 172–3.
26. *DDF*, 1st series, vol. IV, no. 216, Puaux to Paul-Boncour, 15 September 1933.
27. *DGFP*, series C, vol. II, no. 20, memo by official of Department II, 21 October 1933; Gehl, pp. 72–5; Kurt Von Schuschnigg, *The Brutal Take-over: The Austrian Ex-Chancellor's Account of the Anschluss of Austria by Hitler* (London, 1969) pp. 95–6.
28. Gulick, pp. 1112–16.
29. *FO*, Selby to Simon, 9 December 1933 (C10986/420/3).
30. *FO*, Selby to Simon, 23 December 1933 (R37/37/3).
31. *FO*, Clive to Simon, 13 January 1934 (R322/37/3).
32. *FO*, Kirkpatrick to Simon, 28 August 1933 (C7873/7873/22).
33. *FO*, I. L. Henderson to Simon, 7 October 1933, (C9662/429/3); *DDF*, 1st series, vol. IV, no. 199, Sallaud to Daladier, 11 September 1933.
34. *DGFP*, series C, vol. II, no. 149, the Ambassador to the Holy See to the Foreign Ministry, 27 December 1933.
35. D'Amoja, pp. 444–5.
36. Stephen Graham, pp. 200–11, 232–8.
37. *DGFP*, series C, vol. II, no. 92, Lammers to Bülow, 30 November 1933.
38. *DDF*, 1st series, vol. VI, no. 275, Naggiar to Barthou, 2 June 1934.
39. Braunthal, p. 175.
40. Von Schuschnigg, pp. 100–2; E.R. Prince Starhemberg, *Between Hitler and Mussolini* (London, 1942) pp. 121–2.
41. *DGFP*, series C, vol. II, no. 182, Neurath to de Kanya, 13 January 1934.
42. Ibid., no. 322, Foreign Ministry to the State Secretary in the Reich Chancellery, 13 March 1934.
43. *DDF*, 1st series, vol. V, no. 494, Barthou to Rome, Vienna, Budapest, etc., 13 March 1934.
44. Ibid., no. 430, Naggiar to Barthou, 24 February 1934; Aloisi, 21 February 1934, p. 180.
45. Aloisi, 21 February 1934, p. 180.

46. *DGFP*, series C, vol. ii, no. 309, memo by Neurath, 9 March 1934.
47. Ibid., no. 316, the Minister in Austria to the Foreign Ministry, 10 March 1934.
48. *DGFP*, series C, vol. iii, no. 23, Foreign Ministry to the Embassy on Italy, 21 June 1934.
49. *FO*, Kirkpatrick to Simon, 28 August 1933 (C7873/7873/22).
50. *FO*, annual report for 1933 from the Holy See, 1 January 1934 (R153/153/22).
51. Charles-Roux, p. 132; Jasper, p. 227; FO, Wingfield to Simon, 3 January 1935 (R273/81/22); *FO*, Montgomery to Hoare, 8 August 1935 (R4997/81/22).
52. *Opera Omnia*, vol. xxvi, pp. 185–93, speech by Mussolini to the Second Assembly of the Quinquennial of the Regime, 18 March, 1934.
53. Giorgio Rochat, *Militari e politici nella preparazione della campagna d'Ethiopia. Studio e documenti, 1932–1936* (Milan, 1971) p. 40.
54. *DGFP*, series C, vol. ii, no. 368, the Ambassador in Italy to the Foreign Ministry, 29 March 1934.
55. Aloisi, 15 June 1934, p. 199.
56. *DGFP*, series C, vol. iii, no. 23, Foreign Ministry to the Embassy in Italy, 21 June 1934.
57. Gulick, pp. 1437–40.
58. *FO*, Hadow to Carr, 1 May 1934 (R2647/2119/3); *DGFP*, series C, vol. ii, no. 444, Mackensen to Neurath, 10 May 1934; Von Schuschnigg, p. 109.
59. Aloisi, 27 January 1934, p. 177; 27 April 1934, p. 187.
60. Gaetano Salvemini, *Prelude to World War II* (London, 1953) p. 147.
61. *DGFP*, series C, vol. ii, no. 444, Mackensen to Neurath, 10 May 1934.
62. Yet the Archduke Otto confirms that Dollfuss himself was not a monarchist initially. 'It is only in the course of the evolution that he changed his view and in the end was considering favourably the possibility of a monarchy in Austria.' (Archduke Otto to the author, 11 April 1974).
63. *FO*, Montgomery to Simon, 5 May 1934 (R2699/2551/3).
64. *FO*, Montgomery to Carr, 1 June 1934 (R3108/2119/3).
65. *DGFP*, series C, vol. ii, no. 478, Ambassador in Italy to the Foreign Ministry, 1 June 1934.
66. Macartney and Palmer, p. 285.
67. *FO*, memo by Carr, 14 November 1934 (R7265/37/3).
68. *FO*, Selby to Simon, 10 December 1934 (R7081/37/3).
69. *FO*, Hadwen to Simon, 6 September 1933 (C8243/2873/90); memo respecting Italo-Albanian relations, 1925–34, 6 July 1934, (R3775/67/90).
70. *DDF*, 1st series, vol. v, no. 141, Degrand to Paul-Boncour, 15 December 1933.
71. Aloisi, 18 December 1933, p. 168.
72. Ibid., 27 November 1933, pp. 163–4, and 10 January 1934, p. 174.
73. *DDF*, 1st series, vol. v, no. 440, Degrand to Barthou, 26 February 1934.
74. Aloisi, 12 June 1934, p. 197.
75. Ibid., 27 June 1934, p. 200; Skendi, p. 16; *FO*, memo respecting Italo-Albanian relations, 1925–34, 6 July 1934 (R3775/67/90).
76. Aloisi, 3 July 1934, pp. 201–2.

77. Ibid., 31 July 1934, p. 208.
78. Ibid., 14 August 1934, p. 209.
79. Ibid., 20 August 1934, p. 210.
80. Ibid., 15 November 1934, p. 229.
81. Ibid., 24 November 1934, p. 231, and 28 December 1934, p. 240; *FO*, Hodgson to Simon, 27 April 1935 (R2921/878/90).
82. Aloisi, 16 and 20 December 1934, pp. 238–9.
83. *FO*, Hodgson to Simon, 27 April 1935 (R2921/878/90).
84. Macartney and Palmer, p. 327.
85. Aloisi, 1 September 1934, pp. 213–15.
86. Ibid., 7 September 1934, p. 215.
87. Ibid., 3 and 6 October 1934, pp. 224–5.
88. Ibid., 9 October 1934, p. 225, and 14 October 1934, pp. 226–7.
89. Ibid., 14 October, pp. 226–7.
90. *ACS*, Grandi papers, fasc. 3, sotto-fasc. 2, Grandi to Mussolini, 25 July 1931.
91. Aloisi, 24 and 25 December 1934, p. 239.
92. Ibid., 29 December 1934, p. 240.
93. Ibid., 31 December 1934, pp. 240–1.
94. Ibid., pp. 245–6.
95. *De Felice IV*, pp. 519–33.
96. *FO*, Wingfield to Simon, 28 July 1934 (R4265/37/3).
97. *FO*, Wingfield to Simon, 12 January 1935 (R404/404/22).
98. Ernesto Rossi, *Il manganello e l'aspersorio* (Florence, 1958) pp. 230–1; *FO*, Wingfield to Simon, 22 April 1935, (R2740/404/22); Wingfield to Hoare, 11 July 1935 (R4495/404/22).

Bibliography

Primary Sources

(i) *Manuscript collections*
Autografi del Duce, Archivio Centrale dello Stato, Rome.
Chamberlain, Sir Austen, private papers, University of Birmingham, Birmingham.
Collection of Italian Documents, St Antony's College, Oxford.
Grandi, Dino, private papers, Archivio Centrale dello Stato, Rome.
Henderson, Arthur, private papers, Public Record Office, London.
Papers of the British Foreign Office, Public Record Office, London.
Presidenza del Consiglio dei Ministri, Archivio Centrale dello Stato, Rome.
Sargent, Orme, private papers, Public Record Office, London.
Segreteria Particolare del Duce, Carteggio Riservato, Archivio Centrale dello Stato, Rome.

(ii) *Published collections*
Documenti Diplomatici Italiani, 7th series.
Documents Diplomatiques Français, 1st series.
Documents on British Foreign Policy, 1919–1939, series 1A.
Documents on German Foreign Policy, series C.
Exposition of the Malta Question with Documents (February 1929–June 1930) (Vatican City: Vatican Polyglot Press, 1930); the Vatican White Paper on Malta.
Foreign Relations of the United States: 1931.
Mandements, lettres pastorales et circulaires des Évêques de Québec, Vol. XIII.
McLaughlin, Terence P. (ed.), *The Church and the Reconstruction of*

the Modern World: The Social Encyclicals of Pope Pius XI (New York: Image Books, 1957).

Susmel, Edoardo and Susmel, Duilio (eds), *Opera Omnia di Benito Mussolini*, vols XXIII–XXVII (Florence: La Fenice, 1957–9).

(iii) *Correspondence and interviews*

Randall, Sir Alec, correspondence with the author.

Strickland, Hon. Mabel, personal interview, London 9 November 1973.

von Habsburg, Dr Otto (Archduke Otto), correspondence with the author.

Secondary Sources and Memoirs

Aloisi, Baron Pompeo, *Journal (25 juillet 1932–14 juin 1936)* (Paris: Plon, 1957).

Ansaldo, Juan Antonio, *Mémoires d'un monarchiste espagnol, 1931–1952*, trans. Jean Viet (Monaco; Editions du Rocher, 1953).

Askew, William C., 'Italian Intervention in Spain: The Agreements of March 31, 1934 with the Spanish Monarchist Parties', *Journal of Modern History*, vol. XXIV, no. 2 (1952)

Austin, Dennis, *Malta and the End of Empire* (London: Frank Cass, 1971).

Baer, George, *The Coming of the Italo-Ethiopian War* (Cambridge, Mass: Harvard University Press, 1967).

Baeta, C. G., 'Missionary and Humanitarian Interests, 1914 to 1960', in L.H. Gann and Peter Duignan (eds), *Colonialism in Africa 1870–1960*, vol. II: *The History and Politics of Colonialism 1914–1960* (Cambridge: Cambridge University Press, 1970).

Barker, A. J., *The Rape of Ethiopia 1936* (New York: Ballantine Books, 1971).

Bendiscioli, Mario, *La politica della Santa Sede (direttive–organi–realizzazioni), 1918–1938* (Florence: La Nuova Italia, 1939).

——, *Antifascismo e resistenzea (impostazioni storiografiche)* (Rome: Editrice Studium, 1964).

Binchy, D. A., *Church and State in Fascist Italy* (London: Oxford University Press, 1941).

Blouet, Brian, *The Story of Malta* (London: Faber & Faber, 1967).

Boissevain, Jeremy, *Saints and Fireworks: Religion and Politics in Rural Malta* (London: Athlone Press, 1965).

Boveri, Margaret, *Mediterranean Cross-Currents*, trans. by Louisa Marie Sieveking (London: Oxford University Press, 1938).

Bradford, Ernle, *The Shield and the Sword: The Knights of Malta* (London: Hodder & Stoughton, 1972).

Braunthal, Julius, *The Tragedy of Austria* (London: Gollancz, 1948).

Brogan, D. W., *France under the Republic: The Development of Modern France (1870–1939)* (New York: Harper, n.d.).

Brook-Shepherd, Gordon, *The Last Habsburg* (London: Weidenfeld & Nicolson, 1968).

——, *Dollfuss* (London: Macmillan, 1961).

Cannistraro, Philip V. and Edward D. Wynot, Jr, 'On the Dynamics of Anti-Communism as a Function of Fascist Foreign Policy, 1933–1943', *Politico: rivista di scienze politiche*, 38 (1973) pp. 645–81

Cantalupo, Roberto, *Fu la spagna: ambasciata presso Franco, febbraio–aprile, 1937* (Verona: Mondadori Arnoldo Editore, 1948).

Carlton, David, *MacDonald versus Henderson: The Foreign Policy of the Second Labour Government* (London: Macmillan, 1970).

Carocci, Giampiero, *La politica estera dell Italia fascista (1925–1928)* (Bari: Editori Laterza, 1969).

——, *Italian Fascism*, trans. by Isabel Quigly (Harmondsworth: Penguin Books, 1975).

Carr, Raymond, *Spain: 1808–1939* (Oxford: Clarendon Press, 1966).

Carsten, F. L., *Fascist Movements in Austria: From Schönerer to Hitler* (London: Sage Publications, 1977).

Cassels, Alan, *Fascist Italy* (London: Routledge & Kegan Paul, 1969).

——, *Mussolini's Early Diplomacy* (Princeton, N. J.: Princeton University Press, 1970).

Cermelj, Lavo, *Life-and-death Struggle of a National Minority (The Jugoslavs in Italy)*, 2nd edn. (Ljubljana, 1945).

Chabod, Federico, *A History of Italian Fascism* (London: Weidenfeld & Nicolson, 1963).

Charles-Roux, François, *Huit Ans au Vatican, 1932–1940* (Paris: Flammarion, 1947).

Clissold, Stephen (ed), *A Short History of Yugoslavia: From Early Times to 1966* (Cambridge: Cambridge University Press, 1966).

Cole, Hubert, *Laval: A Biography* (London: Heinemann, 1963).

Confalonieri, Carlo, *Pio XI visto da vicino* (Turin: Editrice S.A.I.E., 1957).

Conway, J. S., *The Nazi Persecution of the Churches, 1933–45* (Toronto: Ryerson Press, 1968).

Corsetti, Angelo, 'Dalla preconciliazione ai Patti del Laterano: Note e documenti', *Annuario 1968 della Biblioteca Civica di Massa*, pp. 149–225.

Coverdale, John F., *Italian Intervention in the Spanish Civil War* (Princeton, N. J.: Princeton University Press, 1975).

Craig, Gordon A. and Felix Gilbert (eds), *The Diplomats, 1919–1939*, 2 vols (New York: Atheneum, 1965).

Crankshaw, Edward, *The Habsburgs* (London: Weidenfeld & Nicolson, 1971).

D'Amoja, Fulvio, *Declino e prima crisi dell'Europa di Versailles: studio sulla diplomazia Italiana ed Europea (1931–1933)* (Milan: Giuffré, 1967).

De Bono, Emilio, *Anno XIII: The Conquest of an Empire* (London: Cresset Press, 1937).

De Fabrègues, J., 'The Re-establishment of Relations between France and the Vatican in 1921', *Journal of Contemporary History*, vol. 2, no. 4 (1967) pp. 163–82.

De Felice, Renzo, *Mussolini il fascista*, vol. II: *L'organizzazione dello Stato fascista, 1925–1929* (Turin: Einaudi Giulio, 1968).

——, *Mussolini il duce*, vol. I, *Gli anni del consenso, 1929–1936* (Turin: Einaudi Giulio, 1974).

——, *I rapporti tra fascismo e nazionalsocialismo fino all' andata al potere di Hitler (1922–1933): appunti e documenti* (Naples: Edizioni Scientifiche Italiane, 1971).

——, 'Alcune osservazioni sulla politica estera Mussoliniana', R. De Felice (ed.), *L'Italia fra tedeschi e alleati* (Bologna: Il Mulino, 1973).

Del Boca, Angelo, *The Ethiopian War, 1935–1941*, trans. by P. D. Cummins (Chicago: University of Chicago Press, 1969).

Delzell, Charles F., *Mussolini's Enemies: The Italian Anti-Fascist Resistance* (Princeton, N. J.: Princeton University Press, 1961).

Diggins, John P., *Mussolini and Fascism: The View from America* (Princeton, N. J.: Princeton University Press, 1972).

Dobie, Edith, *Malta's Road to Independence* (Norman, Okla.: University of Oklahoma Press, 1967).

Edwards, P. G., 'Anglo-Italian Relations 1924–1929', unpublished D.Phil. thesis, University of Oxford (1971).

Engel-Janosi, Friedrich, *Il Vaticano fra fascismo e nazismo*, trans. by Enrico Chiavacci (Florence: Felice Le Monnier, 1973).

Evans-Pritchard, E. E., *The Sanusi of Cyrenaica* (Oxford: Clarendon Press, 1949).

Falconi, Carlo, *The Popes in the Twentieth Century: From Pius X to John XXIII* (London: Weidenfeld & Nicolson, 1967).

Federzoni, Luigi, *Italia di ieri per la storia di domani* (Verona: Mondadori Arnoldo Editore, 1967).

Fotitch, Constantin, *The War We Lost: Yugoslavia's Tragedy and the Failure of the West* (New York: Viking Press, 1948).

Gedye, G. E. R., *Fallen Bastions: The Central European Tragedy* (London: Gollancz, 1939).

Gehl, Jurgen, *Austria, Germany and the Anschluss, 1931–1938* (London: Oxford University Press, 1963).

Graham, Malbone W., 'Constitutional Development, 1914–1941', in Robert J. Kerner (ed.), *Yugoslavia* (Berkeley and Los Angeles, Calif.: University of California Press, 1949).

Graham, Robert A., S. J., *Vatican Diplomacy: A Study of Church and State on the International Plane* (Princeton, N. J.: Princeton University Press, 1959).

Graham, Stephen, *Alexander of Yugoslavia: The Story of the King who was Murdered at Marseilles* (Hamden, Conn.: Archon Books, 1972; rep. of the original 1939 ed.)

Grew, Raymond, 'Catholicism in a Changing Italy', E. R. Tannenbaum and E. P. Noether (eds), *Modern Italy: A Topical History since 1861* (New York: New York University Press, 1974).

Guariglia, Raffaele, *Ricordi, 1922–1946* (Naples: Edizioni Scientifiche Italiane, 1950).

——, *Primi passi in diplomazia e rapporti dall'ambasciata di Madrid, 1932–1934*, ed. Ruggero Moscati (Naples: Edizioni Scientifiche Italiane, 1972).

Gulick, Charles A., *Austria: From Habsburg to Hitler*, vol. II: *Fascism's Subversion of Democracy* (Berkeley and Los Angeles, Calif.: University of California Press, 1948).

Hancock, W. K., *Survey of British Commonwealth Affairs*, vol. I: *Problems of Nationality, 1918–1936* (London: Oxford University Press, 1937).

Hardie, Frank, *The Abyssinian Crisis* (Hamden, Conn.: Archon Books, 1974).

Henderson, Nevile, *Water under the Bridges* (London: Hodder &

Stoughton, 1945).

Hess, Robert L., 'Italy and Africa: Colonial Ambitions in the First World War', *Journal of African History*, vol. IV, no. 1 (1963) pp. 105–26.

——, *Italian Colonialism in Somalia* (Chicago: University of Chicago Press, 1966).

——, *Ethiopia: The Modernization of Autocracy* (Ithaca, N. Y.: Cornell University Press, 1970).

Hoptner, J. B., *Yugoslavia in Crisis, 1934–1941* (New York: Columbia University Press, 1962).

Hornyold-Strickland, Henry, 'Strickland, Gerald', *Dictionary of National Biography, 1931–1940*.

Hory, Ladislaus and Broszat, Martin, *Der Kroatische Ustascha-Staat, 1941–1945* (Stuttgart: Deutsche Verlagsanstalt, 1964).

Jackson, Gabriel, *The Spanish Republic and the Civil War, 1931–1939* (Princeton, N. J.: Princeton University Press, 1965).

Jarausch, Konrad Hugo, *The Four Power Pact, 1933* (Madison, Wisc.: State Historical Society of Wisconsin, 1965).

Jasper, Ronald, *Arthur Cayley Headlam: Life and Letters of a Bishop*, (London: Faith Press, 1960).

Jedlicka, Ludwig, 'The Austrian Heimwehr', *Journal of Contemporary History*, vol. I, no. 1.

Jemolo, A. C., *Church and State in Italy, 1850–1950*, trans. by David Moore (Oxford: Basil Blackwell, 1960).

Kirkpatrick, Ivone, *Mussolini: A Study in Power* (New York: Hawthorn Books, 1964).

Lagardelle, Hubert, *Mission à Rome–Mussolini* (Paris: Plon, 1955).

Latourette, Kenneth Scott, *Christianity in a Revolutionary Age*, vol. IV: *The 20th Century in Europe: The Roman Catholic, Protestant and Eastern Churches* (Grand Rapids, Mich.: Zondervan Publishing House, 1961).

Laurens, Franklin D., *France and the Italo-Ethiopian Crisis 1935–36* (The Hague: Mouton, 1967).

Ledeen, Michael Arthur, *Universal Fascism: The Theory and Practice of the Fascist International, 1928–1936* (New York: Howard Fertig, 1972).

Lizarza Iribarren, Antonio de, *Memorias de la conspiracion, 1931–1936* (Pamplona: Editorial Gómez, 1969).

Lockhart, J. G., *Cosmo Gordon Lang* (London: Hodder & Stoughton, 1969).

Longrigg, Stephen Hemsley, *Syria and Lebanon under French*

Mandate (London: Oxford University Press, 1958).

Lowe, C. J. and F. Marzari, *Italian Foreign Policy, 1870–1940* (London: Routledge & Kegan Paul, 1975).

Luke, Sir Harry, *Cities and Men: An Autobiography*, vol. III: *Work and Travel in All Continents (1924–1954)* (London: Geoffrey Bles, 1956).

Lyttelton, Adrian, *The Seizure of Power: Fascism in Italy, 1919–1929* (London: Weidenfeld & Nicolson, 1973).

Macartney, C. A., *Hungary and her Successors: The Treaty of Trianon and its Consequences, 1919–1937* (London: Oxford University Press, 1937).

——, *October Fifteenth: A History of Modern Hungary, 1929–1945*, vol. I (Edinburgh: Edinburgh University Press, 1956).

Macartney, C. A. and Palmer, A. W., *Independent Eastern Europe: A History* (London: Macmillan, 1962).

Macartney, Maxwell H. H. and Cremona, Paul, *Italy's Foreign and Colonial Policy, 1914–1937* (New York: Howard Fertig, 1972; originally published in 1938).

Macek, Vladko, *In the Struggle for Freedom*, trans. by Elizabeth and Stjepan Gazi (New York: Robert Speller, 1957).

Mack Smith, Denis, *Mussolini's Roman Empire* (London: Longman, 1976).

Macro, Eric, *Yemen and the Western World since 1570* (New York: Praeger, 1968).

Marder, Arthur, 'The Royal Navy and the Ethiopian Crisis of 1935–36', *American Historical Review*, June 1970.

Margiotta Broglio, Francesco, *Italia e Santa Sede dalla Grande Guerra alla conciliazione* (Bari: Editori Laterza, 1966).

Martini, Angelo, S. J., *Studi sulla questione romana e la conciliazione* (Rome: Edizione 5 Lune, 1963).

Miccoli, Giovanni, 'La Chiesa e il Fascismo', in Guido Quazza (ed.), *Fascismo e società italiana* (Turin: Piccola Biblioteca Einaudi, 1973).

Monroe, Elizabeth, *The Mediterranean in Politics* (London: Oxford University Press, 1938).

Montgomery, John Flournoy, *Hungary: The Unwilling Satellite* (New York: The Devin-Adair Co., 1947).

Nagy-Talavera, Nicholas M., *The Green Shirts and the Others: A History of Fascism in Hungary and Rumania* (Stanford, Calif.: Hoover Institution Press, 1970).

Ormos, Maria, 'L'opinione del Conte Stefano Bethlen sui rapporti Italo-Ungherese (1927–31)', *Storia contemporanea*, no. 2 (1971).

Pavlowitch, K. St., *La Yougoslavie et l'Italie entre les deux guerres: Les conversations Marinkovitch – Grandi (1930–1931)* (Paris: Editions A. Pedone, 1967).

Payne, Stanley G., *Falange: A History of Spanish Fascism* (Stanford, Calif.: Stanford University Press, 1961).

Petersen, Jens, 'La politica estera del Fascismo come problema Storiografico', *Storia contemporanea* no. 4 (1972).

Quaroni, Pietro, *Diplomatic Bags: An Ambassador's Memoirs* (London: Weidenfeld & Nicolson, 1966).

Randall, Sir Alec, *Vatican Assignment* (London: Heinemann, 1956).

——, 'The Vatican and European Politics, 1922–1945', *The Ampleforth Journal*, Summer 1973.

Rémond, René, 'Il fascismo italiano visto della cultura cattolica francese', *Storia contemporanea*, no. 4 (1971).

Rhodes, Anthony, *The Vatican in the Age of the Dictators, 1922–1945* (London: Hodder & Stoughton, 1973).

Robertson, Esmonde M., 'Mussolini and Ethiopia: The Pre-history of the Rome Agreements of January 1935', in Ragnhild Hatton and M. S. Anderson (eds), *Studies in Diplomatic History: Essays in Memory of David Bayne Horn* (London: Longman, 1970).

——, *Mussolini as Empire Builder: Europe and Africa, 1932–36* (London: Macmillan, 1977).

Robinson, Richard A. H., *The Origins of Franco's Spain: The Right, the Republic and Revolution, 1931–1936* (Newton Abbot: David & Charles, 1970).

——, 'The Parties of the Right and the Republic', in Raymond Carr (ed.), *The Republic and the Civil War in Spain* (London: Macmillan, 1971).

Rochat, Giorgio, *Militari e politici nella preparazione della campagna d'Ethiopia. Studio e documenti, 1932–1936* (Milan: F. Angeli, 1971).

——, 'La repressione della Resistenza Araba in Cirenaica nel 1930–31, nei documenti dell'archivio Graziani', *Il Movimento di Liberazione in Italia* (January-March 1973).

Rogger, Hans and Eugen Weber, *The European Right: A Historical Profile* (Berkeley and Los Angeles, Calif.: University of California Press, 1966).

Rossi, Ernesto, *Il manganello e l'aspersorio* (Florence: Parenti, 1958).

Royal Institute of International Affairs, *South Eastern Europe: A Political and Economic Survey* (London: Oxford University Press, 1939).

Rumi, Giorgio, *L'imperialismo fascista* (Milan: Mursia, 1974).

Rusinow, Dennison I., *Italy's Austrian Heritage, 1919–1946* (Oxford: Clarendon Press, 1969).

Salvemini, Gaetano, *Prelude to World War II* (London: Gollancz, 1953).

Sanchez, José M., *Reform and Reaction: The Politico-Religious Background of the Spanish Civil War* (Chapel Hill, N.C.: University of North Carolina Press, 1964).

Scoppola, Pietro, *La Chiesa e il fascismo: Documenti e interpretazioni* (Bari: Editori Laterza, 1973).

Scott, William Evans, *Alliance against Hitler: The Origins of the Franco-Soviet Pact* (Durham, N.C.: Duke University Press, 1962)

Selby, Sir Walford, *Diplomatic Twilight, 1930–1940* (London: John Murray, 1953).

Seton-Watson, Christopher, *Italy from Liberalism to Fascism, 1870–1925* (London: Methuen, 1967).

Skendi, Stavro (ed.), *Albania* (New York: Frederick A. Praeger, 1956).

Stedler, Karl R., *Austria* (London: Ernest Benn, 1971).

Stambrook, F. G., 'The German-Austrian Customs Union Project of 1931: A Study of German Methods and Motives', *Journal of Central European Affairs*, vol. 21 (April 1961).

Starhemberg, Ernst Rudiger Prince, *Between Hitler and Mussolini* (London: Hodder & Stoughton, 1942).

Suval, Stanley, *The Anschluss Question in the Weimar Era: A Study of Nationalism in Germany and Austria, 1918-1932* (Baltimore, Md.: Johns Hopkins University Press, 1974).

Swindon, Viscount, *I Remember* (London: Hutchinson, n.d.).

Tannenbaum, Edward R., *Fascism in Italy: Society and Culture, 1922–1945* (London: Allen Lane, 1973).

Theodoli, Alberto, *A cavallo di due secoli* (Rome: La Navicella, 1950).

Thomas, Hugh, *The Spanish Civil War* (London: Eyre & Spottiswoode, 1961).

Toscano, Mario, *Alto Adige–South Tyrol: Italy's Frontier with the German World* (Baltimore, Md., and London: Johns Hopkins University Press, 1975).

Von Aretin, Karl Otmar, *The Papacy and the Modern World* (London: Weidenfeld & Nicolson, 1970).

Von Klemperer, Klemens, 'Chancellor Seipel and the Crisis of Democracy in Austria', *Journal of Central European Affairs*, vol. 22 (January 1963).

——, *Ignaz Seipel: Christian Statesman in a Time of Crisis* (Princeton N. J.: Princeton University Press, 1972).

Von Papen, Franz, *Memoirs* (London: André Deutsch, 1952).

Von Schuschnigg, Kurt, *The Brutal Takeover: The Austrian Ex-Chancellor's Account of the Anschluss of Austria by Hitler* (London: Weidenfeld & Nicolson, 1969).

Warner, Geoffrey, *Pierre Laval and the Eclipse of France* (London: Eyre and Spottiswoode, 1968).

Webster, Richard A., *The Cross and the Fasces: Christian Democracy and Fascism in Italy* (Stanford, Calif.: Stanford University Press, 1960).

Woolf, S.J. (ed.), *European Fascism* (New York: Random House, 1969).

Wright, Gordon, *France in Modern Times: From the Enlightenment to the Present*, 2nd edn. (Chicago: Rand McNally College Publishing, 1974).

Zernov, Nicholas, *The Russian Religious Renaissance of the Twentieth Century* (New York: Harper & Row, 1963).

The Press

La Tribuna

Osservatore Romano

Index